D1547281

Irish Tourism

TOURISM AND CULTURAL CHANGE

Series Editor: Professor Mike Robinson, *Centre for Tourism and Cultural Change, Sheffield Hallam University*

Understanding tourism's relationships with culture(s) and vice versa, is of ever-increasing significance in a globalising world. This series will critically examine the dynamic inter-relationships between tourism and culture(s). Theoretical explorations, research-informed analyses, and detailed historical reviews from a variety of disciplinary perspectives are invited to consider such relationships.

Books in the Series
Irish Tourism: Image, Culture and Identity
Michael Cronin and Barbara O'Connor (eds)

Other Books of Interest
Classic Reviews in Tourism
Chris Cooper (ed.)
Dynamic Tourism: Journeying with Change
Priscilla Boniface
Global Ecotoursim Policies and Case Studies
Michael Lück and Torsten Kirstges (eds)
Journeys into Otherness: The Representation of Differences and Identity in Tourism
Keith Hollinshead and Chuck Burlo (eds)
Managing Educational Tourism
Brent W. Ritchie
Marine Ecotourism: Issues and Experiences
Brian Garrod and Julie C. Wilson (eds)
Natural Area Tourism: Ecology, Impacts and Management
D. Newsome, S.A. Moore and R. Dowling
Progressing Tourism Research
Bill Faulkner, edited by Liz Fredline, Leo Jago and Chris Cooper
Recreational Tourism: Demand and Impacts
Chris Ryan
Tourism Collaboration and Partnerships
Bill Bramwell and Bernard Lane (eds)
Tourism and Development: Concepts and Issues
Richard Sharpley and David Telfer (eds)
Tourism Employment: Analysis and Planning
Michael Riley, Adele Ladkin, and Edith Szivas
Tourism in Peripheral Areas: Case Studies
Frances Brown and Derek Hall (eds)

Please contact us for the latest book information:
Channel View Publications, Frankfurt Lodge, Clevedon Hall,
Victoria Road, Clevedon, BS21 7HH, England
http://www.channelviewpublications.com

TOURISM AND CULTURAL CHANGE 1
Series Editor: Mike Robinson
Centre for Tourism and Cultural Change, Sheffield Hallam University, UK

Irish Tourism
Image, Culture and Identity

Edited by
Michael Cronin and Barbara O'Connor

CHANNEL VIEW PUBLICATIONS
Clevedon • Buffalo • Toronto • Sydney

Library of Congress Cataloging in Publication Data
Irish Tourism: Image, Culture and Identity/Edited by Michael Cronin and Barbara O'Connor
Tourism and Cultural Change: 1
1. Tourism–Ireland. I. Cronin, Michael II. O'Connor, Barbara, M.A. III. Series.
G155.I7 I68 2003
338.4'791417–dc21   2002153677

British Library Cataloguing in Publication Data
A catalogue entry for this book is available from the British Library.

ISBN 1-873150-54-7 (hbk)
ISBN 1-873150-53-9 (pbk)

Channel View Publications
An imprint of Multilingual Matters Ltd

UK: Frankfurt Lodge, Clevedon Hall, Victoria Road, Clevedon BS21 7SJ.
USA: 2250 Military Road, Tonawanda, NY 14150, USA.
Canada: 5201 Dufferin Street, North York, Ontario, Canada M3H 5T8.
Australia: Footprint Books, PO Box 418, Church Point, NSW 2103, Australia.

Copyright © 2003 Michael Cronin, Barbara O'Connor and the authors of individual chapters.

All rights reserved. No part of this work may be reproduced in any form or by any means without permission in writing from the publisher.

Typeset by Archetype-IT Ltd (http://www.archetype-it.com).
Printed and bound in Great Britain by the Cromwell Press.

Contents

Contributors

Michael Cronin is Associate Professor and Dean of the Joint Faculty of Humanities, Dublin City University. He was co-editor of *Graph: Irish Cultural Review* from 1986–99. He is co-editor of *Tourism in Ireland: A Critical Analysis* (Cork University Press, 1993) and *Reinventing Ireland: Culture, Society and the Global Economy* (Pluto Press, 2002). He is author of *Translating Ireland: Translation, Languages, Identities* (Cork University Press, 1996) and *Across the Lines: Travel, Language and Translation* (Cork University Press, 2000).

Justin Carville is a lecturer in Historical and Theoretical Studies in Photography in the School of Art, Design and Media at Dun Laoghaire Institute of Art, Design and Media. His writings on contemporary photographic art and Irish photography have been published in *Source*, *Circa* and the American visual arts journal *Afterimage*. His research interests include photography and national identity in Ireland, the relationship between photography, history and archives and the use of photography in memory production. He is currently working on a doctoral thesis in the area of Photography and National Identity in Ireland.

Ruth Casey is lecturing in the Faculty of Tourism and Food in Cathal Brugha St. D.I.T. She is currently researching a Ph.D. in Cultural Tourism with the Department of Sociology in National University of Ireland Maynooth. Her research interests include theories of language and issues of identity in Ireland. Recent publications include 'Virtual Locality' in *Memories of the Present* (Institute of Public Administration, 2000).

Annette Jorgensen is currently working as a researcher in the Department of Sociology, Trinity College Dublin and also teaches Sociology in University College Dublin. Her research interests include identity, tourism, environmentalism, social movements and the sociology of culture.

Moya Kneafsey, having completed doctoral research on tourism and place identity in the 'Celtic periphery' at Liverpool University, moved to Coventry University in 1997 to work on a multi-disciplinary research project examining the promotion of quality products and services through the use of regional imagery in Europe's lagging rural regions. In 1999 she was appointed Research Fellow in Geography at Coventry and has developed a programme of research and teaching revolving around rural tourism and re-localised food systems. She is joint grant-holder of two major EU research projects investigating, first, Integrated Tourism and, second, Food Supply Chains.

Mark McGovern is a Senior Lecturer in the Centre for Studies in the Social Sciences, Edge Hill College, Ormskirk, England. He was co-editor of *Who are the People: Unionism, Loyalism and Protestantism in Northern Ireland* (Pluto Press) and has written widely on Irish cultural politics for journals including *Capital and Class, Political Geography* and the *Irish Journal of Sociology*. He is currently working on the joint production of a community-based oral history book telling the story of the victims of the conflict in a nationalist community in North Belfast due for publication in 2002.

Máirín Nic Eoin is a lecturer in the Department of Irish, St. Patrick's College, Drumcondra. She has published widely on different aspects of Irish-language literature and culture. She is author of *An Litríocht Réigiúnach* (An Clóchomhar, 1982), *Eoghan Ó Tuarisc: Beatha agus Saothar* (An Clóchomhar, 1988), *B'ait Leo Bean: Gnéithe den Idé-eolaíocht Inscne I dTraidisiún Liteartha na Gaeilge* (An Clóchomhar, 1998).

Barbara O'Connor is Senior Lecturer and Programme Director of the Communications Degree in Dublin City University. She has published widely on aspects of Irish cultural identity. She is co-editor of *Tourism in Ireland: A Critical Analysis* (Cork University Press, 1993) and of *Media Audiences in Ireland: Power and Cultural Identity* (University College Dublin Press, 1997). She is currently working on a study of the role of popular social dance in Irish culture.

Juliette Péchenart is a lecturer in the School of Applied Language and Intercultural Studies, Dublin City University. She has acted as language consultant to CERT, the national tourism training authority and is co-author of *Parlez tourisme* (Gill and Macmillan, 1997). She is currently President of the Applied French Association.

Stephanie Rains holds a BA in Communication Studies from Dublin City University and a Higher Diploma in Arts Administration from University College Dublin. She has held an Assistant Lectureship in Communications at Dundalk Institute of Technology, and has published articles on cultural policy and cultural tourism within Ireland. She is currently researching a

PhD. at Dublin City University on Irish-American diasporic representations of Irishness within popular culture.

Eamonn Slater is a lecturer in the Department of Sociology, National University of Ireland, Maynooth. He has contributed to a number of publications on the cultural impacts of Irish tourism. He is co-editor of *Encounters with Modern Ireland* (Institute of Public Administration, 1998) and *Memories of the Present* (Insitute of Public Administration, 2000).

Spurgeon Thompson is Assistant Professor in the Department of Arts & Sciences, Cyprus College, Nicosia, Cyprus. He holds a PhD from Notre Dame University and has contributed to a number of publications in the area of Irish studies. He is currently preparing his critical study of the role of heritage tourism in the construction of Irish national identities for publication.

Bernadette Quinn (MA, National University of Ireland Maynooth, PhD, NUI Dublin) is a geographer who lectures in the Faculty of Tourism and Food, Dublin Institute of Technology. Her research interests include local – global interactions in the shaping of tourism places, festivals and festivity, and tourism as an agent of cultural change. She has published a number of articles on these themes and is currently undertaking comparative research on the relationship between tourism and festivity in Italy and Ireland.

Introduction

Tourism has been and continues to be a major shaping force in Irish society. General and specialist interest in Irish tourism parallels the increasing importance of tourism within the Irish economy and culture. The de-differentiation of society which we referred to in the introduction to *Tourism in Ireland: A Critical Analysis* (1993) has gained momentum and has resulted in the increasing imbrication of tourism in many areas of social and cultural life. Indeed, one could claim that tourism is a prism through which we can see other social, cultural and political scenarios being played out. Because of this we feel that the current volume on tourism is as much about issues of central concern to sociologists, cultural critics and those concerned with the future direction of Irish society as it is to tourism studies or tourism policy narrowly defined.

In the ten years since the publication of *Tourism in Ireland: A Critical Analysis* a number of developments have taken place both in the field of tourism studies itself and within Irish society which make it timely to return to the topic once again. In the interim a number of key tourism texts have been published in Ireland and elsewhere. Within Ireland there has been considerable expansion of the field of tourism research and the publication of a number of diverse contributions to the analysis of Irish tourism. There is the valuable and insightful volume from the Geography Department in the National University of Ireland, Maynooth, *Irish Tourism Development* (1994), edited by Proinnsias Breathnach. Other works of note include *The Heritage of Ireland* edited by Neil Buttimer, Colin Rynne and Helen Guerin (2000) which offers a rich and diverse exploration of heritage in Ireland and is a welcome and significant contribution to the fields of tourism and heritage studies. The focus of the volume is on the mapping of the field, the organisation and management of heritage, and on policy issues mainly. It is the first major volume of its kind to be published on Irish heritage and is a welcome addition to the field. James Deegan and Donal Dineen's *Tourism Policy and Performance* (1997) is a study of the political economy of Irish tourism and provides an analysis of the economic, political and policy aspects of Irish tourism and is also a benchmark publication.

Alongside publications in tourism studies it is also heartening to see a more concerted research effort on the subject with the development of post-graduate courses and the establishment of research centres research such as the Dublin Institute of Technology's Tourism Research Centre. Taken together, these publications and research initiatives represent a major move forward in the area of tourism studies.

In this volume we have sought to address and develop the discussions and issues which were presented in the 1993 volume. The emphasis contin-ues to be on a cultural analysis of tourism in Ireland, specifically in relation to imagery, representations and identity. The issue of identity has become increasingly important and questions of who we are and where 'we' are going has been raised ever more frequently in a society which has experi-enced massive and rapid social change over the last decade.

Tourism is much more than the sum of its infrastructural parts and to see the tourism sector in Ireland as simply a ready source of income and labour is to both underestimate its real significance and limit critical readings of its impact. The Irish *wirtschaftswunder* of the late 1990s through extensive deregulation and privatisation and substantial foreign investment has meant the accelerated integration of the country into the global economy (McSharry, 2000). In the language of economists and policy-makers, Ireland is now one of the most 'open' economies in the world. Openness implies access, movement and hospitality, traditionally watchwords of tourism development. When during the foot-and-mouth crisis tourism chiefs repeatedly declared that Ireland was 'open for business', the phrase was particularly apt in the context of the close links between tourism and dominant economic practices. These links take two forms. Firstly there is the continued importance of place in the global economy. In contrast to the wilder speculations of cyberhype and the dystopian predictions of cultural critics, the new IT-driven global economy has not dispensed with geogra-phy. Location, location, location is not only the mantra of real-estate gurus but it is also a strategic factor in corporate policy. As Manuel Castells notes in a discussion of major European metropolitan areas in *The Rise of the Network Society*, tourism and travel are generally an integral part of the new economic structure (Castells, 1996: 401).

The young, urban professionals who make up the knowledge-generating élite of the new economy are attracted to locations where working hard is rewarded by playing hard in the form of appropriate tourism and travel facilities. Being a tourist in one's own or someone else's country is seen, then, less as a form of alienation than as an attractive perk for deciding to locate highly mobile skills in one place rather than another. This explains why the much-vaunted incompatibility between the adver-tising campaigns of the Industrial Development Authority (IDA) and the

Irish Tourist Board was, in fact, no such thing. They were complementary not contradictory. Critics failed to see how Ireland could present itself in IDA advertising as a progressive, modern economy and at the same time, in tourism advertising, offer the image of a lackadaisical pre-modern culture, inhabited mainly by old men and (rusting) bicycles. Yet, what the modernists were unable to anticipate was that it was ultimately the pre-modern that would attract the post-modern.

Despite the increase in tourism research a recurrent difficulty in responses to tourism in Ireland is that they often settle into a depressing binarity. Either tourism is seen as a 'Good Thing' which brings in money, creates jobs and facilitates regional development or it is seen as intrusive, exploitative and uniquely destructive in its commodification of peoples and their cultures. The pressure on commentators if they do not subscribe to the former view is to fully embrace the latter. But economic reductionism and cultural apocalypticism both fail to do justice to the complexity of a country's engagement with tourism which does not invariably produce the monochrome responses predicted by its supporters and detractors.

The binary moral evaluation of tourism is mirrored in more recent debates on the related issue of globalisation. Indeed, the concept of globalisation can be seen as germane to tourism studies as tourism by its very nature involves some form of cross-cultural contact between people from diverse locations or different kinds of 'ethnoscape' in Appadurai's terms. Debates on globalisation have tended to offer absolutist accounts frequently based on a political-economy critical frame without reference or with only minimal reference to the cultural processes and practices involved in the interplay between the local and the global. In developing a critical perspective on tourism development in Ireland and elsewhere, it is important to take into account not only the views of the actors themselves but also to allow both tourists and tourism providers a critical reflexivity that is not the sole prerogative of tourism commentators. In the last volume we regretted the dearth of ethnographic research which we see as one of the most appropriate ways of examining the relationship between the local and the global in tourism, more specifically the relationship between the 'hosts' and 'guests'.

The Local and the Global

We explore the issue of the relationship between global and local identities and the constructions of the meaning of place in the first part entitled 'Changing Places: The Local and The Global in Tourist Communities' which consists of three contributions by Moya Kneafsey, Ruth Casey and Bernadette Quinn. This part opens with Kneafsey's chapter which sets out to explore the complex interplay between tourists, musicians, publicans and local residents at pub sessions in an area of North Mayo. She takes issue with some of the more negative characterisations of commodification and claims that because she is addressing issues of live music rather than reproduced music in the form of a CD for instance, we must the address the musical meanings which are created. She borrows the concept of 'inalienable possessions' from Weiner as something which can be 'shared yet never completely given away'. Kneafsey argues that at certain moments the tourist and musicians are in a symbiotic relationship to the extent that the tourists provide an appreciative audience for the pub sessions in the relative absence of local enthusiasm for traditional music. However, the picture she paints is more complex and she also highlights the ways in which ironically the tourists do not have the ability to engage with the music in the ways which the musicians appreciate. This symbiotic relationship between musicians and tourists is overlain by more formalised relationships between 'performers' and 'audience'. She draws a distinction between playing and performing and uses Revill's concept to characterise the experience of playing in which musical meanings are constituted by heterogenous combinations of human and non-human entities and are perceived through a variety of senses. In their polite, silent and intent listening, the gaze is the main way in which tourists interact with the music and in their failure to react in a more knowledgeable way, their presence has the effect of turning the playing of 'a few tunes' into a more formal performance which is often resented by the musicians who do not see themselves as performers in this formal sense. Kneafsey indicates that this tendency is also evidenced in some local publicans who see the sessions as a good way of boosting profits. She points to the ways in which the musicians themselves tend to resist this process of formalisation by various means including ignoring set starting and finishing times, the tunes played, lack of communication with the audience and resistance to being moulded easily into a commodification model. However, she does acknowledge that there has been an increase in 'gigs' but that sessions still exist. She is also quick to point out that research in this area has just begun and that more definitive work would require more qualitative and longitudinal studies of the relationship between all the actors involved in the situation.

Quinn's chapter also engages with the complex inter-relationships between different agents who produce tourism places – locals, artistic élites, both local and extra-local, and tourists – in her analysis of two arts festivals which have become tourist attractions: the Wexford Opera Festival and the Galway Arts Festival. She critiques the relative absence of the role assigned to human agency in tourism studies which leaves intact the frequently crude dichotomy between tourist and locals with the balance of power in favour of the tourist and the local being presumed to be the passive victim or acted-upon. She transcends this binary opposition by tracing the way in which local artistic élites developed networks with extra-local players to achieve their artistic purposes and how the role of these agents combined with other factors of time, location etc. to lead to the emergence of two distinct festivals. She points to the neglect of agency in tourism studies and claims that agency is all important in understanding the way in which places are 'authored landscapes' and that their meanings emerge and change in the way in which tourism is implicated in influencing the meanings and experience of place. In the early days of the two case-study festivals the networking between the local and extra-local networks was crucial in initiating and controlling the festival landscapes in such as way as to involve local residents in different (and arguably minor in the case of Wexford) ways, as volunteer workers in the case of Wexford and as performers and spectators/audience in the case of Galway. What is crucially important in Quinn's piece is that she highlights the cross-class alliances between local and extra-local agents and the need to differentiate between different and, at times, opposing local interests.

She claims that tourism increasingly has the power to 'overwhelm local initiatives' and that local interests are being increasingly overlooked in the emphasis on image and marketability. Tourism, thus, remain an important way of reproducing 'place'. As an activity, it leads to a change in the meaning and experience of place for those people who are local and those who visit. In many instances, local artistic elites find themselves struggling with the agents of tourism. The needs of locals which had previously been catered for in distinct ways in the two festivals is coming more and more under pressure from the forces of tourism/tourism agents who are subject to a growing emphasis on packaging and marketability.

The construction of the meaning of place and the role which tourism plays in this process links the focus of both Kneafsey and Quinn's contribution with Casey's chapter based on an ethnographic study of Ballygannive, a community in the Burren area of Co. Clare which is heavily economically dependent on tourism. As a starting point she uses Robertson's (1992) claim that globalisation involves the 'invention' of localities and the use of global processes for local purposes. She goes on to explore the again complex and varied relations between the permanent local residents and 'outsiders' (which include visitors, 'blow-ins' and tourists) and argues that one of the main consequences of the influences of global processes on the locality is the development of an 'environment culture' which is manifested both in the locals' attitudes towards their own lifestyle and in their attitudes towards Ballygannive itself.

In contrast to the stereotypically negative role attributed to 'outsiders' in local areas she concurs with Brody's (1973) classic study in conferring a positive role on 'outsiders' in terms of affirming the values of their place to local inhabitants. Outsiders of various categories play a pivotal role in the creation of local awareness of their own difference. This is achieved as a consequence of learning and internalising how the various natural resources in the area are used by the various categories of tourist. Locals learn what aspects of their environment can be selected out for the 'tourist gaze' and learn to see it as others see it – as special, exotic, unique and so on. These attitudes are not only internalised but are also manifest in behaviour which results in the land and other natural resources being socially 'constructed' and commodified by the locals to be sold as 'green products' elsewhere in Ireland and abroad. Casey sees the tourist, therefore, as generating a self-reflexive and commodifying attitude on the part of the locals and local–tourist encounters are increasingly commodity-driven because locals have learned the value of their environment from the global market and actively engage in global networking to market their products.

While Casey does emphasise the positive influence of 'outsiders', she also acknowledges that the development of an 'environment culture' has a downside. This side is evidenced in a movement towards the privatisation of space and the commodification of the ambient countryside. The new aesthetic values which have emerged have also created tensions within the community in terms of dissatisfaction with the negative visual impact of the caravan sites connected to the aesthetic of not visually pleasing and the practical problem of water shortages. Casey's evaluation of the globalisation process tends towards the positive end of the pole but she also finds that the 'environment culture' is not without its problems as manifested, for example, in the conflict over land use in a situation of increased commodification of land use in the area. There are two opposing views, then: the presence of a tourist leads to increased commodification of the area but also provides the locals with livelihoods in an area where depopulation has been rife.

The contributions to this part serve to highlight the complexity of the process of globalisation. While there are tensions between the contributions in terms of a moral evaluation of the impact of globalisation we do not finally offer a definite normative evaluation. There is certainly a tension between contributions in terms of their assessment of the relationship between the local and the global. However, what each of the contributions serves to contest is the bounded nature of the two concepts of 'local' and 'global'. For example, Kneafsey claims, on the basis of her ethnographic study of the practice of playing traditional Irish music in North Mayo, that the two concepts are interlinked. Quinn in her comparative study of the Wexford Opera Festival and the Galway Arts Festival points to the social-class-based alliances between locals and non-locals in initiating and developing the festivals which serves to debunk the myth of the locals as a romantic harmonious category. Ruth Casey, in her analysis of the networks in a rural coastal community, indicates very clearly the different types of social relatioships. In evaluative terms Casey's piece tends towards the positive pole but with the acknowledgement that the culture is not without its problems as manifested, for instance, in the conflict over land use in a situation of increased commodification of land use. None of the three authors is didactic in terms of their political evaluation of the globalising process . What is useful is that they take on board the complexity and indeed divergent and, at times, contradictory aspects of the process. The emphasis is on both agency and structure. Their approach is particularly useful for grounded studies in highlighting structures within which people operate, the forces working upon them, the agency of different groups and power differentials within 'local' communities.

Performing Heritage

A factor which has brought Irish tourism centre-stage has been the increased importance of aesthetic components in the production of goods and services in the developed world. Whether it has been the phenomenal expansion of media empires, the exponential growth in advertising budgets or the borrowing of operational paradigms from areas of cultural creativity (music, cinema) by conventional, mainstream industries, the aestheticisation of both production and consumption has become a marked feature of our age (Lash & Urry, 1994). If consumers are famously creatures of choice, then the decision to buy is more a matter of persuasion than conviction but persuasion is always more effective if it carries the aura of conviction. Hence, the appeal is to wishes, aspirations, needs (real or imaginary), which are grounded in cultural rather than utilitarian contexts. It is the aesthetic component (picture, sound, cultural allusion) which will often be decisive in the choice between competing products and services. This new economy of signs affects Irish tourism in its specific relation to the cultural industries on the island. The use of a hit song from the Irish rock group The Cranberries as the theme music in a highly stylised promotional video for Irish tourism rather than the more conventional strains of uileann pipes and merry fiddles is a significant departure from previous practice. The international success of artists like U2, Sinead O'Connor, Van Morrison, The Cranberries and, more recently, Boyzone and Westlife have made contemporary Irish popular music a prominent cultural export. In effect, what the soundtrack tells us is that all cultural products, irrespective of the intentions of the artists, become a form of tourism advertising. When the U2 lead singer, Bono, promised Irish ministers that he would tell his US fans that it was okay to come to visit Ireland, despite the foot-and-mouth outbreak, he was, in a sense, merely making explicit what is implicit in tourism strategy. In a world of aestheticised production and consumption, cultural industries (music, film, dance) are indispensable allies so that it is often increasingly difficult to tell the creative (River)dancer from the (tourism)dance (Cronin & O'Connor, 2000: 165–84).

The concern with globalisation continues in the second part entitled 'Performing Heritage: The Globalisation of Tourist Products and Practices' but the emphasis in this section is not on locality *per se*, although place is still an important implicit motif but rather on the products and practices of an aestheticised tourist landscape. This section includes three chapters dealing with three different aspects of heritage which have gained increasing popularity over the last decade as part of the tourist sector, i.e. Irish dance, heritage centres and Irish theme pubs.

The importance of the Irish pub in promoting Ireland in the tourism landscape is the focus of Mark McGovern's chapter in which he traces the historical and contemporary association of the Irish with a distinctive drinking and pub culture. He identifies a number of factors which have shaped the representations of the Irish drinking culture as the establishment of a 'stage Irish' persona in Victorian Britain; the identity branding of Irish-produced alcohol products such as whiskey and stout from the 19th century onwards; dominant perceptions of Irish migrant culture; the rise of the Irish theme bar in the 1990s as a strategy for increasing product sales; and the public and social nature of drinking in Ireland.

What, then, are the distinctive perceived characteristics of the 'Irish pub' which make it so attractive to tourists visiting Ireland and, in the case of theme pubs globally, to the 'non-travelling tourists' in places in mainland Europe, America and the Far East? There is the association of the Irish pub with a social centre creating opportunities for the tourist to have the 'craic' which may be seen as a combination of easy conviviality, sociability, witty conversation and music. Authentic folk music, an atmosphere of easy conviviality, the sense of a collective, communal existence and a supposed ethnically-specific verbal dexterity and conversational skill emerge as 'key motifs defining the objects of tourist consumption that can readily be accessed through the pub'. McGovern argues that what is expected and perceived to be available for the visitor is precisely those elements of culture which are lacking in their everyday life, i.e. a break from a work-oriented, modern world, which can engage with people in an easy and relaxing fashion which he terms as 'cultural hedonism'. Pubs provide an opportunity to 'consume' Irish people and culture – a combination of having a good time/enjoying the craic while simultaneously gaining a 'worthy' cultural experience.

McGovern argues that the tourist demand for the elements which they have come to expect and the heavy codification of pub iconography of what pubs will have on offer has led to a commodification of 'craic' and an arena for 'stage authenticity'. This, in turn, will lead to cultural performances within the pub being shaped by tourist expectations in a way which might be regarded as a modern version of the 'stage Irish' persona of the Victorian era; and that this will be an arena through which Irish people will 'construct, negotiate and contest their sense of self'. It is interesting to compare McGovern's conclusions with Kneafsey's in that her findings did indicate an increase in 'gigs' as opposed to 'sessions' but she is more sanguine in that she highlights the ways in which musicians develop strategies of resistance to the commodification.

A feature uniting tourist cultures from Ireland to Hawaii and Cuba is the prominence given to dance. A common theme in negative representations of cultural globalisation is to view the relationship between tourism and dance as uniquely exploitative, the dances and dancers being commodified in the McDisneyisation of the tourism industry. In her analysis of a regular Irish-dance show in a Dublin pub, Barbara O'Connor takes issue with the oversimplifications of the negative globalisation approaches. O'Connor sees these as frequently overlooking the crucial opinions of the actors themselves. A tendency to stress issues of ownership and control means that the element of agency in human performance gets overlooked and content is almost invariably privileged over process.

The spectacular success of shows like *Riverdance* and *Lord of the Dance* have made dance into a critical component not just of the selling of Ireland to tourist markets but of the tourism experience itself. Indeed, in the energy, vitality and inventiveness of the dancing presented in these shows, there is seen to be an image of a new Ireland which has effected an attractive synthesis between tradition and innovation. In eliciting the views of the dancers themselves, O'Connor shows how dancing for tourists was used in an enabling sense by the dancers to promote a positive sense of self and to embrace aspects of their own cultural traditions. She underlines the fundamentally dialectical nature of the relationship between performers and audience (and how this can go badly wrong). In contrast to other critics, she does not conclude that participation is a prerequisite of tourists' experiential engagement with dance but shows how certain kinds of dance experience are enhanced rather than diminished by spectatorship. In bringing the actors back into discussions of tourism and globalisation, O'Connor wants to give a voice to those who are silenced as much by tourism's critics as they are by tourism's apologists.

O'Connor in her chapter on dance in tourist settings argues that the globalisation of Riverdance, while leading to the adoption of certain choreographic styles and looks has not rendered this kind of dancing 'inauthentic'. Based on her interviews with dancers in a Temple Bar venue, she claims that 'experiential authenticity' must be included in any analysis of this cultural performance and that to dismiss Riverdance on the basis of a political-economy analysis alone would be to miss the point. These studies exemplify the advantages of a holistic approach which is particularly appropriate to the study of culture where the emphasis is on the construction of meanings and the role of human agency in forging and negotiating cultural patterns and identities in everyday life.

The marked success of Irish pubs and Riverdance companies in all five continents of the world is a telling indicator of the capacity of cultures not only to be *toured* but to go *on tour*. If spatial fixity has been seen as a defining characteristic of tourism – you have to consume tourism on the (beauty) spot – then the Irish pub and Riverdance phenomena suggest that the site of tourism consumption may not always coincide with the site of tourism production. For this reason, it will become increasingly important to develop transnational perspectives on tourism phenomena. This is not simply a matter of comparative studies, though these of course are much needed and help to put paid to myths of national 'exceptionalism', but it is a question of Irish tourism not being confined to Ireland and of needing to understand an Irish tourist experience which begins in an Irish pub in Sydney and is prolonged after the visit to Ireland in the Guinness Tavern in Paris. Herein, perhaps, lies the distinction between a *diasporic culture*, the culture of the historical Irish diaspora, as a source of roots tourism and a *touring culture*, whose membership is not predicated on ethnic affiliation and which makes Irish 'tourism' a much more pervasive activity than that accounted for by visitor statistics to Ireland. In addition, transnational perspectives would help to offset a tendency in certain strands of globalisation theory to dwell on centre–periphery diffusion of cultural practices and allow us to examine what elements of peripheral touring cultures move centre-stage. But it is also worth remembering the important role of diasporic culture in the creation of tourist imagery referred to in McGovern's, O'Connor's and Rains' contributions and indeed the relationship between diasporic and touring culture in the linking of the past and present, of the there and the here which runs through the volume.

In a country which has experienced rapid economic growth in a relatively short period of time, the question must inevitably be as it moves from the present into the future, what to do with the past? One response to change is schismatic modernism, the joyful repudiation of the pig in the parlour and of Irish history as the nightmare from which the young modernist has finally awoken. There is another response, which has involved not so much a jettisoning of, as an obsessive engagement with versions of the past in the form of heritage. John Urry and Scott Lash make a distinction between two experiences of time in late modernity, glacial time and instantaneous time. Instantaneous time is that of space–time compression, of financial transactions circumnavigating the globe in seconds. Glacial time is the immensely long, gradually changing, evolutionary relationship between human beings and nature (Urry & Lash, 1994: 242). If we introduce a third concept of 'historical time' to express a human sense of duration over recorded time, then it becomes apparent that the greater the pressure to work in the instantaneous time of the new economy, the greater the desire to play in the historical time of heritage and the more important the context of glacial time in the presentation of tourist destinations. In other words, the 'acceleration of just about everything' in the words of the US science writer, James Gleick (1999), leads to a desire to protect and preserve historical time in the form of buildings, heritage centres and interpretative centres and to enshrine glacial time in the image of Ireland as the Green Isle, an eco-friendly sanctuary from the wasting breath of the industrial revolution.

Representations of the past through heritage is the theme of Eamon Slater's structural analysis of the heritage centre on Inis Mor on the Aran Islands. He suggests that the way in which it is constructed militates against a knowledge of the local people and their social and cultural history but invites instead an engagement with the icons and artefacts which promotes a temporary sentimental response. If heritage is importantly about pleasure and a visualisation of the past that can be readily consumed by visitors to heritage centres, then it follows that space will take precedence over time in representations of culture and narrative will be subordinated to visual imagery. Museums borrow their aura from the objects physically present in the space of the museum but Slater demonstrates the powerful proprietary scope of the pictorial which through images brings the whole island into the centre. In this way, the aura generated is that of the collective (and selective) visual representations of a culture.

If the experience of the heritage centre is one of an individualised, silent sojourn the silence is not only on the part of the viewer but also of those viewed. They are presented through the words of others, rarely in their own words. Not only everyday objects but time itself becomes exotic. As Slater demonstrates, the use of black and white images reduces experiences from different historical periods to one undefined past, emptying time from the visual. As with the shortcomings in the presentation of historical information, the visitor to the heritage centre is often powerless to challenge specific particular interpretations or indeed make any overall sense of what s/he sees. There is the occasional invitation to speculation, but the framing of the question is such that genuine answers are neither sought nor expected. If the rambler became an iconic figure in representations of the 19th century countryside, it is the *flâneur* or urban stroller whom Slater views as emblematic of the construction of heritage in late modernity. In the compressed artificial landscape of the heritage centre the strollers are let loose but rarely are they left to their own interpretive devices.

The Power of the Gaze

The twin motifs of 'power' and 'the gaze' have been central in framing discussion of tourist/native encounters. Both of these issues are addressed in the part entitled 'The Power of the Gaze: Negotiating Tourist and Native Identities', which provides a micro-analysis of the interpersonal cultural contact between locals and tourists and includes two chapters, one histori-cal and one contemporary. Emphasis on the pervasiveness of the tourist gaze can often lead to a wholly passive representation of the objects of the gaze as downtrodden, unreflective and manipulated. Máirín Nic Eoin chal-lenges this view in her exploration of the responses of writers in the West Kerry Gaeltacht to the tourist phenomenon. Nic Eoin looks into the repre-sentation of tourists and tourism in the writings of Tomás Ó Criomhthain, Seán Ó Criomhthain, Eibhlís Ní Shúilleabháin and Pádraig Ó Cíobháin. What emerges is a highly nuanced set of responses to tourism in an area which has been a tourist destination for both internal and external tourists for many decades. The Irish-speaking locals are fully able to distinguish between encounters which are enriching and authentic at some level from those which remain exploitative and culturally insensitive.

Language enters the picture, of course, but not in predictable oppositions. If later writers bemoan the linguistic indifference of English speakers who treat the area as an exotic parenthesis in Anglicised Ireland, the Gaeltacht writers are also often uncomfortable with the behaviour and expectations of Irish speakers or language learners who indulge in their own form of predatory tourism. Here again, as is apparent in the analysis of Pádraig Ó Cíobháin's writings, the native can turn predator and simulate the practices of the hedonistic and objectifying tourist. Although, writers like Pádraig Ua Maoileoin have been deeply critical of native complicity in pandering to the tourist stereotype, Nic Eoin points out that this indigna-tion can be the flipside of an excessive idealisation of rural culture or native life, a tendency to quarantine cultures in a space outside of history. Nic Eoin also wonders whether the celebration of particular forms of inde-pendent travelling in opposition to mass tourism might not have seriously damaging effects at a linguistic level as a more intimate mode of contact leads to even greater pressure on language communities in a relatively weak or endangered state.

Jorgensen too deals with the notion of power involved in constructing the other in her ethnographic study of tourists on guided trips to Glendalough, Co. Wicklow. She takes up the argument advanced by Urry (1990) of how the tourist gaze is constructed and critiques of his work which suggest that rather than the tourist themselves having control of the gaze it is the powerful professionals in the tourist industry such agents, guides, hotel employees and guide-book writers who control this process. Jorgensen examines the balance of power in the construction of the 'tourist gaze' – i.e. how the tourists actively negotiate the meaning of Irishness with the tour guide and with fellow passengers on the spot and how they both reinforce and reconfigure prior images and stereotypes from other sources such as tourist brochures. While Jorgensen discovers that the negotiation of meaning is complex, the cultural resources which tourists bring to bear are independent of the tour guide's influence, while simultaneously the tour guide depends on already existing touristic discourses for his / her guiding narratives. Though dealing with flipside of the coin as regards the issues of power in relation to cross-cultural contact, the conclusion of both pieces is that the issues are more complex and multifaceted than some of the earlier studies would have us believe, that power is present but that it is not something which can be attributed *a priori* and that one needs to explore the discursive resources at the disposal of the participants within the wider context of their structural power positions.

Imagining Ireland

In the fourth part entitled 'Imagining Ireland: The Construction of Tourist Representations', the contributors explore the particular importance of representations in cultural contexts for the development, reception and experience of tourism. In looking at how writers, film-makers and photographers have interacted with tourism, the contributors show how few areas of aesthetic expression in Ireland have remained unaffected by the tourist presence.

Michael Cronin's chapter provides an analysis of the changing discourses in Bord Fáilte's tourist publication, *Ireland of the Welcomes*, since its first publication in 1952 and charts its evolution from literary journal to colour supplement. For Cronin, one of the most striking characteristics of the early writing was its literary quality achieved by of the engagement of acclaimed Irish writers such as Brendan Behan, Sean O'Faolain and Benedict Kiely. The critical stance adopted by these writers towards aspects of Irish cultural and political life did not in any way mar the tourist representation. Indeed, Cronin argues that it was precisely because of this that their writing possessed an enhanced accuracy and legitimacy. A number of identifiable discourses were present in the pages of the magazine in the early years. The Irish talent for talk was foregrounded, presenting the 'word' itself as a tourist attraction. In a country which did not boast a wealth of material culture 'sightseeing could give way to eavesdropping'. Egalitarianism was also identified in the offering of leisure pursuits such as sailing and horse-racing to tourists (typically lower-middle-class British visitors) which would have been regarded as élite pursuits at home. The potentially delicate relationship between tourist and native in a situation of obvious material inequality was reconciled by emphasising the non-material, in particular, the culture and nobility of the common people and thus allowing the 'debased physical realities to be subsumed into a more prestigious frame of reference'.

Cronin sees a number of changes in discourse since the early 1950s. The early more egalitarian discourses have given way to a 'Merchant–Ivory nostalgia' , an embracing of the Anglo-Irish tradition and an emphasis on 'Big House' tourism which is in line with the policy to attract high-spend tourists. Modernisation itself is not problematic. One response is to see it in terms of an improved delivery service to tourists, better quality of food, a greater variety of leisure activities and so on. And the other way is to 'create a history outside history'. This is achieved by a number of processes including the avoidance of any large-scale historical narratives, the fetishisation of place and the local and the representation of Ireland as a 'timeless arcadia' the province of fairytale and myth. While the discourses have changed, so too have the writers. The writing is now done mainly by freelance journalists and Cronin points to the irony of a situation in which literature is enlisted by the magazine in an era where the pen has been superseded by the 'microphone and notepad'.

Cinema emerged in the modern period as a powerful rival to photography's claims to capture elsewhere for the traveller. An important constituent group of tourists to Ireland over the years has been Irish-Americans returning to the land of their forebears and Stephanie Rains analyses the evidence of film to see what it tells us about the connection between the Irish-American diaspora and Ireland as a tourist destination for that diaspora. By the time tourism from the USA to Ireland began to emerge as a significant phenomenon, most of the US tourists were second-, third-, fourth-generation Irish-Americans who had had no direct, first-hand experience of Ireland prior to their visit. The images and impressions they had of Ireland would have been conveyed either through story or pictures. The primacy of visual and oral narratives helps to explain the marked difference in Irish tourist promotion films produced for the British and American markets. Whereas the former were largely concerned with presentation of place and provision of information, the latter were highly stylised with fictional characters, story lines and a variety of visual cues which pointed to the centrality of narrative in the Irish-American (re)appropriation of native place.

Although films like *The Quiet Man* have often been derided as expressing a quintessential Hollywood kitsch which has informed Irish-American touring practices, Rains argues for a more complex reading of the film and a more sensitive approach to the real dilemmas of a diasporic population returning to the land of original departure. In effect, *The Quiet Man* constantly points up the tension between diasporic imagination and Irish reality and underscores the very real difficulties in attempting a genuine 'homecoming'. In subsequent travelogues, there is a repeated counterpointing of the traditional and the modern not only to reassure the visiting tourist that the hired car will actually be there when they arrive in the premodern Arcadia but to enact or to anticipate the difficulties of the Irish-American tourist in dealing with time that has passed not only for his/her family but also for the country they left. Hence, the Irish-American tourist experience has to be radically reconsidered. Rather than treating it simply as the naive embrace of anti-modern romanticism, Rains shows how in the crucial area of filmic represention, there is a complex and subtle attempt to reconcile diasporic memory with the realities of a contemporary Ireland.

Justin Carville, for his part, explores the relationship between tourism and natural history in Ireland, with specific reference to photography. One of the dilemmas faced by the Victorian middle class was how to deal with leisure. Upper-class wastefulness and lower-class dissolution were both blamed on the perverse effects of free time. The importance of natural history was that it provided the middle classes with an opportunity to go touring but with the necessary alibi of scientific curiosity and self-improvement. Hence, the popularity of naturalists' field clubs in all the major Irish cities in the Victorian and Edwardian period. Conspicuous application and dedication would be the hallmarks of the Irish professional on tour. Photography, previously the domain of wealthy aristocrats, became more accessible in the Victorian period and was soon recruited to the cause of amateur natural history. The advantage of the camera over the pencil and paintbrush is that it would present the real unadorned, the photograph would be the picture as reality itself. In this respect, it was seen as radically different from the staged vignettes of tourist photography.

Carville shows, however, that the manner in which the boundaries between the conventions of 'picturesque' photography and 'scientific' photographic shots of the amateur naturalists were, in fact, remarkably fluid. Furthermore, the naturalists were not content just to take photographs of the flora, fauna or landscape. They repeatedly took photographs of themselves in the landscape, thereby affirming a cultural and visual mastery over a world that had previously been exclusively associated with the peasantry and the aristocracy. In analysing the work of William Lloyd Praeger and Robert T. Welch, Carville points to the importance of middle-class tourism and an associated visual culture in the social construction of nature in late 19th and early 20th century Ireland. The legacy of the amateur naturalists has proved to be enduring in that many tourist responses to and representations of the Irish landscape are still framed by the work of the erstwhile members of the socially ambitious Irish field clubs.

Tourism Policy

Approaches to tourism policy are frequently framed in terms of economic imperatives or short-term political pragmatism. Only too rarely are they related to broader societal questions. In the final section entitled 'Tourism Policy: Historical and Contemporary Issues', Spurgeon Thompson and Juliette Péchenart examine the fundamental connections between tourism policy and the very terms within which Ireland has been defined in two very different historical periods, the early 1920s and the late 1990s.

Spurgeon Thompson takes a critical look at tourism development in the early years of the Irish Free State. He examines, in particular, the activities of the Irish Tourist Association (ITA) founded in 1925 and the points of view expressed in the ITA journal, *Irish Travel*. Thompson sees Irish tourism in the period as the classic expression of a post-colonial élite dependent for patronage and favour on the former colonial power. Not only was Ireland heavily dependent on Britain for agricultural markets but the country also created a legacy of dependency in the tourism sector by its almost exclusive focus on the British market. In order for the project of attracting British tourists to succeed, it was important to sanitise, normalise and depoliticise representations of a country which only years earlier had been engaged in open warfare with the British state. It was this task that was embarked upon by the ITA in its publications and promotional campaigns.

Thompson shows how the staunchly pro-Free State political views of the ITA board members diverged radically from those of the ITA staff, all of whom were either former or still active members of the anti-treaty IRA. It was these staff members who would be responsible for producing much of the promotional and advertising literature on Ireland for the British market in the latter half of the 1920s. Notable in the early period was the reticence of ITA employees like C.S. (Todd) Andrews towards the whole tourism enterprise who saw it as the perpetuation of national flunkeydom. Dissenting views in the early years were not common, though, in the publication of Irish-language articles in *Irish Travel* and brief attempts to encourage Irish internal tourism, Thompson detects a move to frustrate a uniquely depend-ent position for tourism in the new state.

The breakdown of traditional distinctions between 'natives' and 'new-comers' is the concern of Juliette Péchenart's chapter in the context of non-Anglophone employees in the tourist sector. Recent expansion of the tourism sector has led to a skills shortage particularly in the hotel and catering areas which has resulted in the recruitment of workers from abroad starting a trend that is likely to continue. The former policy efforts regarding the acquisition of appropriate linguistic skills by Irish employees concentrated on teaching Irish employees languages such as French, Spanish, German and so on to enhance communication between hosts and guests. This has now been transformed into a concern with teaching non-Anglophone employees English in an attempt to facilitate communication between the two groups. Concern has been expressed about the lack of proper job training and sometimes low levels of competence in English and the absence of any tests of linguistic competence. In the light of these changes, Péchenart identifies a number of challenges for policy-makers: proper job training, linguistic training and testing of linguistic competence and the imparting of intercultural skills. The latter is regarded by Pechenart as crucial because of the importance of the personal encounter in service sectors such as tourism and the potentially detrimental effects of culturally inappropriate behaviour in such encounters. This is particularly true in a country like Ireland where traditionally tourist expectations include wel-coming and friendly behaviour and while Pechenart states there is some evidence to suggest that there is now some playing down of 'people' and more on 'scenery and landscape' as themes, friendliness is still considered to be an essential ingredient in the tourist package. In order to alleviate a general anxiety about a deterioration in the quality of interaction between tourists and host the changes must be dealt with in a positive and inclusive manner by putting appropriate training programmes in place for employ-ees in the tourist sector in an increasingly multilingual and multicultural Ireland.

The chapters in this volume demonstrate the fundamental relevance and importance of tourism in the construction of local, national and global identities. Rather than treating tourist phenomena in isolation, this book has sought to express the complex interplay of tourism with a wide range of social, economic, political and historical forces. There is no easy agreement between contributors in relation to the overall merits and demerits of tourism. And this is appropriate in that we are dealing with a complex and multifaceted phenomenon which necessitates eclectic and nuanced methodological approaches. A concern of the volume has not only been to focus on structure but also to give voice to the agents involved in tourism. In particular there is an emphasis on culture and identity as concepts which are constructed in the context of both continuous social interaction and the construction of meaning in everyday life.

References

Appadurai, A. (1996) *Modernity at Large: Cultural Dimensions of Globalization*. Minneapolis: University of Minnesota Press.

Breathnach, P. (ed.) (1994) *Irish Tourism Development*. Maynooth: Geographical Society of Ireland.

Brody, H. (1973) *Inishkillane: Change and Decline in the West of Ireland*. London: Allen Lane.

Buttimer, N., Rynne, C. and Guerin, H. (eds) (2000) *The Heritage of Ireland*. Cork: Collins Press.

Castells, M. (1996) *The Rise of the Network Society*. Oxford: Blackwell.

Cronin, M. and O'Connor, B. (2000) From Gombeen to Gubeen: Tourism, identity and class in Ireland, 1949–99. In R. Ryan (ed.) *Writing in the Irish Republic: Literature, Culture, Politics 1949–1999* (pp. 165–84). London: Macmillan.

Deegan, J. and Dineen, D. (1997) *Tourism Policy and Performance: The Irish Experience*. London: International Thomson Business Press.

Gleick, J. (1999) *Faster: The Acceleration of Just About Everything*. London: Little Brown and Company.

Lash, S. and Urry, J. (1994) *The Economies of Signs and Space*. London. Sage.

McSharry, R. (2000) *The Making of the Celtic Tiger: The Inside Story of Ireland's Boom Economy*. Cork: Mercier Press.

Robertson, R. (1992) *Globalization: Social Theory and Global Culture*. London: Sage.

Urry, J. (1990) *The Tourist Gaze: Leisure and Travel in Contemporary Societies*.

Part 1

Changing Places: The Local and the Global in Tourist Communities

Chapter 1

'If It Wasn't for the Tourists We Wouldn't Have an Audience': The Case of Tourism and Traditional Music in North Mayo

MOYA KNEAFSEY

Introduction

Traditional music is often used as an important, if contested, signifier of Irish national identity. For instance, Ireland is one of the only countries in the world to have a musical instrument, namely the harp, as its national symbol (Vallely, 1999). Contemporary tourism images, appearing in brochures, postcards and books, reinforce the association of Ireland with traditional music and dance and encourage tourists to expect at least some exposure to the sounds of the nation that produced *Riverdance*. This expectation is enhanced through television travel programmes about Ireland that inevitably portray mountains, lakes and empty beaches accompanied by the wistful strains of the pipes or whistle and show musicians playing in a cosy local bar, pints of Guinness prominently displayed.

Not only are visitor numbers to Ireland increasing at a rapid rate, with a massive 7.1 million tourist arrivals predicted by 2003 (Bord Fáilte, 1998) but the audience for various forms of recorded 'Irish music' is also growing (Thornton, 2000). There has also been a huge increase in the number of summer schools and festivals offering classes and competitions in a wide variety of instruments, singing styles and dance, as well as lectures, recitals and pub music sessions. One of Dublin's newest tourist attractions is Ceol,[1] described as an 'interactive Irish music encounter' and 'a celebration of a living tradition'. Similarly, the Dublin musical pub crawl has proved highly popular, with tickets being sold to approximately 6–7000 tourists a year (Quinn, 1996). Not only does traditional music, therefore, act as a general backdrop to various representations of Ireland but there is evidence to suggest that significant numbers of people include listening to or playing traditional music[2] within their holiday activities.

Despite the growth of tourism in Ireland, the evident interest in traditional music on the part of tourists and the gradual recognition that music can be a valuable component of the Irish tourism product, little research has been published on the relationship between tourism and traditional music. Indeed, this may be indicative of a more general 'absence of critical discussion' of the subject of tourism in Ireland (O'Connor & Cronin, 1993). Yet the interface between tourism and traditional music raises a whole series of questions regarding the impacts and sustainability of cultural commodification, the ways in which visitors and local people construct meanings of authenticity and tradition and the ways in which tourism influences shifting geographies of musical production and consumption. My aim in this chapter, therefore, is to present an introductory discussion of some of these issues through a focus on just one aspect of the traditional music–tourism relationship, the pub 'session'. This is probably the setting in which most visitors to Ireland consume the performance of live traditional music and it is an interesting cultural practice to examine in that it retains a sense of spontaneity and mystique which distinguishes it from many contemporary forms of entertainment. The discussion is based on fieldwork undertaken in North Mayo and should be seen as an attempt to, first, prompt further research on this rather neglected topic and, second, contribute to the development of a theoretically-informed body of work investigating the sociocultural and economic influences of tourism in Ireland more generally. In order to do this, I draw on notions of 'culturalisation', commodification and recent theories of the construction of musical meanings. Using these ideas, I suggest that during the summer season, *symbiotic relationships* between musicians, tourists and publicans are constitutive of the meanings attached to the pub sessions held in North Mayo. However, the summer session is gradually being re-defined as a 'gig' and these delicate relationships of symbiosis may be replaced by *formalised relationships* between 'performers' and 'audience'. This increased formalisation, however, does not necessarily indicate the complete commodification of this cultural practice. Rather, it is necessary to recognise that some of the socio-musical meanings that are currently attached to the session by locals, publicans and musicians enable it to 'defy' or evade commodification in any consistent sense.

The Traditional Music and Tourism Interface: Conceptualising Complexity

Traditional music is the older dance music and song in Ireland. According to the Irish Traditional Music Archive (Vallely, 1999: 403) it is, above all, the music of a living popular tradition. It incorporates a large body of material from the past but this does not form a static repertory – rather it is always changing through shedding material, the re-introduction of neglected items and the composition of new items. Change, however, is slow and takes place within generally accepted principles. It is essentially oral in character in that song and instrumental music have been carried in memory – largely independent of writing and print. Even today, with more printed music available, most musicians learn through imitating more experienced performers. Within this context, the session functions as an important opportunity for musicians to meet and exchange tunes. Although it may be popularly perceived as a very old and thus 'authentic' cultural practice, playing together seems to have happened first amongst emigrant musicians in early 20th century America. Pubs generally became an important feature of Irish social life only after the Second World War and from the late 1940s, emigrants imported the idea of sessions from Irish pubs and clubs in England. The session began as a purely amateur event but around the mid-1970s publicans began to pay one or two musicians to turn up on a regular night. It is estimated that there are now more than 1500 pub sessions weekly, many in some way commercial, with half of them running throughout the year (Vallely, 1999).

Whilst research has been conducted into the revival of local festivals (Aldskogius, 1993; Boissevain, 1992; Ekman, 1999), relatively little work has focused specifically on the use of music as a tourist attraction. In the case of Ireland, Quinn (1996: 393) has conducted preliminary work on blues, arts and opera festivals, but affirms that it is '[A] difficult task, and one which requires extensive further research attention, understanding the nature of the music–tourism relationship, and in particular, under-standing how music is affected in the process of tourism consumption'. The conceptualisation of the relationship between tourism and traditional music presents a considerable challenge, not least because both practices can be theorised from a multitude of perspectives drawing from a variety of disciplines including tourism studies, cultural studies, sociology, geog-raphy, anthropology, ethnomusicology and popular music studies. Furthermore, as Lau (1998: 116) argues, 'we must recognise from the outset that a universal theory of tourism is highly impractical and virtually impossible because the nature and mode of interaction between society and tourism varies significantly from place to place'. He continues that the study of tourism should be grounded in the 'context and specificities dictated by particular social and historical conditions'. Recognising this, I propose some initial conceptual foundations upon which an understand-ing of the relationship between tourism and traditional music in just one place in Ireland might be constructed. I suggest that starting points can be found in the literature concerning cultural tourism, cultural commodification and the construction of musical meanings.

The 'Culturalisation' of Touristic Practices and the 'Commodification' of Cultural Practices

A useful point of departure is provided by Rojek and Urry (1999), whose underlying aim is to demonstrate that tourism is a cultural practice and that tourism and culture hugely overlap. For instance, they note the increased 'culturalisation' of tourist practices, which is most obviously seen in the growth of 'cultural tourism'. In Ireland, cultural tourism has been particularly developed in the form of heritage attractions, interpretive centres, parks and monuments (O'Donnchadha & O'Connor, 1996). However, traditional music is now being recognised as an important part of the tourism product and a recent report (Ó Murchú, 1999) recommends a comprehensive assessment of the potential of Irish traditional music, song and dance in cultural tourism. Interestingly, July 2000 saw the re-introduction of 'Seisiún', a nationwide scheme of traditional music and dance, for the first time in over a decade. Organised by Comhaltas Ceoltóirí Éireann, the aim of Seisiún is to help visitors to find the 'hidden Ireland' by providing a 'music trail' of 'native entertainment' in specified locations across the country over a seven-week summer period.

The current chapter is concerned with the following question: What are the impacts of the increased 'culturalisation' of touristic practices upon existing cultural practices? This question is usually framed in terms of debate over the commodification of culture and resulting issues of authenticity, meaning and ownership. Craik (1997) for instance, asks whether culture has merely become a convenient marketing ploy or whether a fundamental change in the nature of tourism has occurred. Her central argument is that any modification of the culture of tourism is only short term. Drawing on the work of Silberberg (1995), she casts doubt on the existence of many 'true' cultural tourists and suggests that, in fact, a significant number of tourists are actually 'culture-proof'. Furthermore, cultural tourism incurs disbenefits that will undermine rather than enhance recent governmental and institutional commitments to cultural development. One of the reasons for this is that the cultural experiences offered by tourism are consumed in terms of prior knowledge, expectations, fantasies and mythologies *'generated in the tourist's origin culture* rather than *by the cultural offerings of the destination'* (Craik, 1997: 118; emphasis in original). In short, she implies that cultural tourism developments can threaten longer-term cultural integrity. There is a sense that market values subsume everything and local people risk losing the 'authentic meanings' of their culture by performing for outsiders.

Countering this view, some more recent local-level studies demonstrate that issues of meaning, ownership and power relations are important in discerning whether cultural integrity – however this may be defined – is maintained. Lau (1998), for instance, demonstrates that in the Chinese context it is important to examine the different ways of understanding the term 'traditional'. To Chinese musicians the term is applied to any music that has existed for a period of time and this is reflected in concert-playing styles and repertoire. This is in contrast to western connotations of 'authentic', 'pure' and 'ancient.' Lau suggests that the majority of tourists do not know about this difference in emphasis or its implications for performance. Rees (1998), however, problematises this assumption by pointing to the existence of tourists dismayed by professional troupes and in search of more 'traditionalist' concerts. Nevertheless, from the Chinese perspective, control over the content of cultural production remains firmly with the hosts. Importantly, Lau also highlights the ways in which tourist performances are intertwined within the Chinese state's perception of post-Mao nationhood and modernity and local perceptions of identity. Lau's focus on contextualising tourism within the 'social and historical moment' is important, although the resulting account has a structuralist flavour, whereby performers are conceptualised as 'actors' or 'players' in the 'show whose script is written in the narrative of society'. There is a sense that performances are 'determined' and 'pre-disposed' by the political economic and social forces at work at national and global levels. I hope to develop a more fluid interpretation whereby the meanings of cultural productions are seen as being continually constructed and contested through processes mediated by individuals and institutions operating at multiple geographic scales. The key strength of Lau's work is his attention to the meanings that are attributed to music by performers and I argue that this provides a clue to understanding the impact of the 'culturalisation' of tourism in the sphere of Irish traditional music. More specifically, it is necessary to focus on how musical meanings are constructed through the complex interplay of tourists, musicians, publicans and local residents.

The Construction of Musical Meanings

Some powerful theoretical insights into this process are provided by Revill's (1998) work on hybridity, identity and networks of musical meaning. He draws on Actor–Network Theory to argue that 'musical meaning is produced through a cultural geography consisting of heterogeneous networks of practices, institutions and artifacts that together make music at once an imagined and a material entity' (p. 198). Specifically, he refers to Michael Callon's thesis that all human and nonhuman entities are potential actors, which have 'the capacity to make connections with others, thereby producing networks of social meaning' (p. 201). Revill proposes that this approach is useful for the study of music because 'it enables the diverse elements of musical communication – from patterns of sound and embodied gestures, to technical skill in instrumental virtuosity or dance, to written scores, to theoretical treatises, to recordings of performances – to be considered together as mutually constitutive of musical meaning' (p. 202). Music is thus always both at once a social and a technical activity. Revill suggests that one of the most controversial aspects of Callon's work – the idea that all intermediaries, human or non-human, have agency – is best interpreted as 'a set of potentialities that reside in the nature of the object rather than any form of self-reflexive action' (p. 211). This can be described as 'a tendency towards multivalency that allows the artifact . . . to resist or escape definition within any particular network'. This relates most closely to the quality of music, which, in Said's words, allows it to 'travel, cross over, drift from place to place in a society, even though many institutions and orthodoxies have sought to confine it' (cited by Revill, 1998: 211). This point can be illustrated through reference to the contested history of traditional music in Ireland. Different actors have struggled to attach different meanings to a cultural practice which has enormous mobility. For instance, to many clergy in the early decades of the 20th century, it was seen as an accessory to immoral social behaviour. At the same time, some politicians associated it with subversive political activities such as raising funds for the IRA. They combined to pass the Public Dance Halls Act of 1935, which introduced strict licensing controls which, according to critics, almost resulted in the eradication of music and dance in some areas. At the same time, traditional music also faced competition from fashionable new music imported from America and England. In contrast to these modern, urban cultural practices, traditional music was denigrated by many as the expression of unsophisticated and primitive country folk (Vallely, 1999: xv). Nevertheless, the 1960s era of protest songs and civil rights movements saw a revival of interest in traditional music. This, in itself, prompted another battle for definition, as musicians tried to distinguish 'authentic' Irish music from popular folk song (e.g. Bob Dylan), Irish 'ballad groups' and political ballads. More recently, traditional Irish music has experienced another surge in popularity, this time re-defined in the context of a new, highly commercialised 'Celtic craze', which began in the late 1980s (Hale & Payton, 2000).

There is thus a long and complex history of struggles to define, defend or control the meaning of 'traditional music'. This history illustrates the

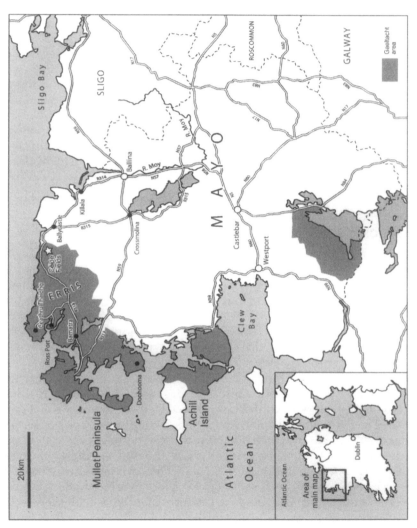

Figure 1.1 The study region of north Mayo

'ability of music to escape or defy the meanings assigned to it' (Revill, 1998: 212). The point is that any consideration of what happens to traditional music when it is juxtaposed with tourism must take into account the intricate relationships through which musical meanings are (de/re)constructed. In order to open up these complex issues in relation to some empirical research findings, I now turn to the case of traditional music sessions in North Mayo. For the purposes of this research, I decided to focus on the three coastal towns of Ballycastle, Killala and Ballina (see Figure 1.1). This was partly dictated by the availability of sessions but it also allowed me to build upon qualitative research already conducted on aspects of tourism, culture change and identity in North Mayo (Kneafsey, 1998, 2000). Crucially, it enabled me to draw on experiences and knowledge gathered over a decade of playing in sessions during fieldtrips and holidays to the area. The main research techniques were participant observation at sessions during the summer of 2000, plus qualitative interviews with musicians, publicans and tourists.

Introducing North Mayo: Tourism and Musical Practices

County Mayo as a whole is firmly located, both geographically and symbolically, in the West of Ireland. This region has, over time, been portrayed as a repository of national identity (Nash, 1993), the heartland of linguistic and cultural traditions. According to Bord Fáilte statistics, the county received 288,000 out of a total of 1,071,000 overseas tourists to the West Region (covering Counties Galway, Mayo, Roscommon) in 1998. It is estimated that this generated IR£50 million in revenue against a total of IR£236.6 million for the West Region as a whole (Bord Fáilte, 1999). Although tourism development in County Mayo has concentrated around the hotspots of Westport and Achill, there has been a discernible growth in the number of visitors to North Mayo, especially to the towns of Killala and Ballina. The latter, in particular, now offers an improved range of accommodation facilities and both towns also host heritage days at which traditional music features prominently. The situation is different in areas further West. Despite the flagship Céide Fields Visitor Centre, which in 1998 received 40,104 visitors (Tourism Development International, 2000), the scenic stretch from Ballycastle to Ceathru Thaidhg provides few facilities for tourists and remains relatively inaccessible. The area suffers from a lack of adequate basic infrastructure such as good roads, consistent water supplies and reliable waste treatment facilities. Although the county population is becoming increasingly urbanised, North Mayo is still a predominantly agricultural and rural area, which supports small and comparatively isolated communities, including those in the fragile Erris

Gaeltacht. In fact, as urbanisation proceeds at an ever faster rate around the main population centres, these areas seem increasingly marginalised in comparison. According to census figures, the number of people employed in agriculture, farming and fishing has fallen substantially from 13,206 in 1981 to 7963 in 1996. Unfortunately the census does not show numbers employed in tourism but the estimated 32,090 employed in tourism in the West Region gives some idea of the relative importance of the industry (Tourism Development International, 2000).

The Music and Musicians of North Mayo

Although never as renowned as the East Mayo–Sligo border area, with its well-documented tradition of fiddle and flute-playing, nor the more recently famous town of Westport, North Mayo was once well known for its melodeon players. Up until the 1930s traditional music was strong in Mayo but then a number of factors militated against it, as in other areas of Ireland. These included the Dance Halls Act (Vallely, 1999), the growth of show bands and emigration. With 111,524 inhabitants in 1996, the county has never recovered its pre-famine population of 388,887 in 1841. The impact of mass emigration on the musical life of small rural communities cannot be underestimated – most of the noted Mayo musicians of the early 20th century emigrated to America or England. This long history of emigration has an important 'feedback' effect, in that many visitors to the county are, in fact, 'exiles' returning home. Many of them are of a generation that left the region at a time when the native culture, including the Irish language and music, was often associated with backwardness and failure. Both were largely abandoned in favour of the English language and American country and western music. The returning exiles have not, therefore, generated a great demand for traditional music, which may help to explain why it has been relatively slow to reassert itself in some places.

This said, small groups of musicians did get together to keep the tradition going. In the absence of large numbers of tourists, much depended on finding publicans who shared a love of the music. In the early 1980s, sessions emerged (now ceased) in the small village of Rossport in what is probably the last mainly Irish-speaking pub in North Mayo. The sessions were attended mainly by older musicians from Ceathru Thaidhg, Rossport, Doohooma and Barnatra. At about the same time, sessions were encouraged by a couple of publicans 30 miles up the coast in Killala. Talented young accordion players from the village met up with musical families from the nearby coastal townland of Lacken. More recently, new traditional music venues have been established in Ballina since the town hosted the Fleadh (a festival of Irish music) in 1997 and 1998. Many of the younger players are now internationally demanded for live performances and recordings. They had emerged as tourism slowly began to grow in the area and the interest in Irish music became a world-wide phenomenon. Suddenly these young musicians, barely in their twenties, were in demand at the Paris Hilton on St Patrick's night or found themselves touring America and the Far East. As Stokes (1994) remarks, 'musicians often live in conspicuously translocal cultural worlds' and it is notable that the majority of musicians encountered during the research had spent long periods of time living and working outside Mayo. Indeed, at times, there was hardly a musician left because many of the younger ones left to complete their third level education.

Looking back over a period of ten years or so, it is possible to identify a shifting core of about ten established musicians who have kept sessions going in the study area. These include several accordion players, a piper, a couple of flute players, a banjo player, a fiddle player and a couple of singers/guitarists. By established musicians, I mean those who play in regular sessions more or less throughout the year in the study area and who are paid to play (approximately €35–51 a night), at least during the summer. The personnel within this core may vary from month to month, as individuals leave periodically to play in festivals and concerts and teach at summer schools throughout the world. However, most of these core players eventually return to the locality where their main source of income is to be found. Their occupations include school teacher, fisherman, carpenter, electrician and plasterer. There is a striking lack of female players active in pub sessions, although further research is required to establish why this is so. Of these musicians, only one could be described as truly professional, in that he makes his living from teaching, performing and playing and, unusually, has a higher education qualification in music. In fact, he has recently secured a contract with Riverdance and it seems likely that his music will take him away from the locality in the near future.

In addition to this core of established musicians, there is another layer of locally based but more transient musicians. This includes, for example, the group of six or so post-Leaving Certificate students, including a predominance of young women, who established a session in one of the Ballycastle bars during the summer of 2000. As the landlord noted sadly though, there was every chance that they would 'disappear to the four corners of the world', as many previous players had done. It also includes visiting musicians, friends and relatives, who stay in the area for anything from one night to a period of weeks, plus local residents who play in sessions sporadically, largely because work and family commitments prevent them from playing more often. There is also a number of family groups consisting of school-age musicians who spend the summer playing gigs, often under the management of their parents. When all these additional layers are added, the number of musicians active in some way in the pub session environment rises to almost 40 and it must be remembered that this is just within the area a single researcher was capable of covering effectively during a five-week period. Although this may seem like a lot, local publicans complained of a shortage of regular and committed musicians. As one Ballina publican said, 'Really and truly it's very hard to pick and choose. You have to take what you can get to a certain extent.' Similarly a publican from Ballycastle pointed out: 'There's not that many musicians and they're well sought after'. The core musicians may play up to five nights a week in venues around North Mayo and beyond. By mid-season many of them are already 'jaded' and evidently finding it difficult to sustain their creative momentum. They usually welcome visiting players who will help inspire them with new tunes and songs.

Tourists and Musicians: A Symbiotic Relationship

As stated earlier, this chapter is concerned with the impacts of tourism 'culturalisation' on cultural practices. More specifically, I am interested in how tourism may be affecting the practice of traditional music within the context of the session. In the case of North Mayo, I suggest that the relationship between musicians and tourists can currently be described as one of symbiosis. A striking theme to emerge consistently from interviews and observations was that tourists provide a supportive audience for musicians. Indeed, out of 32 randomly selected visitors, 60% wanted to hear or play traditional music as a prime part of their visit. Most of the others were more 'culture-proof' individuals who thought it would be 'nice' but not essential. Only two people positively did not want to hear traditional music, these being an Irish couple who said 'In fact, if we saw it we'd avoid it' and did not wish to be interviewed. This part of the research was very exploratory but tourist interest in traditional music was confirmed by observations at sessions and conversations with publicans and musicians. In some instances, almost the entire audience was composed of visitors. The situation was captured by one established local musician who, half-jokingly, suggested that 'if it wasn't for the tourists we wouldn't have an audience'.

The presence of the tourists is given increased importance by the relative absence of consistent local interest in traditional music. As one Killala publican said, apart from a few local 'diehards', traditional music appeals to 'foreigners mostly'. Another respondent, this time a bar manager in Ballina, stated that 'it appeals, in my opinion, more to visitors than it does to Irish people themselves . . . mainly Americans – and English people coming back home'. Two young musicians, regular players in Killala, one night confirmed that local people are 'worse' than the tourists: 'The tourists come in and actually show interest in your music; the locals come in and in the majority of cases they turn their back. They turn their back on you.' As we sat in the bar and looked around us, one of the musicians said, 'You can see all the people that was listening to us tonight are not Irish'. Two other musicians who live in the Erris Gaeltacht related a story about their unsuccessful attempt to play traditional music in one of the larger towns in Erris, where the people 'hate' the music. They also talked about their plans to get a session going in their nearest pub. They were a little apprehensive about how the locals would receive them but wanted to try because the lack of a session close to home means that they currently have to make a round trip of 50 miles to play in Killala.

Quite why local attitudes towards traditional music are so antipathetic is a question which requires more research. Various opinions were expressed about this during interviews, although it must be said that respondents usually found it difficult to explain. According to some musicians, people in some areas just are 'not musical' and there is not much to be done about that. Other observers thought it could be a case of local people 'taking it for granted' or 'familiarity breeding contempt'. It may also be a sort of 'cultural hangover' from the time when Irish traditional music and language were undermined through economic and social marginalisation and years of emigration. *Riverdance* may have popularised Irish music and dance across the world but the associations with an old and previously denigrated cultural heritage may persist in certain rural areas. Interestingly, it is in the more wealthy urban centres that traditional music is currently more widely played. Sessions in small rural communities are few and far between, especially in the Erris Gaeltacht.

To summarise, what appears to be happening is that tourists and musicians are currently existing in a symbiotic relationship. This confirms Lau's (1998: 132) observation that 'tourism and its impact can no longer be categorically interpreted as a form of exploitation; rather, they assume the role of a transnational network of exchanges in which the locals and the tourists are directly and indirectly fulfilling each other's needs'. The tourists, through their sheer physical presence, provide support and encouragement for the musicians. For their part, the musicians provide a seemingly authentic cultural experience for the tourists. This relationship assumes particular importance within the context of relationships between musicians and locals which, in some cases, are ones of antibiosis. However, the tourist–musician symbiosis shows signs of changing. Ironically, the changes are occurring largely *because* of the way in which tourists consume the session, as shown in the following section.

'There's No Sessions Any More, Only Gigs': From 'Playing' to 'Performing'

Despite the fact that core musicians usually receive payment for playing, they try to retain the idealised notion of the session as the chance for 'a few tunes' and 'a bit of craic'. The session is an inherently social event and is about more than simply listening to or playing music. Other sounds are also constitutive of the session – the instruments being tuned and warmed up, fragments of half-remembered tunes, the conversations between musicians, the shouts, laughter and talk drifting in from the spaces beyond that in which the musicians and listeners share their attention to music. Moreover, not only is this an aural experience, it is also intensely visual and sensual in other ways. For instance, the expressions on the musicians' faces as they concentrate on their playing, the smell of cigarettes, the taste and effects of alcohol, the bodily presence of other people are all integral to the actual experience of the session. To link back to Revill's work, musical meanings are thus constituted by heterogeneous combinations of human and non-human entities and they are also perceived through a variety of senses.

A really good session requires not only good musicians and a good rapport between them but it also needs the presence of listeners who possess appropriate social and musical knowledge. As Revill (1998: 200) suggests, 'rather than trying to understand musical meaning in terms of more or less fixed semiotic systems, we should look to the inherently social qualities of music as the key to understanding musical meaning'. Socially and musically knowledgeable listeners can distinguish when it is necessary to turn their full concentration on the music and when it is enough to let the music slip into the background. They know when to offer either loud encouragement or respectful silence. They know the musicians and they know the tunes, airs or songs in which they excel. These listeners do not really conform to conventional understandings of an 'audience' in the sense that they do not adopt a formal or spectatorial relationship with the musicians. Rather, both listeners and musicians are engaged in a creative process, whereby the shape and meaning of the music is negotiated through inter-personal, mutually appreciative relationships, the ultimate goal being the achievement of a 'mighty session'.

Although there is no doubt that tourists present an appreciative audience, they do not usually have the social and musical knowledge required to appreciate the music in the way that the musicians would like. As one tourist said, 'All the tunes sound the same'. The musicians recognise this. In the words of a young accordion player, tourists 'don't know the difference' between tunes, and they think traditional music is Enya, The

Pogues, Hot House Flowers and Danny Boy – the 'haunting sounds' and 'diddle-de-oy-zone'. It irritates him when tourists ask him to play Danny Boy and he will usually reply that he does not know that one and then play something else. He hoped that one day a new generation of tourists would emerge who would be able to ask him to play 'the Roscommon Reel or a couple of Donal Lunny or Frankie Gavin tunes'. (Interestingly, Donal Lunny is often not regarded as a strictly 'traditional musician'. This highlights the contested constructions of the term 'traditional' to be found among musicians as well as audiences.) Until that day, however, tourists who lack the socio-musical knowledge which would enable them to respond emotionally and behaviourally in the way that musicians would prefer, resort to consuming the session largely through the medium of 'the gaze'. This, in turn, allows the tourists to position themselves as 'audience' and is observable in the way they sit around the musicians, watching very closely and quietly, often taking pictures or video-taping events and clapping at the end of each set of tunes. They often do not participate fully in the other sensorial aspects of the session such as drinking, smoking and talking. As one musician joked, 'They'll buy you a drink and then sit around sharing a coffee'. It is likely that for the majority of tourists, the role of audience is familiar, being the one they most commonly adopt in their consumption of music in their own lives. Craik's (1997) conviction that tourists consume culture in terms of knowledge and expectations *generated in their own origin culture* appears to be correct in most cases. Yet many musicians are not comfortable with the role of 'performer'. Sometimes, the heaviness of 'the gaze' is just too much. One night in Killala, a tourist video-recorded the entire evening – about three hours of music. A couple of days later, in another bar, one of the older musicians started complaining about that tourist with the video, joking that you 'couldn't blow your nose!'. Another said of the same session that it is 'more like a concert now'.

Ironically, therefore, it seems that although the spontaneity and informality of the session probably attract tourists, their tendency to *watch* the musicians (often quite intently) and offer applause at the end of each set of tunes begins to turn the event into a 'performance'. This inevitably becomes more formalised than a group of musicians simply gathering to 'have a few tunes'. At this point it is important to emphasise the difference between 'playing' and 'performing.' The majority of musicians perceive themselves as doing the former rather than the latter and, indeed, few of them have any particular training in performance skills. Thus, they do not identify themselves as performers, yet they do require people to listen. So although musicians may sometimes be rather disparaging of those tourists who evidently have little knowledge of the music, they do need their physical presence in order to create the right atmosphere.

Publicans who recognise that traditional music can attract tourists into their bars are also encouraging the transition towards 'performance'. The newer gigs tend to be held where the more commercially minded of these publicans are trying to establish more formalised and regularised entertainment for the visitors. In some cases they know little and care less about the music itself. For instance, one bar manager in Ballina admitted that he is not 'fussed' about the music. As he bluntly stated: 'Well it's all economics at the end of the day. They [i.e. the musicians] have to be paid, we have to get the punters in. If they're not there, we can't afford to pay.' Another manager who started traditional music in order to 'busy the pub up' described himself as 'not a major traditional fan', especially 'the really heavy traditional music'. He also felt that consumers do not like the 'pure traditionalist' music and that 'you have to make it appealing, like Riverdance' so that people would 'sit down and have the craic'. Some of the bands he had tried before were 'too traditional' but the family group he had just taken on were more suitable. They played standard sets of well-known tunes, interspersed with popular pub songs such as Wild Rover, Whisky in the Jar etc. However, he had no illusions about what it takes to keep the music going: 'If it fits in and does well, we'll keep it up. If it doesn't we might try something else, y'know. That's the nature of the game.'

Thus music in these cases is constructed as a commodity, as a 'thing which can be exchanged for money on a systematic basis' (Lovering, 1998: 32). If it does not sell, it will no longer be produced. This construction of musical meaning tends to converge with the touristic tendency to regard the music as a performance. These changes are so pervasive that one musician lamented: 'There's no sessions anymore, only gigs'. He was making a clear distinction between the spontaneous, participatory, socio-musical experience of the session and the commercialised, performance orientation of the gig. This leads to the final issue that I wish to consider, namely the question of whether the session has, as this comment seems to suggest, become a commodified cultural event. In the following section, I tentatively suggest that the nature of the musical meanings that are attached to, and constructed through, the session may enable it to resist or defy commodification.

Defying Commodification?

So far, I have argued that the symbiotic relationship between tourists and musicians is being overlain by more formalised relationships between 'performers' and 'audience'. Yet, whilst this may be so during the summer months, this does not necessarily mean that the session is being commodified. What does appear to be happening is that a distinction is emerging between 'sessions' and 'gigs'. The latter correspond more closely to the notion of a commodity and are emerging mainly in bars in the larger urban settlement of Ballina. The musicians who play gigs tend to be younger in age and are often family groups. These gigs co-exist with sessions that retain characteristics which defy commodification. Three observations suggest that the sessions are not yet commodified. First, one of the engines that usually drives commodification is the desire to make profit. Yet for the musicians, financial gain is rarely the main motivation for playing in sessions and there is no direct monetary relationship between musicians and tourists. For the publicans, profit-making is, of course, a general motive but the sessions are not regarded as highly lucrative. As one longstanding host of sessions gruffly put it, 'It's not really viable. But I do it.' Some of the publicans cited non-commercial reasons for hosting traditional music. For instance, a Ballycastle publican recognised that although music is 'good for tourism', it is also necessary to encourage the younger musicians to play: 'If I don't give them a chance to play – if they don't start playing somewhere and get encouragement they'll never get off the ground you know?' Another publican, this time in Ballina, pointed out that the music is 'very important. Summer time and winter time, all year round. It's very important. For our kids to see and hear it. And to keep the tradition going.' Amongst these respondents there was a sense of responsibility to the tradition, a sense that their role was to encourage the younger people in particular to take an interest.

Second, as Lovering (1998: 34) notes in reference to the music industry, commodification is dependent on public systems of regulation – 'markets will only work if they are framed by laws, by routinised behaviours and by industry "technology standards".' Such considerations do not apply to the session. For example, there is little regulation in terms of the professionalisation of musicians. Publicans find out about musicians through word of mouth and often face 'headaches' and 'heartache' in trying to secure regular and timely attendance. Moreover, musicians are often contemptuous of the idea that sessions should start a little earlier in order to conform to visitors' preferences. Publicans also have to deal with squabbles between musicians who fall out over differences in style and approach. As one publican said, she has a 'love–hate' relationship with the musicians. Another rather embittered publican felt that there is a lot of 'snobbery' amongst musicians, not only towards other musicians but also towards the listeners. He criticised the musicians who 'don't entertain', but just want to sit and play, making no concession to the consumers, without whom the session would not exist. Moreover, his attempts to encourage the musicians to engage with their audience were rebuffed. His comments were considered to be an unacceptable encroachment on the musicians' autonomy. From the musicians' point of view, relationships with publicans are often just as informal. For instance, the question of money is often shrouded in mystery. As one older musician described,

> The publicans pay them fees at the end of the night and it's a fee that is never negotiated. The publican gives them a certain sum, the musicians don't even look at it, put it in their pockets and they won't look at it 'til they go home. Maybe not then either, maybe the first time they want to buy a pint.

There is thus a definite sense in which both publicans and musicians seek to resist moves to regularise and formalise the session. The sessions which last longest in one place are those which are founded upon friendships between musicians and publicans and personal preferences for certain venues and 'the crowd that's in it'.

Third, Lovering also suggests that to be a commodity – something that is exchanged for money on a systematic basis – individual musical constructions must be capable of being parcelled up in ways that allow mass production and mass sale. Such a description cannot (yet) be applied to the sessions in North Mayo, which are not mass produced or mass consumed. Moreover, each is a unique, unrepeatable and unpredictable event and retains social meanings that are at odds with capitalist constructions of the commodity. These meanings, in effect, subvert the forces of commodification. Drawing on Revill's ideas, it can be argued that the session is thus able to evade incorporation into regularised, formal relations of production and consumption. Indeed, 'Seisiún', the scheme mentioned earlier, is the musical construct, which most closely meets the criteria of a commodity. It presents a regularised, structured and choreographed performance, which starts at a specified time and for which an entrance fee is charged. As such, it is quite different to many of the sessions which occur in North Mayo.

Conclusions

This chapter has been concerned with the relationship between tourism and traditional music. More specifically, I have attempted to examine how one musical practice, the session, responds to touristic impulses towards commodification. On the basis of fieldwork, I have suggested that current symbiotic relationships between tourists and musicians are being replaced with more formalised relationships between 'audience' and 'performers' and the move towards 'gigs' as opposed to 'sessions'. However, the trend towards gigs does not necessarily replace the sessions, which retain meanings that defy commodification. At this point, it must be stressed that the research presented here is specific to a particular sub-regional context and it is likely that different relationships exist between tourists and music in different places. For example, the situation in North Mayo differs from that of music spaces such as Doolin or Galway city, where the numbers of tourists are greater and music has become more highly commodified. As such, there is a need to develop a more detailed understanding of the relationship between tourism and changing geographies of musical production and consumption as they are played out across different sociocultural and economic terrains.

Whilst I have begun to identify some of the ways in which musical meanings are constructed through the session, the research has also raised questions which require more qualitative, longitudinal investigation. For instance, the tourists' voices have remained comparatively quiet in the account presented here. I have focused mainly on the effects of tourism upon musical meanings and practices but what are the effects of these meanings and practices upon tourists? The participants in this research were selected at random, with the intention of gaining a preliminary idea of the extent of tourist interest in traditional music, their success in accessing music and their perceptions of it. More systematic research is needed to find out how tourists' responses differ in relation to age, gender, nationality, ethnicity and so on. How do tourists construct meanings of tradition and authenticity in relation to music? The term 'tourist' itself is something of a generalisation, particularly within the Mayo context, where many 'tourists' are also 'exiles' or their descendants, returning to their roots. How do these distinctions influence the ways in which visitors relate to traditional music and how do they help to shape musical practices and performances?

Finally, one of the most intriguing areas for further research is the matter of local attitudes. Although I have demonstrated that tourists are perceived as the most appreciative audience for traditional music in the summer and that, in some cases, locals will actively snub traditional musicians, this is not to say that there is no local support *at all*. After all, sessions do continue when the tourists are no longer present, although they are not as numerous. There are also instances when locals offer exactly the kind of support that musicians thrive on. By way of illustration, during the Ballina Heritage Day (July 2000), there was an afternoon session at which a crowd of 'country people'[3] gathered around the musicians. They obviously knew the tunes and whooped, shouted, clapped and stamped as the music changed tempo and key. The musicians took heart from the encouragement and played with ever more energy. The tourists stood around the edge of the circle, gazing in, trying to take photographs between the heads of the locals pressing in around the musicians. Was this a glimmer of an appreciation of traditional music and musicians that often seems to lie hidden behind a veil of antipathy and neglect? Moreover, is it correct to characterise these attitudes in this way? An alternative reading of the situation might suggest that dominant local responses to traditional music could be described in terms of 'embarassment' about a twee, touristic version of Irishness which is plainly at odds with the daily lived experiences of many inhabitants. Or, is it a case of tourists unwittingly appropriating Irish music for their own purposes and effectively excluding local residents from participating in their own cultural practices? This seems unlikely, given the decline of traditional music in Mayo during the 20th century and the fact that its revival has coincided with the growth of tourism over the last two decades.

These are questions for further detailed research but it seems clear that spatially-embedded power relations between musicians, tourists and locals are of fundamental importance. In many ways, the locals hold the balance of power in that if they were to abandon traditional music completely, the publicans would find it difficult to host sessions. Every publican who was interviewed stressed the importance of retaining his or her local clientele. In the summer months the balance of power may tip in favour of the musicians and tourists – in that the publican needs both of them in order to boost business – but this is only a seasonal adjustment in the usual configuration of local power relations. Thus any conclusions regarding the changing nature of the relationships between musicians, tourists and publicans, in turn, have to be understood within the context of contested local constructions of musical meaning and identity. Whilst the research has only just begun to uncover some of the complexities of these deep-running local attitudes, there can be no doubt that they exercise a profound influence on the practice of traditional music when the tourists have gone home.

Acknowledgements

This research was inspired by many wonderful musical experiences in Mayo, during which many musicians and publicans made me feel welcome. Amongst these, special thanks are due to Brian and Maeve Gallagher, Victor Alexander and Sean MacHale. Thanks also to Greta Byrne for permission to interview tourists at Céide Fields and Tom and Angie Hayes for keeping me going with cakes and coffee during the process! Particular appreciation is also due to Seamus Duffy who provided me with much valuable information concerning the history of traditional music in North Mayo and to Anthony McCann who provided a valuable critical reading of an earlier draft of this chapter. Finally, I am grateful to the musicians, publicans and tourists who agreed to be interviewed and to the Geography Department at Coventry University for providing financial assistance.

Notes
1. The Irish word for music
2. From now on, traditional music signifies 'Irish' traditional music unless otherwise indicated.
3. A term which is often used locally, particularly in relation to inhabitants from rural parts of Erris.

References
Aldskogius, H. (1993) Festivals and meets: The place of music in summer Sweden. *Geografiska Annaler* 75B(2), 55–72.
Boissevain, J. (ed.) (1992) *Revitalizing European Rituals*. London: Routledge.
Bord Fáilte (1998) Business Plan 1998–2003. Dublin: Bord Fáilte.
Bord Fáilte (1999) *West Facts '98*. Dublin: Bord Fáilte.
Craik, J. (1997) The culture of tourism. In C. Rojek and J. Urry (eds) *Touring Cultures: Transformations of Travel and Theory* (pp. 113–36). London: Routledge.
Ekman, A. (1999) The revival of cultural celebrations in regional Sweden: Aspects of tradition and transition. *Sociologia Ruralis* 39(3), 280–93.
Hale, A and Payton P. (eds) (2000) *New Directions in Celtic Studies*. Exeter: University of Exeter Press.
Kneafsey, M. (1998) Tourism and place identity: A case study in rural Ireland. *Irish Geography* 31(2), 111–23.
Kneafsey, M. (2000) Tourism, place identities and social relations in the European rural periphery. *European Urban and Regional Studies* 7(1), 35–50.
Lau, F. (1998) Packaging identity through sound: Tourist performances in contemporary China. *Journal of Musicological Research*, 17, 116–28.
Lovering, J. (1998) The global music industry: Contradictions in the commodification of the sublime. In A. Leyshon, D. Matless and G. Revill (eds) *The Place of Music* (pp. 31–56). New York: The Guilford Press.
Nash, C. (1993) The West of Ireland and Irish identity. In B. O'Connor and M. Cronin (eds) *Tourism in Ireland: A Critical Analysis* (pp. 86–112). Cork: Cork University Press.
O'Connor B. and M. Cronin (1993) (eds) *Tourism in Ireland: A Critical Analysis*. Cork: Cork University Press.
O'Donnchadha G. and O'Connor B. (1996) Cultural tourism in Ireland. In G. Richards (ed.) *Cultural Tourism in Europe*. Oxford: CAB International.
Ó Murchú, L. (1999) *Tuarascáil ar Cheol Tíre na nÉireann*. Dublin: Government Stationary Office.
Quinn, B. (1996) The sounds of tourism: Exploring music as tourist resource with particular relevance to music festivals. In M. Robinson, N. Evans and P. Callaghan (eds) *Culture as the Tourist Product* (pp. 383–96). Northumberland: Centre for Travel and Tourism.
Rees, H. (1998) 'Authenticity' and the foreign audience for traditional music in South West China. *Journal of Musicological Research* 17, 135–61.
Revill, G. (1998) Samuel Coleridge Taylor's geography of disappointment: Hybridity, identity and networks of musical meaning. In A. Leyshon, D. Matless and G. Revill (eds) *The Place of Music* (pp. 197–221). New York: The Guilford Press.
Rojek, C. and Urry, J. (1997) *Touring Cultures: Transformations of Travel and Theory*. London: Routledge.

Silberberg, T. (1995) Cultural tourism and business opportunities for museums and heritage sites. *Tourism Management* 16 (5), 361–5.

Stokes, M. (ed.) (1994) *Ethnicity, Identity and Music: The Musical Construction of Place.* Oxford: Berg.

Thornton, S. (2000) Reading the record bins: The commercial construction of Celtic music. In A. Hale and P. Payton (eds) *New Directions in Celtic Studies.* Exeter: University of Exeter Press.

Tourism Development International (2000) *Dispersing Tourism Growth in the West* (a report for the Western Development Commission, Ballaghademeen, Co. Roscommon).

Vallely, F. (1999) *The Companion to Irish Traditional Music.* Cork: Cork University Press.

Chapter 2

Defining the Local: The Development of an 'Environment Culture' in a Clare Village

RUTH CASEY

Situating Ballygannive

Ten miles equi-distance from the nearest major towns lies the village of Ballygannive, in the Burren, Co. Clare. Upon entering the village, the traveller is immediately struck by its scattered ribbon dwelling, which stretches for nearly two miles. The road begins shortly before the river and extends the length of Ballygannive, flanked by various businesses and houses, to fork at the entrance to the local national school, and to merge again at the local pub and post office. There the traveller follows the road to the furthest end of the village, where it disappears behind a bend. One pub, one shop with adjoining post office, a restaurant, a church, a national school, two caravan sites, a horse-riding centre and five bed-and-breakfast (B&B) houses comprise the facilities available.

Gradual development of Ballygannive as a tourist location started in the latter part of the 1970s and the early years of the 1980s. The village boasted one B&B in 1972, with the addition of two more in the late 1970s, this number growing to five in the early 1990s. 1975 marked the year when a group of charismatics first started coming to Ballygannive to reside in the larger caravan site. The development of holiday homes started in the early 1980s, at a time when the caravan site began to cater for an influx of families, mostly from Limerick and Dublin. Now, in 2001, the site boasts just over 150 caravans, 50 of which are occupied by charismatics with small families for the duration of the Charismatic Week in July, with nearly 70 left unoccupied.

Drystock farming continues to be the main source of income for the residents of Ballygannive but on a part-time basis only. Current market trends coupled with a declining patriarchal system, previously the stronghold for the farming community in Ireland, have contributed to a decline in practice. With a drop in population, the farming land is either left to local friends in the village or sold at a premium price to visitors to Ballygannive. The consequences of this structural change are illustrated by the increasing number of holiday homes built at an uneven ratio to the number of permanent local residences in Ballygannive, 250:150.

Past literature tends to depict tourism as an agent of degenerate change, focusing on the resultant 'cultural decline and widespread anomie' (Scheper-Hughes, 1982) or 'community atrophy' (Brody, 1973: 30). Frank McDonald made disparaging reference to the impact of tourism in Ireland in a series of articles in *The Irish Times* (18, 20 and 21 August 1998), entitled 'The Trouble with Tourism'. The huge increase in the number of holiday homes in Ireland – but more specific to this analysis – in the western region of Ireland has raised some interesting issues. With the increase in demand for houses in scenic coastal areas, the long-term implications for more remote and isolated villages such as Ballygannive in Co. Clare has become a contentious issue, as documented by *The Sunday Tribune* (31 May 1998), which reported on a study conducted by CEA Economist, Kevin Heanue, in North West Connemara. Findings relayed a figure of up to 60% of houses being owned by 'temporary residents'. Heanue argues that these residents originate from the urban middle class, whose perspective on issues pertaining to the environment, agriculture and land use is reflected in differing practices, values and political outlook from those of the full-time local. This difference is exacerbated by an increasing affordability gap in house prices for the permanent local residents, who are struggling to compete on an international market. While acknowledging the long-term implications of the housing crisis for more remote and smaller villages in the west of Ireland, a much neglected contributing factor towards the urban migratory movement of young population is lack of employment. In an earlier DART report on Caernarfonshire in England (1978: 6), the danger of confusing the inability of local people to compete on the housing market with the cause – the lack of employment opportunities in parts of the country – was pointed out. Heanue's 'anchor' for economic stability is rooted in this fundamental difficulty. Significantly, it stated that levels of local organisation and club membership amongst second homeowners were relevant in areas of increased holiday-home ownership.

In a recent study conducted in Ballygannive, Co. Clare, the 'outsiders' or 'temporary residents' have created a sense of solidarity and cohesion amongst community members through the coordination of local events and activities with the permanent local residents. This study attempts to revisit the findings of Hugh Brody in 1973 entitled *Inishkillane, Change and Decline in the West of Ireland*, while adopting a hypothetical-deductive approach in order to address two fundamental issues of tourist related impact: first, the attitude of the permanent local residents of Ballygannive to their own lifestyle pattern, and second, the attitude of the permanent local residents towards Ballygannive itself. These questions provided the framework for exploring Brody's concept of 'seasonal reversal' at the peak of the tourist season and in the aftermath of Christmas in Ballygannive.

This chapter will discuss the tourist impact on Ballygannive, but, more significantly, how in modernity, the presence of holiday homes has clearly affected the way in which the permanent local residents are now related to their hinterland in a learned internalised attitude gained from a 'dual community' scenario whereby the indigenous population of Ballygannive live alongside a holiday-home population of 'outsiders'. Crucially, it is how this learned internalised attitude towards Ballygannive has become manifest in the behavioural pattern of the locals, which has instigated a process conceptualised as 'environment culture'.

Types of Tourist Impact

Roland Robertson's (1995) argument that globalisation 'has involved the simultaneity and the interpenetration of what are conventionally called the global and the local . . . ' is particularly relevant to an understanding of the global impact upon Ballygannive. He contends that the concept of globalisation involves the 'invention' of localities in opening up the possibility of mobilising and manipulating global processes for local purposes. Extending the barriers of this notion still further, one could argue that a consequence of the influence of global processes on locality has been the emergence of an 'environment culture'. Central to an understanding of this concept is the attitude of the local towards his/her hinterland which has been learned, from the local/tourist interaction. The incorporation of this concept into the consciousness of the local or non-local is reliant upon this interpenetration of global and local at ground level and the application of knowledge or skills based upon that experience in relating to the hinterland – on a community and environment level. How effectively this application is carried out by the local is determined by the degree of tourist/global impact and, critically, by the way in which the local perceives his/her hinterland with that consciousness. By implication, conceptualisation of the attitudinal change of the local towards Ballygannive envisages behavioural change as a by-product of an 'environment culture'.

With farming steadily declining, the permanent local residents of Ballygannive have come to depend upon tourism as the chief source of income. While the tourist season is reasonably short, Ballygannive receives a small trickle of tourists throughout the year. As Ballygannive is built along the Clare coast road, the passing traveller is defined by the locals in terms of the level of contact which s/he will have with the locality. As 'outsiders' to the area, they are categorised as visitors, blow-ins and tourists respectively. Within the boundaries of this categorisation, the tourist is objectified and defined by the locals according to the relevant encounter and degree of contribution, economically and socially, to the host community of Ballygannive. The type of tourist differs according to the particular season and the type of accommodation in which s/he will stay. The summer months herald an influx of families, students and groups who will travel through the village as one fixed median point en route to the nearest major destination town. Located at different points on the sand dunes and at the furthest bend in the road are the caravan sites. The mobile homes are owned by families from Limerick, Galway, Cavan and Dublin, some of whom sub-let at various intervals during the summer. The caravan site appeals to the family or visitor who wishes to spend two months or more in the region. At night, the pub is dominated by a festive atmosphere of shared encounters between local and tourist. By day, the beach provides a safe haven for children, enabling a type of 'resort holiday'. With a communal atmosphere created by a nexus of caravans and tents bound together by the river and the sea, the caravan-site tourist will embark on a 'collective gaze' of the community and of Ballygannive itself.

In contrast to the caravan sites, the B&B tourist will pay only a fleeting visit. Their specific needs and predisposed requirements frame their time subjectively around particular aspects of Ballygannive in the interest of the romantic gaze. Therefore, minimum contact will be made with the local community. In most cases, this type of tourist will maintain loyalty to the particular B&B, returning as 'visitor' to the guesthouse the following summer season. The continued level of contact between visitor and local redefines the category of tourist and enables a flow of information communication in terms of global networking based on social and commercial interests.

The coach tourist represents a category of tourist exclusively interested in the scientific features of Ballygannive. Two local residents of the area travel around the Burren with a group of tourists from Denmark, Germany and Italy highlighting particular sites of interest. The clear movement to and from the bus around the various sites allows for an 'environmental gaze' (Urry, 1990: 191). The didactic manner of the tour guide frames the tourist gaze around the selection of sites to be gazed upon. In turn, the interpenetrative impact of the relationship between tour guide and tourist enables local learning of the uniqueness of Ballygannive through networking amongst the various nationalities with differing specialised environmental interests. For instance, one local youth spoke of the students who attend a summer art course in the Burren. She described how they would sit on the beach and draw aspects of the landscape. The collective gaze of the local community upon the art students, the coach tourists, the B&B tourist and the caravan-site tourist is closely linked to a learned understanding of how the natural resources of Ballygannive are used by the various categories of tourist.

A Public Celebration

Summer, for the permanent residents of Ballygannive, begins at Easter with the advent of holiday-home owners. There is an increased sense of activity with the onset of the hay season for the farming community alongside the approach of the tourist season. With a full house, the pub will not close until well into the small hours of the morning, welcoming the trade and the buzz characteristic of this season. This portrait of a pub in the height of the tourist season bears striking similarities to Brody's description of the same in Inishkillane in 1973.

With more hours of light, more activities seem possible. In the past two years, the locals have pressed Bus Éireann for a more frequent service through Ballygannive. One local youth insisted that this was surely an indicator of the increasing levels of tourist flow through the village. Ironically, however, busier hours for the local community ensures relatively little contact with the visitors (notwithstanding contact through local services) until the evening when most people congregate in the pub for a night of music and drink. It is during the summer that events, which are constructed to lure tourists rather than to provide entertainment for the locals take place. The Wildlife Symposium provides such an example, as its lecture-style format affords a specialised insight into aspects of wildlife on the Burren. The symposium is held for one week in May and September in Ballygannive, which has the tendency to lengthen the tourist season at both ends of the summer. Although the local community is freely invited, few if any locals turn up with the result that the Symposium is heavily dominated by Americans, Germans, the Dutch and French.

Both the Wildlife Symposium and the Fishing Competition have been organised by Peter Hennessy, a permanent local resident of Ballygannive. In former years, the shore-angling festivities were a major attraction, attracting fishermen from Ireland and abroad for two weeks in June and July. Another feature of the summer is the Matchmaking Festival held annually in Lisdoonvarna. In former days, the knock-on effect of this event was a spread of tourists out to Ballygannive. Of late however, the festival has diminished in attraction as has its impact on Ballygannive.

Dominating the season's excitement is the annual arrival of the charismatics to Ballygannive. The 'Charismatic Week', which is held during the second week of July, attracts young and old from Cavan, Limerick, Cork, Dublin, Belfast, America, Germany and France. Underpinning the week is the idea of leaving home comforts behind in order to 'Camp with the Lord'. Celebration of the mass begins in the dunes, where a procession of charismatics walk barefoot to the church reciting decades of the rosary. The pilgrimage over the stones re-enacts the ideology of suffering connected with the Catholic Church. During the prayer meetings in the marquee and then again at evening time in the church, the priest actively encourages the pilgrims to walk the beach or climb the mountain in order to seek spiritual renewal through the elements. The charismatics learn to release their suffering in a collective discourse with the environment. At one stage during the week, mass is held in the open air, where the group are led either upstream or to the dunes, where the pilgrims will congregate for meditation and prayer overlooking the ocean at sunset. Towards the latter part of the week the priests arrange themselves at intermittent points down the stream to hear confessions. The group engages in this sacrament sitting on a rock amongst the rushing water.

The success of the week is ranked in terms of the charismatics' ability to commune with the elements in a mantra of 'Walking with the Lord'. A fundamental aspect of this spiritual discourse is the process of sacralisation, the framing and elevation of aspects of the landscape that are encountered during the masses, confession and prayer meetings. The tourist embarks on a journey as a true modern pilgrim, seeking authenticity in other 'times' and other 'places' away from his/her everyday life (MacCannell, 1976: 107). Of crucial significance is local involvement in this ritual of prayer and gaze, which includes an organised trip up the mountainside to build an altar of stone. Through participation in this process, the locals are accepting and endorsing the outsider definition of Ballygannive as a place of spirituality.

Each of the different events organised during the tourist season clearly impact upon how the local community then relates to Ballygannive in a specialised manner. Through guiding or being guided through the green roads, onto the beach or up the mountain, the locals participate in a learning process of the salient and unique quality of Ballygannive as place and then of their enhanced lifestyle quality by virtue of living in Ballygannive. This is clearly expressed in the local description of Ballygannive as 'a wonderful place to live' and has implications for how the local community then relates to its environment.

There is an important difference between Brody's use of the concept of 'seasonal reversal' in 1973 and its use by the permanent local residents of Ballygannive in 2001. While Brody's concern focused on the differing mood swings of the locals of Inishkillane according to summer and winter respectively, the locals of Ballygannive use time as a major factor in their ability to fully participate in the activities available, both in the summer at the height of seasonal employment and during the winter. Summer is characterised by high levels of social interaction between returning visitors or friends and locals, which is then compared against winter, a 'boring' time.

Central to the process of 'seasonal reversal' is the concept of 'cyclical change'. While recognising the positive impact of tourism on Ballygannive in the summer, it does not necessarily follow that the winter season is characterised by its direct opposite in the marked absence of both tourists and local youth. Instead, what is becoming apparent is a pattern of toil and hard labour during the height of the farming and tourist season, with a period of rest that marks the winter season. When indicating a preference for the summer or winter season, each of the locals explained in turn that while the summer season was more appealing, both in terms of a bigger community and more hours of light, they were equally content to witness the advent of winter, equating it with a time of rest and time to themselves after the busy extreme of the summer season.

> It's nice to have the change of being busy in the summer and very quiet in the winter . . . By the end of one season you're sort of ready to . . . ready for change'. 'If you are involved in tourism, or one thing or the other, you'd need the winter to . . . regenerate your energies for the next . . . the next year.

In addition to the public activities of the community in the summer time, there is an interesting movement towards private celebration of the life of the village.

A Private Community

October to March marks the winter season. As the B&Bs close their doors, the pub becomes quiet, the lifeguards leave and the atmosphere in the community is relaxed. There is a significant change in community life, through the emptiness of each holiday home and the marked absence of local youth, which is particularly visible at mass times on Saturday evening and Sunday morning. The very late opening hours of the pub is also indicative of this absence of the indigenous population. A local youth stated that life in Ballygannive at Christmas was 'very boring', explaining that nobody of her own age group was around. Another local emphatically pronounced Ballygannive as 'miserable', while a returning elderly local described how the village looked 'washed out' after the storms at Christmas.

Opinions differ in descriptions of Ballygannive during the winter months but one local encapsulated her definition of the village as being a truly wonderful place to live in as a busy mother of three children but unimaginably dull and lifeless without children. This presupposes some type of work pattern which involves a social setting such as Ballygannive's national school. In the past year, the national school has witnessed drama and singing classes taught by the local schoolteachers of which it boasts two. A recent addition to this repertoire has been fiddle classes, taught both locally in Ballygannive and surrounding villages by a non-local. Set dancing has experienced a huge revival in the west of Ireland, practised with equal fervour and popularity in MacDavitt's pub, where classes are offered to all. A non-local from Holland has been teaching Irish dances to the locals for the past three winters with such success that classes were also offered to the national school.

The close of the summer season thus offers leisure-time in abundance with the advent of winter. Unlike Brody's portrait of the heavy loneliness of the bachelors huddled close together for comfort in the bar, Ballygannive's permanent residents are not despondent, lonely or dejected through self-reflexivity. One local equates the success story of the community to act cohesively with the organisation of activities in the hands of newcomers to Ballygannive. Crucially now, it is the outsider influence within the indigenous community which is pushing for and organising these events.

> It's [the community] growing. In terms of doing and organising things and people co-operating. When I came here first it was different. You'd start something and it would last two weekends and eh, people would just, wouldn't go any more. But now it's different.

By drawing a distinction between past and present efforts, a clear differentiation is drawn between the influence and impact of the 'outsider' community on the locals. The outsiders in Ballygannive are promoting and supporting 'traditional' activities within the community. Significantly, it is the influence of the outsiders which is creating the community feel, to extend beyond attitudes (as observed by Brody of Inishkillane) to include internal events and activities.

> People like myself and people, y'know that have children in the school, that have moved in. They're very enthusiastic and they want things moving and they want things happening ... I think it's young – newer people in the area who are very good at organising it. Whereas people

years ago just didn't be bothered 'coz 'twas too much hassle. I suppose
I would have hated the sight of it when I came here first. They – the fact
that there was nothing happening. That seems to be changing now.

The type of 'seasonal reversal' which is evident here can be divided into
the summer season characterised as an outward-looking community (i.e.
towards external events) and the winter season as an inward-looking community in an essentially positive manner. Events such as the Wildlife
Symposium and the Charismatic Week which are organised through
global networking during the summer months are dominated by visitors,
clearly portraying a community amongst tourists. Throughout the winter
months the locals look to newcomers – of returning locals or different
nationalities who have settled in the area – to initiate and organise activities. Effectively, this new type of 'local' to Ballygannive has created an
inverted atmosphere within the local community intrinsically linked to a
concept of 'community among tourists' expressed through the winter-time
activities of fiddle and set-dancing classes.

Central to the 'public' activities of the summer season and the 'private'
activities of the winter season is an understanding of how the locals relate
to and use the resources at hand in fulfilment of an 'environment culture'.
During the tourist season, the locals provide entertainment for the tourists
through the pub which invites bands from outside the locale; the Wildlife
Symposium which offers a specialised insight into the Burren; the riding-
centre which provides horse-riding lessons and treks through parts of the
Burren. The significance of the winter lies in the way in which the locals are
using the resources such as the riding-centre, which they have provided as
an attraction for tourists, for their 'private' activities to occupy themselves
during the 'long hours of winter-time'. Local use of resources extends to
reproduction of events for personalised enjoyment in winter, in an articulated learned definition of how tourists or outsiders relate to the
environment.

> Well, in the summer months, it would be virtually all tourists. And
> then in the winter, eh, it would be . . . it would be 80% all locals I'd say.

The nature of the religious experience – the full participation of lay and
religious communities – underpinning the Charismatic Week which is
organised by a non-local priest for charismatics nationwide and globally
has prompted a local priest of the community to organise an Easter Vigil in
a broadly similar style. This event occurs on an annual basis, set in a
deserted ruin at the foot of the mountain. People from around Ireland congregate from the early hours of the morning to celebrate mass in the old
abbey amongst the spirits of the dead. It was the practice of the parish priest

in previous years to ask the local community of Ballygannive to walk to mass for the month of May in celebration of the Blessed Virgin Mary. The aim behind this idea was to provide a mechanism whereby the community could meet through walking the green roads together, while simultaneously taking the time to notice the awakening of the Burren in Spring.

A number of different processes must be noted here to understand of the significance of the winter activities. First, the important role played by outsiders coming to the area in providing an integrative mechanism for the local community during the winter period. The knock-on-effect of this medium extends to the contribution of the parish priest, who as a result of his heightened awareness of the beauty of the area has sought to change the attitude of the community by impacting upon the behavioural pattern of the locals by organising the walk to mass. Second, there is the way in which one of the local priests of the community has incorporated the idea of celebrating mass in a style similar to that of the Charismatic Week, within the context of the winter activities. Third, local use of such tourist activities as the riding centre demonstrates how the locals are exposing themselves to aspects of the Burren which they have specifically chosen for visitors to the area, thereby constructing their local area in terms of the 'romantic gaze'.

Practical Problems

During the course of the interviews conducted during January and February, some tensions and potential conflict amongst the locals were noted. As some of these tensions became articulated, it was evident that the inward-looking nature of the local community during the winter facilitated a build-up of pressure, which often became problematic straining the fabric of the community.

At the heart of this tangled web of inter-relationships, conflictual relationships are exacerbated by the strain of a declining indigenous population. The ability of these tensions to counteract the cohesive nature of the community is only offset against the ability of outsiders to provide an integrative function in the winter through set-dancing and fiddle classes, and an exciting diversion in the summer.

Co-existing alongside these covert tensions is the equally covert level of dissatisfaction inwardly expressed in relation to the two caravan sites. The first covers a large section of the river which runs the length of the site onto the beach. The many caravans stretch far and wide over the sand dunes and are a prominent feature against the landscape of the area. The second caravan site is smaller in size, holding up to 20 caravans and is located at the far end of the village. Both sites are distinct upon the horizon, identifiable from many angles in the village. Murmured dissatisfaction in this regard is directly related to a greater awareness of how outsiders value the area in terms of its physical features and geological worth. As the orientation of Ballygannive is towards the sea, the sweeping view of the dunes and beach is interrupted by the sprawl of caravans which comprise the larger caravan site. Over two-thirds of these caravans remain untended throughout the year, while a small scattering of caravans in various hollows in the dunes, have been left derelict. The mass presence of these man-made structures across the landscape of the Burren has provoked some disquiet among the community regarding the preservation of the natural landscape. Local recognition and attempts to facilitate the romantic tourist gaze of both the community and of Ballygannive is central to the internal concern about the aesthetic impact of the caravan site. Queries have been raised concerning the degree of economic contribution, which the caravan site continues to make towards the local economy. The ability of the caravan site to run almost self-sufficiently has also generated some tension within the community. Local concern about the caravan site thus moves from the aesthetic to its economic contribution to the community as a whole.

Co-existing alongside these tensions is the problem of water shortage which occurs on an annual basis during the height of the tourist season. Obviously the consequences of this are disastrous, for both the farming and tourist sectors. The Water Scheme was established in order to deal with this problem, comprising a committee of outsiders and permanent local residents. The proposed solution costs in excess of €127,000. As a result, each resident, permanent or temporary, must pay a due equivalent to the amount of water used. The caravan site is least affected by this problem due to its advantageous location beside the river and at the start of the central water supply. As the bulk of the tourists tend to stay in the caravan sites, this is viewed as one of the more problematic aspects of tourism, giving rise to annoyance amongst the locals for the subsequent inconvenience. In mid-July of 1993, Ballygannive experienced a severe water shortage. As the tourist season was at its peak, articulated tension within the community was directed towards the large caravan site which was busy catering for the charismatics. They were requested to reschedule their week of prayer to the second week in July, instead of the third, as had been their tradition. This partially resolved the water shortage problem, however, it continues to affect the local community both economically and socially.

An 'Environment Culture' Created

The locals' description of Ballygannive in summer and winter, indicates how outsider definition of the area (given in terms of its geological and botanical worth) has been internalised and reproduced. The resultant 'environment culture' is the 'product' of a learning process whereby the interpenetration of tourist/local has played a major role in how the local community now relates to its environment as expressed through the public and private activities of summer and winter respectively. One of the consequences of the 'environment culture' and central to it is the process of demarcating the landscape as a separate entity from the surrounding hinterland – in effect, the 'commodification of countryside spaces'. By cordoning off an area of the landscape, the local entrepreneur constructs an aesthetic discourse for the tourist. Through this spatial practice of demarcation, the bounded landscape is defined by the local as an object of cultural appropriation, which the tourist is required to pay for the privilege of gazing upon. A sequence for this process can be drawn up as follows:

Phase 1: Seeing the land as an object
Phase 2: Separating it off from other users
Phase 3: Controlling access
Phase 4: Charging for access
Phase 5: Signposting the new commodity

Fundamental to this process is the framing of the setting which encompasses the landscape. This is an ongoing process whereby the raw materials of Ballygannive and its surrounding hinterland are being socially 'constructed' and commoditised by the locals, to be sold as a 'green product' in its natural state to visitors from both locally in Ireland and abroad through global networking.

A signpost beckons the traveller off the main road to follow the river upstream to the Nature Reserve. This has been nurtured and maintained by a local botany enthusiast, Peter Hennessy. According to Hennessy, this area alone holds up to 150 unique species of flora, specific to the Burren. It is also home to an array of wildlife including pine-martens, stoats and otters, in an area hemmed in by the road on one side and by the river on the other. This reserve is currently licensed to the Burren Conservation Trust, which has the intention of opening it to the public under the management of a tour guide. A wooden cabin stands at the entrance of the reserve, beyond which three notice boards direct the visitor's gaze towards the various types of rock, flora and fauna which can be seen in the reserve. Throughout the walks in the reserve, specific flowers and items of interest are labelled on a wooden plaque, while wooden benches are arranged at intermittent points for the weary traveller.

Two processes are clearly evident here. The separation of land by wooden posts around the boundary and a barrier blocking entry to the site not only demarcates the space as salient in its content but also, crucially, serves to privatise the land as the exclusive property of the local. The public now views the landscape at the convenience of the local and must pay in order to understand what they are seeing.

Exploring this concept further still, there is the notion of the 'learning holiday'. With specific reference to the German and Dutch tourists who travel by coach through Ballygannive, Cotter explains how their specialised interest in gardening has led them to Ireland. Cotter operates as a tour guide, showing tourists specific sites of interest in the area, incidentally guiding their collective gaze towards the same. The very idea of guiding tourists around the site ensures that the tourists pay for the privilege of gazing upon the natural landscape. By indicating specific sites upon which to gaze, the tour guide is yet again marking the terrain as a space both exotic and unusual in its aspect. However, Cotter goes beyond this still by remarking that the whole concept of 'guiding the tourist' should be carried through to the classroom environment where it would operate almost as an internal garden through illustration of the various flora on the overhead projector and blackboard. Within this context, the tour guide becomes the teacher, teaching a specialised knowledge of the flora.

Macnaghten and Urry (1998: 191) comment in some detail on the marketable qualities of the countryside emerging from popular conception of the same as the object of a 'romantic gaze'. They state that commodifying processes in the countryside are occurring in indirect forms, such as guided visits to nature reserves and specific sites, pony trekking using different routes such as 'green roads' up the mountain and by the beach, and caravan sites in dominant areas of beauty. Different modes for spatial and temporal access to the countryside may also be linked to non-direct forms of payment. Macnaghten and Urry contend that further diversification of spatial practices based around countryside activities may engineer further specialisation of outdoor pursuits such as mountain-climbing, rock-climbing, caving, swimming and walking. Commodification of the countryside ensures that the landscape will be increasingly consumed as a spectacle, as images and symbols become transformed into saleable commodities. A consequence of this will be the divorce of these saleable qualities from their social and historical contexts, with the subsequent general loss of the local distinctiveness of countryside places. At worst, countryside spaces become spectacles devised by marketing strategies, earmarked as 'attractions' where the environmental qualities of countryside places become identified as commodities, specifically devised to enhance their economic value (Macnaghten & Urry, 1998: 192).

Urry (1998:192) states that in order to preserve a 'green' image, the cultural landscape must become a landscape of signposted, saleable commodities or attractions which are dotted about the countryside and which increasingly structure people's movement through it. Emerging social spatialisation of the countryside defines the same principally as a resource to be utilised for tourism. According to Urry and Macnaghten, one's relationship with the qualities which tempt people to the countryside in the first place is separated from the leisure subject (the visual space of representation) but where they are also increasingly likely to have to pay for these managed qualities so as to maximise the economic opportunities that exist in the countryside for a growing tourist industry (the spatial practice of commodification). This operates as a level of rhetoric expressed via the marketplace.

In Ballygannive each tourist–local encounter is commodity driven, from the pub to horse-riding, to learning about the flora. It is an expression of the awareness of a product based on knowledge gained from the global market and of the technical process which then accesses that product through global networking. By guiding the gaze of the tourist over aspects of the landscape, the locals have effectively defined an 'environment culture' based around its 'constructed' exotic and salient quality. The endeavours of the Charismatic Week to instigate a process of 'sacralisation' whereby the tourist pays homage to the landscape in spiritual discourse with the elements; and the use of tour guides both in the context of the coach tours and the Nature Reserve deliberately structure the tourist's movement through the landscape, while the pre-selected routes used by the riding centre bring the tourist off the beaten track onto the 'green roads' up the mountain, into the more hidden and therefore exciting parts of the Burren.

Faced with a pluralisation of value systems and lifestyles, the locals in Ballygannive adopt a self-reflexive attitude which differentiates between their indigenous culture and a globalisation of cultures. However, central to the understanding of this self-reflexive attitude of the locals, both with respect to Ballygannive and to their self-perception as a community, is the way in which the 'Other' has positively impacted on the former. Inasmuch as the difference of the outsiders is highlighted in the school through art and crafts, the outsider use of the physical features of Ballygannive for caving and walking positively affects the locals' awareness of their own difference. The local priest summarises this pivotal argument:

> And eh, I think to see people [tourists] parking ... their car ... here in the church ground and taking out their sticks and walking up the hill y'know . . . Think that it kind of forces people to say, 'What are they doing out? What's so special about this like?' ... It's just something they take for granted. And em ... probably ... forget that they have a beautiful place here that's heaven to so many people.

It is crucial to note how, in Ballygannive, as in Inishkillane, the role of the tourist has become a reassuring one vindicating the lifestyle pattern and choices of the locals.

They [tourists] say it's beautiful and you somehow feel responsible for how beautiful it is.

The ability of the tourist to influence the attitudes of the locals positively both towards themselves and Ballygannive must not be underestimated. It may be useful to think of it within the context of a progression from the demoralised frame of mind of the locals of Inishkillane, as identified by Brody (1973), to a heightened awareness and commodifying attitude on the part of the locals of Ballygannive.

Cordoning Off the Landscape

One of the more striking instances of outsider impact on Ballygannive has been local claim to ownership of terrain. Temporary conflict between the riding centre and the large caravan site illustrates such an instance. It was the practice of the riding centre to bring riders from the beach onto the sand dunes as part of a trekking route. The owner stated that the route was seen to be encroaching upon the land of the caravan site and, consequently, the riding centre was requested to stop using that particular route. The articulated conflict between the caravan site and riding centre indicates the value attached to the land and space, through the competition between the families staying in the caravans and horses for the same spatial area. The land has been revalued by outsider interest, both in terms of aesthetic discourse and monetary value, which has effectively privatised local interest in Ballygannive as a place. Brody (1973: 144) described how 'urban conceptions of success and home' had created the self-continued household which stood as 'lonely farm houses . . . apart from one another' (1973:144). Twenty-six years later, not only has the household become individuated, the land has also become contested terrain and, crucially, it is cordoned off to the exclusion of others. This phenomenon is apparent at macro (outsider) and micro (permanent local resident) levels.

According to Shaw and Williams (1994: 231), the construction of the countryside as a zone of consumption results in a number of sharp contradictions. Foremost amongst these is the privatisation of the land which severely constrains accessibility. Brody (1973) noted this when he talked at length of the alienating process which was an accompaniment to the process of household privatisation. The social constructions of the landscape popular in the 1990s and, more significantly, at the end of the 20th century as images of the pastoral idyll and production zone are in direct conflict with the continued growth of holiday homes.

Following alarm concerning the safety of large industrialists in Ireland, a German resident planted trees and erected electric fences around the boundary of his property in Ballygannive. Shortly after, a Dutch resident and British resident also planted trees around the boundary walls of their properties. Outsider use of trees must be understood within the context of Slater's (1993:24) examination of 19th century travel books in Ireland, in which he refers to the 'native gaze' as a variant of the 'picturesque'. Slater explores the role of trees, which were used as boundary fences on landlord estates, but which also symbolically screened the estates from being viewed. In so doing, it is remarked that the tree in the garden of the picturesque was acting as a theatrical prop to the viewing process itself. As the essential feature of the picturesque was about viewing, views were manufactured by using trees to close off or open up views of the landscape (Slater, 1993: 37). Effectively, the trees were set at fixed points in order to eliminate any sign of indigenous life from the view of the landlord, while simultaneously framing aspects of the landscape for the same.

The significance of outsider use of trees to screen aspects or whole parts of their property lies in the construction of a romantic view but, more crucially, in the construction of the ideology inherent in that view to the exclusion of others. In modernity, increasing numbers of people have sought to build their holiday homes in an area that affords solitude, privacy, and a personal, semi-spiritual relationship with their environment (Urry, 1995: 85). Urry (p. 180) remarks that the countryside appears to be 'closer' to nature; that there is a relative absence of people; and that there is a non-mechanical environment (1995:180). Bound up within the gaze of the tourist or outsider is visual consumption of the landscape. The construction of boundary trees effectively demarcates the terrain as the private space of the outsider. What is crucial to note in Ballygannive is how this process has been interpreted by the local community. In one case upon the death of a German property owner, a permanent local resident bought the property and removed the trees and fencing.

> . . . I think the Germans in particular when they come, they're inclined to put up fences and seal themselves off . . . They both died and em, that house has been bought by a local and all the trees are gone.

Of fundamental importance is the way in which the locals saw themselves as being cut off from a part of their own village landscape. The death of the German demonstrates local reaction: an attempt to retrieve their land and, by connection, their space.

However, of greater significance is the growing movement towards the privatisation of space amongst the locals. Emerging conflict within the community indicates a sharpening awareness of the landscape – gained through outsider impact – and increasing claims to ownership of the land. The gradual process of privatisation in Ballygannive can be traced to local reaction against outsider attempts to urbanise their space. There was an initial movement amongst the locals towards viewing trees as a necessary tool for sheltering vegetables and crops from Atlantic gales. The cement walls and gates constructed by outsiders was seen in the past as excluding devices to hide their property from public view. The local community has adopted this practice to afford privacy between households. Of crucial importance is how the spatial practice of privatisation of the landscape has been learnt from the presence of outsiders in the area and provides yet another example of the locals' learned attitude towards the land.

Representing Ballygannive – Local and Outsider Perspectives

Local and outsider representation of Ballygannive is quite similar in style, indicative of the interpenetrative mode of the community. Both rely heavily on global networking amongst friends and returning visitors to signpost the area. An elderly local described how he leaves Ballygannive every winter for four months, travelling around parts of America visiting friends who make a return visit to Ireland during the summer months. Likewise, other businesses explained how they would maintain contact with visitors coming to the area. The link of friendship provides the greatest mechanism for both local and outsider representation of Ballygannive, as illustrated through the degree of networking evident in the Wildlife Symposium, organised by a local, and the Charismatic Week, which is organised by an outsider.

Tee-shirts bearing emblems of the Wildlife Symposium are circulated both during the conference and while visiting friends abroad. In the same way, recordings of the music and the sermons of the Charismatic Week are circulated amongst friends, both in Ireland and abroad, aiding the construction of spiritual discourse linked to the environment on a global level. The attempt to recreate a personal space for the continuation of spiritual renewal for the charismatic on a year round basis is a deliberate one. Outsider representation of the experience of spiritual discourse keenly associated with Ballygannive and its location in the Burren is encapsulated within the literature with titles such as 'Camp with the Lord' or 'The Pilgrim's Progress'. A brochure from one B&B house describes Ballygannive in terms of a leisurely pace of life:

A cosy village set between the golden sandy beaches from which it takes its Irish name, and the gentle sloping hills of the Burren.

The tone is quite deliberate in its evocation of peace and tranquillity. Crucially, the choice of adjectives used indicates ease with 'Mother Nature' and ease with the local residents, who incidentally have signposted themselves under the caption of 'cosy'. Both events illustrate the very real way in which local and outsider are using the landscape to construct the collective or romantic tourist gaze.

Conclusion

This chapter has attempted to explore issues relating to tourist development in a rural community in the west of Ireland, specifically the development of an 'environment culture' as a consequence of the interpenetration of the local and global. It was argued that the development of a 'dual community' has presented a radical challenge to locals' self-perception and local perception of Ballygannive, which in turn is manifest in changes in behaviour. An examination of the locals' relationship to aspects of the landscape, the urbanisation of countryside spaces and the global representation of Ballygannive as village evidenced the emergence of an 'environment culture'.

Note

This text is based an analysis from a series of cyclical in-depth interviews, conducted during the summer and winter.

References

Brody, H. (1986) *Inishkillane: Change and Decline in the West of Ireland*. London: Allen Lane.

Curtin, C. (1996) Back to the future? Communities and rural poverty. In C. Curtin *et al.* (eds) *Understanding Rural Poverty*. Dublin: Oak Tree Press.

Heanue, K. (1998) The affordability gap for housing in peripheral rural areas. In *The Sunday Tribune*, Dublin.

MacCannell, D. (1976) *The Tourist: A New Theory of the Leisure Class*. New York: Schocken Books.

Macnaghten, P. and Urry, J. (1998) *Contested Natures*. London: Sage.

MacDonald, F. (1998) The Trouble with Tourism. *The Irish Times* (18, 20 and 21 August). Dublin.

Robertson, R. (1995) Globalisation: Time–space and homogeneity and heterogeneity. In M. Featherstone, S. Lash and R. Robertson (eds) *Global Modernitites* (pp. 30–1). London: Sage.

Scheper-Hughes, N. (1982) *Saints, Scholars and Schizophrenics: Mental Illness in Rural Ireland*. California: University of California Press.

Shaw, G. and Williams, A.M. (eds) (1994) *Critical Issues in Tourism: A Geographical Perspective*. Oxford: Blackwell.

Slater, E. (1993) Contested terrain: Differing interpretations of Co.Wicklow's land-scape. *Irish Journal of Sociology*, 3.

Urry, J. (1990) *The Tourist Gaze: Leisure and Travel in Contemporary Societies*. London: Sage.

Urry, J. (1995) *Consuming Places*. New York: Routledge.

Chapter 3

Shaping Tourism Places: Agency and Interconnections in Festival Settings

BERNADETTE QUINN

Introduction

In the contemporary era local places seem exposed to more and faster change than ever before. The difference between places seems to be diminishing and debates as to whether 'cultural homogenisation' or 'reconstituted difference' best describes the changes affecting place feature prominently in recent social science and humanities literatures. Local places are linked to regional, national and supra-national spheres through multiple connections. Tourism is one important globalising force, linking places into the wider world and influencing the changing meanings of place.

This chapter is broadly concerned with examining how tourism is implicated in changing the meanings of place. The type of tourism places selected for enquiry is arts festivals turned tourist attractions. The arguments draw on doctoral research conducted into the Wexford Festival Opera and the Galway Arts Festival. It construes tourism places as phenomena forged through local – extra-local interactions, explores the complicated roles played by both place-based actors and tourists and analyses the tourism places ultimately reproduced.

Conceptualising Local and Extra-local Inputs in the Shaping of Tourism Places

In much of the tourism literature there is an implicit assumption that tourism exists as an all-powerful, virtually 'placeless' phenomenon that, by definition, affects change, causes impacts and creates effects on 'defenceless' local places. Chang *et al.* (1996) have remarked that the relationship between the global and the local is often portrayed in the tourism literature as unequal, with global forces exerting considerable influence over local conditions in creating and shaping tourism products. This view dominates the political economy literature where, as Chang *et al.* (1996) have paraphrased, the prevailing argument sees metropolitan corporations and market conditions determining the pace and form of tourism development around the world, with local actors playing only peripheral roles. Meanwhile in the very sizeable body of literature devoted to analysing the impacts of tourism, there seems to be an assumption that extra-local tourism forces and externally-derived tourists represent the dynamic elements in the process with destinations, host economies and resident populations existing merely as passive receptors of change. The literature's very preoccupation with analysing the 'impacts of tourism' on people, places, cultures, societies and economies within tourism research suggests this.

This privileging of the global, and the presumption that structure prevails over agency, reflects a failure to appreciate the ability of human agents to initiate development, mediate and harness external tourism forces and capitalise on place-specific characteristics and resources to influence the shape of local tourism places. Undoubtedly, the globalisation of the tourism industry has advanced relentlessly since the 1950s. However, individual entrepreneurs, family businesses and small companies remain to the fore in shaping tourism developments in 'local' tourism resorts and regions across the world. Furthermore, since at least the mid 1980s, local people in countless locations have become extensively involved in 'community-based' tourism planning and development initiatives. Thus, the opportunity for individuals, small firms and community groups to mould, or at least to influence the shape of tourism landscapes is very significant. Murphy (1983) and Blank (1989) both implicitly pointed to the role of agency with the reminder that the 'destination' is actually the 'host community'. More specifically, Barnes and Hayter (1992) emphasised the role of individual agency in shaping a tourist destination in a Canadian context. Elsewhere, Morris and Dickinson (1987) pointed to the ability of a few local developers to manipulate community organisations in the pursuit of their economic agenda; while Reed (1997: 567) has commented on the 'pivotal role that the actions of individuals can have at the local level' in tourism development. Yet, with few exceptions, the literature is remarkably silent on the role of agency.

However, neither arguing the force of the global nor defending the power of the local in isolation is adequate. Tourism is a classic example of a phenomenon that pivots on a local–global dynamic. Local–global interactions underpin the transformation of places existing as 'local' places into 'international' destinations; of dwellers into tourists; and they create the links between the producers of tourism products and services consumed in

situ, and globally active multinational corporations. Historically, concep-
tualising these interactions has not been a priority for tourism researchers
and yet enquiries here could produce truly meaningful insights into how
tourism places are shaped.

In recognition of this, some recent tourism literature has begun to rethink place. Chang *et al.* (1996) and Milne (1998), for instance, argue that
tourism must be viewed as a 'transaction process incorporating the exogenous forces of global markets and multinational corporations as well as the
endogenous powers of local residents and entrepreneurs'. This line of
argument draws attention to the interplay between formative forces and
invites interest in exploring the hitherto neglected role of agency in mediating global forces. Hence, as Oakes (1994) has argued, the roles played by
human agents in shaping local places is being accorded increasingly more
significance in the tourism literature.

Exploring Agency – Insights from Festival Settings

Tourism researchers have long understood that resident and community groups in tourism places cannot be regarded as homogeneous (Ryan &
Montgomery, 1994). However, few attempts have been made to analyse
this heterogeneity or to investigate individuals'/sub-groups' active
involvement in tourism. Insights into the role of agency in tourism settings
can be gleaned from the humanities and social science literature on festivals. Festivals represent complex cultural phenomena that humans, for
centuries, have engaged in to invest cultural practices with specific
meanings, to celebrate their beliefs and to assert their identity. Recent years
have seen public festivities being created and revived on an unprecedented
scale (Manning, 1983) and the accompanying upsurge of research interest
has been preoccupied with the relationships between people, space and
power.

A commonly asserted tenet is that there is very little that is natural or
spontaneous about festival spaces. Studies of the Notting Hill Carnival
(Jackson, 1988), St Patrick's Day parades (Marston, 1989), community festivals (Smith, 1996), urban festivals (Guichard-Anguis, 1997), and the Rio
carnival (Lewis & Pile, 1996) among others repeatedly show them to be
authored landscapes where dominant individuals and groups lay out
dictates transforming and stimulating the contestation of space. In sharp
contrast to this literature, tourism research on festivals has appeared
largely uninterested both in the contentiousness of relationships in festival
settings and in the possibility that festival landscapes bear strong signs of
authorship. Too frequently, it fails to look beneath the 'stage-managed'
veneer of festivals and in so doing seems to undermine the significance of

festivals as cultural acts which people engage in to make statements about who they are and about how and where they live.

This chapter presents case-study research that draws on both literatures. The research methodology employed a combination of approaches to collect primary data within a framework that was predominantly qualitative in design. The findings reported here draw mainly on an analysis of archival material held by the Arts Council of Ireland; semi-structured interviews with 'key informants' involved in the festival organisations and in the arts scene in the two places; and two questionnaire surveys, containing both closed and open-ended questions, which were administered to resident populations in Wexford ($N = 166$) and Galway ($N = 138$) during the 1996 festivals.

Festivals as Tourist Attractions

Wexford (current population 15,000) is a medium-sized county town located some 100 miles south of Dublin on the south-east coast. In 1951, when the newly independent Irish state was engrossed in the weighty task of modernising itself, the town ambitiously launched an opera festival dedicated to a repertoire of what it described as 'rare and unjustly neglected opera'. The individuals behind the venture came from among the town's middle classes and specifically comprised a group of local opera devotees accustomed to gathering in each others' drawing rooms to enjoy opera and to travelling to the UK and further afield for the opera seasons. While its focus on 'rare opera' was novel, it was in essence a very conventional undertaking in that its preoccupation with the 'high' arts was unequivocal. Partly because of this, it was immediately understood and attractive to powerful sections of society and to institutions both at local and national level, including the Arts Council, the government, the national media and Bord Fáilte. In the intervening years the festival has become established as the premier international event on the Irish arts calendar. In the late 1990s, it annually attracted approximately 20,000 people during a three-week period in October / November.

The Galway Arts Festival, founded in the Western Region's capital city (current population 57,095) in 1978, was launched by a group of students led by Ollie Jennings. Dedicated to celebrating the work of artists from within the Western Region, the festival founders enthusiastically epitomised the unorthodox in Irish arts at the time. Operating on a very informal basis and developing innovative artistic policies, the Galway Arts Festival represented a form of agency that was historically little understood and, in consequence, relatively ignored by national institutions. In line with contemporaneous cultural thinking throughout Europe, it sought to further sociopolitical goals through the arts with programmes that confused the boundaries between 'high' and 'low' arts (literary theatre on the stage alongside visual theatre on the streets) and contested conventional notions of what constitutes appropriate arts spaces (unorthodox venues used include a tent, warehouses, garages, shopping centres and public spaces). Its peripheral geographical location, non-élite social origins and particular ideological underpinnings, promoted its autonomy. If Wexford hosts the most internationally renowned event on the Irish artistic calendar, it is Galway that hosts the most nationally renowned one. In the late 1990s the festival annually attracted fee-paying audiences in excess of 60,000 as well as an estimated 90,000 people to free events over a 15-day period in July.

Creating a Semblance of 'Community'

The Wexford and Galway festivals were both founded by outstanding individuals of vision, determination and charisma who had a strong interest in the arts. Both were equipped with strong leadership qualities and left very different but enduring marks on the festival landscapes. In Wexford, the intention was to establish the festival as an internationally recognised centre of opera production and early tasks revolved around recruiting singers and artistic personnel. The emphasis was on recruiting singers, artistic personnel and, of course, repertoire, from the UK and continental Europe. However, an equally important task was to expand the initiative away from its narrow social origins and make it a meaningful proposition for the local residents as a whole. The festival founders were acutely aware of the need to ally their ambitions with those of other interest groups in the town and recruitment to the Festival Council reflected this need. The inaugural Council of 1951 included a local Teachta Dála, the Honorary Secretary of the Chamber of Commerce, the town's mayor and leading clerics from the town's religious communities. All of these figures represented means through which the festival could garner financial, political and community support.

It was essential to the very survival of the festival that the support of the local population at large be forthcoming. Opera is extremely costly to produce. Corporate sponsorship of the arts was not yet common and the prospects of receiving adequate funding from the state in the early 1950s were poor. Initial appeals for local people to act as beneficiaries met with very positive responses. Financially, local residents and businesses were generous. In 1957, for instance, a deficit of IR £3500 was cleared by means of a silver circle to which local people had contributed approximately 50%. In other capacities, hundreds of locals enthusiastically lent their support. Volunteers emerged to sing in the opera chorus and to contribute in numerous ways to the production (including wardrobe, make-up, lighting, set painting and construction, stage and technical management). By the festival's third year, 1953, the townspeople were very actively engaged in producing the festival, as the following *Irish Press* (26 October 1953) commentary suggests:

> the 1953 festival is above all, a product of voluntary effort on the part of the Wexford man in the street, his wife and family, and his fellow workers and friends. Shop-keepers large and small, and the householders in the fashionable and humbler quarters alike . . . have come out in a spontaneous drive to give these famous narrow streets a look of gaiety and colour they never had before.

These 'behind-the-scenes' spaces became over time a crucial part of the Wexford festival landscape. They constituted the domain in which local people's creative energies could flourish in uncontested fashion, where they could demonstrate their support for the festival and express their stakeholder status. In return for their voluntary efforts and for investing something of themselves in making the festival happen each year, they earned the opportunity to purchase tickets for the opera dress rehearsal performances. They also earned the satisfaction of witnessing 'their' festival achieve national and sometimes international critical acclaim. The voluntary support that continues to sustain the festival today stands as one of its most symbolic features.

Officially, in its programming, practices and symbols, Wexford fits comfortably among the ranks of élite arts festivals. However, it simultaneously projects itself as a venture that enjoys the unqualified support of local society in general. From the outset, the festival organisation publicly insisted that 'everybody connected with the organisation of the festival would feel very badly if the Wexford people did not look upon it as their festival' (Festival Council member quoted in the *Wexford People*, 25 October 1952). Yet a sense of ownership was not to be cultivated through involving locals in artistic or audience domains. Unlike the Galway Arts Festival, Wexford is not acclaimed for having fostered local artistic creativity. Local people have assumed performance roles here only infrequently. Neither has local people's stakeholding role been truly developed through their participation in an audience capacity. The cultural vision which propels the festival forward does not privilege local people as members of the audience. Prioritising a local audience would have exerted a downward pressure on ticket prices that would have impeded the festival's pursuit of its over-riding artistic objectives. Thus, 'front of house' space has been, and continues to be, reserved largely for visitors. Building a sense of local ownership of the festival was founded, instead, on involving people in behind-the-scenes capacities.

The basis of the relationship between the Galway Arts Festival organisation and the people who live in Galway has been quite different and much simpler to that which evolved in Wexford. Most obviously, the Galway festival has been staged unambiguously for local people. Prior to the 1990s no effort was made to attract non-Galway audiences. In spite of this, townspeople were not asked to develop their stakeholding in the initiative by providing financial or in-kind support of any nature. The decision to establish a festival was only taken once state funding had been received from the Arts Council. The balance of financial requirements was then generated through the box office. The costs of production were minimised by employing ingenious ways of acquiring vacant city spaces and transforming them into venues. For many years, the festival did not seek support from the city's business community. It was not until 1987, when the organisation was 10 years old, that a serious sponsorship drive was launched. Furthermore, the founding members of the organisation themselves assumed total responsibility for the administrative and managerial undertakings involved in staging the event. Just as no serious overtures had been made to the business community for financial support, no attempt was made to generate voluntary support for the festival among the residential community at large. In effect, the organisers of the Galway festival functioned as if they were professional arts administrators, except that they were not being paid. It was not until 1990, when the expanding festival was 13 years old and in the early stages of professionalising, that a formal strategy to attract voluntary support for the festival was launched.

In general, the festival organisers made just one overt demand on Galway residents – that they come to the arts events staged and engage themselves as audiences in the festival process. Making the prospect of audience involvement as appealing as possible for local people was an unparallelled priority. Festival events were housed in familiar settings: poetry readings took place in schools, art exhibitions in parochial halls and visual theatre on the streets of the city; admission prices were kept to a minimum and many events were admission free; a broad range of art forms to cater for diverse artistic preferences was staged. Specifically, the engagement of locally based artists and musicians was actively sought in the production of the event. A prominent aim of the Galway Arts Festival was to create a platform where local creativity would find a place to express itself. To this end, the festival organisation used its knowledge of the local arts scene, cultivated contacts with individuals based both in the city and in the Western Region more widely, and engaged locally and regionally based artists on a commercial basis to produce the festival programme.

This notwithstanding, the Galway festival organisation's view of the local people and local art was not as inclusive or as 'community based' as this analysis might suggest. Undoubtedly, much effort was made to draw local people into the cultural arena being constructed but part of the process involved marginalising certain groups and certain artistic ideologies. From the mid-1980s onwards, for instance, the national theatre for the Irish language based in Galway, An Taibhdhearc, was conspicuous by its absence from the arts festival programmes. From the festival's perspective, the work of Siamsa, the company based in An Taibhdhearc, has been 'incompatible' with the artistic direction taken by the festival. The festival manager's explanation for this is that Galway is a product-driven festival: 'If it's there we'll have it' (McGrath, 1997). However, the history of the Galway festival demonstrates that very rarely did it rely on a 'product' presenting itself for inclusion in a programme, one of its acknowledged achievements is that it has created 'products'. A similar and more commented upon situation exists in relation to the lack of space created for classical music and its audiences in the festival programme. Thus the semblance of inclusiveness which attaches to the Galway Arts Festival can be easily unravelled to reveal a more complex agenda.

Constructing a Role for Tourists

If the boundaries of local involvement were carefully carved out in the Wexford case, the role envisaged for tourists was as deliberately construed. From the very earliest years, tourism was consciously construed as an instrument for advancing the artistic aims of the festival. Tourism was never an explicit goal. Indeed, Walsh was quoted as saying that 'I think the confusion of tourism and the arts is a bad thing' (*The Irish Times*, 23 October 1963). However, it was viewed as a means to an end and was determinedly and effectively promoted. By 1959, 60% of audiences came from outside of Wexford, with 20% from Dublin, 13–15% from the rest of Ireland and 25–27% from overseas (*The Irish Independent* 24 October 1962). By 1989, 85% of audiences originated outside of Wexford, with more than one-third coming from abroad in the 1990s (O'Hagan *et al.*, 1989). Very importantly, these tourist flows sustained the venture financially in a way that serving a local market could not. Furthermore, the policy of attracting outsiders served an extensive range of interests ranging from the local level (the business community, politicians, opera devotees) to the national level (the Arts Council, Bord Fáilte). The festival's status as a successful tourism attraction was an important factor consolidating support from these institutions.

Tourism played a role in the Galway Arts Festival in the sense that it influenced the early decision to alter the timing of the festival from Spring to Summer. However, this was as much to capitalise on Galway people's increased leisure time as it was to capture a visiting audience. In telling fashion, historical data pertaining to audiences at the Galway Arts Festival in the pre 1990 period are non-existent. However, relative to Wexford, efforts to market the event were much more concentrated on attracting local audiences and it is reasonable to suggest that the audience profile was much less spatially diverse. In fact, the disinterest in attracting audiences beyond Galway city and county is a defining trait of the early festival. Since 1991, however, this has changed. The festival's growing reputation as the leading arts festival in the country has inevitably stimulated visitor flows and the festival organisation is now actively marketing itself to visiting audiences. In 1994, it was estimated that 40% of audiences came from outside of Galway city and county, with 15% coming from overseas (Envision Marketing Consultants 1994) Nevertheless, the festival remains committed to privileging local audiences. In an address delivered at the 1997 festival, the international marketing manager of Bord Fáilte emphasised the festival's great tourism potential. Adverse local reaction to this address elicited a swift response from the festival organisation ensuring local people that while tourist audiences were welcome, the festival would continue to prioritise local needs.

Networking and Mediating: Forging Tourism Connections

The argument thus far is that there is nothing natural or inevitable about the way the two case-study festivals evolved. They both show clear signs of having been purposefully constructed according to well-defined agendas intended to further specific interests. In Wexford, the festival architects can be seen to be constructing an artistic endeavour that was to be produced by local people but to be performed and enjoyed largely by others. In Galway, the entire concern was to serve a range of local needs, although not all interest groups were equally privileged. These findings support those of Farber (1983: 40), who, in a study of a community-based festival in Canada, demonstrated how the festival was designed and structured by leading members of the community as a 'symbolic representation of the asserted, believed and controlled community identity'. However, the authorship of key individuals in manipulating the festival production process and in successfully harnessing local approval for its vision has not proceeded unproblematically in the two case-study sites. Beneath the semblance of community that attaches to both festivals lies a series of tensions dividing various interest groups and shaping local people's engagement with the festivals. These tensions have come into perspective ever more clearly as the two festivals have intensified their interactions with agents and structures emanating in extra-local spheres. Critically implicated in the divisions that characterise the relationships between people in these festival sites has been the arrival of visitor flows. The key questions to be answered in this context are: how has tourism emerged as a force of influence in these festival places and how is tourism affecting the meanings being produced there?

Developing an understanding of the relationships which the festivals subsequently developed with external places must take as its starting point an analysis of Wexford and Galway themselves. The characteristics of the two places are critical in explaining both the networking tendencies exhibited by the organisations and the effectiveness of local agents in negotiating external forces. Both festivals were 'products' of their place and could not have emerged in their constituent form anywhere else. Their respective geographical locations were enormously formative factors. Wexford's historical links with the Anglo world, promoted by its location on the south east coast, can be forwarded in partial explanation of the festival's willing embrace of the conventions and values of the European 'high brow' musical world and of British models of festival development. Pragmatically, the ease of access to Britain by air (via Dublin, some 80 miles north of Wexford) and particularly by sea (via Rosslare, 10 miles east of Wexford) facilitated the development of contacts between the festival organisers and opera professionals in places like Glyndebourne and Covent Garden. As the festival developed, this factor was crucial in fostering the growth of British audiences and in establishing Wexford as part of the British opera circuit around which British casting directors, opera critics and other influential gatekeepers journeyed.

The Galway festival landscape equally manifests evidence of the city's longstanding identity as a place with strong cultural associations yet one which has stood on the margins of the more modern, eastern part of the country dominated by Dublin. The concern to promote locally sourced arts for the benefit of local audiences was an attempt to stimulate what it considered to be a dormant artistic creativity and to challenge the capital city's dominance of the Irish arts landscape. Its preoccupation with the West did not mean that its vision was myopic or parochial. Over time its programming became increasingly internationalised, yet its inspiration continued to be simultaneously drawn from its locale.

Contained within the very founding ambitions of the Wexford festival was a desire to shake off its status as a 'local' festival and to operate within an international sphere. Ironically, the critical factor propelling it into a series of relationships with external forces was its place-specific, historically-rooted middle-class origins. The key festival architects had emerged from the town's social élite, an élite that can trace its origins back to the town's particular heritage as a prosperous and cosmopolitan trading port (Furlong, 1991). These social origins bestowed on the actors both the inclination to advance their initiative through networking and a series of critical advantages in doing so. They had close connections to those in powerful positions and opportunities for mobilising public support at the local level. Equally, they had deep levels of appreciation of the 'high' art form being promoted, connections with leading figures active in the national music and opera scene, and familiarity with how the international opera world operated. The fact that an overwhelming proportion of the Wexford festival's audience comes from outside of Wexford is testimony to the organisation's longstanding efforts to market the festival, particularly in the UK. As early as the 1950s, the Festival Council was coordinating schedules with the cross-channel ferry companies and holding press conferences in London. By 1961, festival publicity material was being distributed through the international offices of Aer Lingus , British Rail, Coast Lines and Bord Fáilte. Currently, Wexford Festival Opera holiday packages are distributed through an international network of tour operators.

The lack of interest displayed by the Galway Arts Festival in expanding the spatial reach of its activities stands in marked contrast. Its particular dedication to cultivating local and regional creative imaginations produced an orientation that was much more spatially contained. The networking strategies that took it into extra-local spheres were primarily concerned with artists and artforms. It was not until the 1990s that marketing efforts were extended beyond the local and regional levels. Then the festival altered its ticket distribution systems to develop extra-local audiences. It began to advertise in the national press and on national radio and efforts to win sponsorship from major companies intensified. Gradually, a visitor audience materialised, although it did so in a way that can only be understood in the context of general tourism growth in the city during the 1990s. The festival's engagement with tourism evolved in a way that was neither deliberately stimulated nor controlled by the festival organisation.

Tourism's Role in Reproducing Cultural Meanings

The Wexford festival represents a model tourism event. Audience capacity is regularly achieved, sizeable flows of high spending tourists are generated and the difficulties associated with the low season are eliminated during the several weeks encompassing the festival. The volume of tourist flows is very manageable because of the festival's modest audience capacity (the Theatre Royal seats just 550), and the type of tourists attracted. Overall, tourism effectively complements the aims and vision of the festival. Without it, Walsh's original dedication to producing rare opera to a high standard of excellence could not have been sustained.

While tourism has served the dominant vision shaping the Wexford festival landscape, the arrival of visitor flows thwarted the ambitions which many local people had for involving themselves in the festival. As early as 1952 a local newspaper reported that 'such was the demand for seats that hundreds (of local people) were unable to gain admission' (*Wexford People* 8 November 1952). The following year the same newspaper wrote of the need to extend the season 'so that local people can still share in a thing that many travel to see from foreign parts' (*Wexford People* 17 October 1961). Gradually, the failure of the festival to accommodate local people in its audiences contributed to a waning interest in the venture. The most tangible sign of this was that between 1958 and 1964 the number of festival subscribers fell dramatically from 800 to 250. The focal point of local interest in the festival began to shift from the opera performances to what has subsequently become known as 'The Fringe'. By 1961, the *Wexford People* was reporting that 'for many, the Festival Forum is the best part of festival week. It is open to the public and is known as a fringe event' (*Wexford People* 30 September 1961). A survey of local respondents ($N = 166$) during the 1996 festival found that while almost 60% attended a fringe event, just less than 17% attended an event on the main opera programme. Meanwhile, just 7.2% had attended an opera. Other survey data record that involvement in voluntary and performance capacities has declined over time, while contemporary attendance has greatly declined relative to audience capacity since the festival's early period.

That the Wexford festival is not designed with the local population in mind was well recognised by the local population surveyed in 1996. Respondents repeatedly demonstrated an understanding of the festival as a phenomenon that includes and excludes people on the basis of social standing reinforced by place of residence. For a minority, exclusion was accepted without question. However, for the majority, exclusion was an issue and opinions on the festival ranged from stoicism to extreme anger: 'The opera is only for "big" people, it has always been that way. I'd like to go but that's the way it is.' Many resented exclusion: 'Local involvement has gone . . . it's out of our hands'; 'Too much hoity toity, should be open to everyone'; 'Why doesn't Wexford get bigger? It's not accessible enough, there's a need to bring the arts to the public rather than *vice versa*'. A minority could not contain their anger: 'It's catering for a tone deaf élite'; 'It's not a people's event, just to keep people happy they throw in a few fringe events'.

The sense of exclusion from the festival landscape expressed by local survey respondents was palpable and was heightened by a strong self-awareness of their own historical store of musical talent. Yet the contentiousness which this divided landscape inevitably produced has never inspired a radical resistance to the cultural meanings and the social ordering reproduced by the festival. Instead, it has been a question of local people slowly, over time, withdrawing support from the back and side stages of the festival production zone, and steadily resigning themselves to the realisation that their very sizeable interest in the 'high' arts has to find expression outside of the festival arena. This quiet yielding of space to the visiting festival audiences and the acquiescence to the meanings produced by the festival have been promoted by the festival's 'compensatory system' (including the fringe festival and the opera dress rehearsals) which effectively renders local compliance and support. Tourism has also played a critical role in this respect. The economic rewards generated by tourism are very significant. Furthermore, the sizeable inward flow of middle- and upper-class visitors is part of the process which 'puts Wexford on the map' as one respondent put it and partially explains the overwhelming sense of pride that local residents feel in the festival.

The implications that the arrival of tourists has had on the cultural meanings produced in Galway are more ambiguous than in Wexford. For its first decade, tourism had no role to play in the festival. Thus the festival landscape that evolved was one in which local people, in the main, could freely engage and feel completely at home. The decision to target tourists in the 1990s, while it offered a means of expanding audiences and thus generating more income, immediately problematised the festival's objectives. The historical privileging of Galway residents and the place of Galway was now altered and the control which local residents traditionally felt over the festival has become threatened. Recent transformations have not gone unnoticed. One of the festival founders has been reported as saying: 'the festival has to make up its mind what it is, whether a big established arts festival where the level of credit card booking is a measure of its success, or whether it redefines itself in terms of the community' (Breathnach, 1999). Meanwhile, among the local population, there is a sense that the festival's acknowledged close relationship with the people of Galway has been weakened. While almost 53% of the locals surveyed during the 1996 festival ($N = 138$) attended at least one festival event and satisfaction levels were generally high, voices cautioned against the type of development path being taken by the festival. 'The festival must be kept as it used to be: meeting the needs of ordinary Galwegians.' It must 'maintain identity . . . it needs to be careful about this . . . shouldn't go too alternative'. There was a concern that the festival is becoming too 'elitist. This is the image they want to put across for people outside of Galway'. Many local people sense that they are being distanced from the artistic core of the festival, and are conscious of the various mechanisms (credit card booking, the ending of the season ticket scheme, productions that are considered too 'arty') through which this process is advancing. These findings could be interpreted in the light of social exchange theory, as advocated by Getz (1994) and others, as a means of understanding residents' attitudes to tourism. It holds that 'residents who view the results of tourism as personally valuable and believe that the costs do not exceed the benefits, will favour the exchange and support tourism development' (Jurowski *et al.*, 1997: 3).

It is significant that the tourism profile associated with the festival does little to promote local acquiescence to local people's changing status. To begin with, the festival's timing coincides with the height of the tourist season and takes place in Ireland's third largest tourism centre. The city welcomes one million tourists annually and the timing of the festival serves to compound any social and environmental problems already existing in the city (Galway Chamber of Commerce, 1996). It also limits the economic benefits that the festival can generate for the city's hospitality sector because this is when capacity sales are at or near saturation. Furthermore, the festival has not proven itself capable of generating sizeable flows of tourists who come to the city with the singular intention of experiencing the festival, unlike in Wexford. Nor is it likely that the relatively youthful visiting audiences are particularly high spenders (Envision Marketing Consultants, 1994). Thus, it appears that in materialising into a tourist attraction, the Galway Arts Festival is becoming involved in an activity over which it cannot possibly exert control. This relates in part to the extensive scale of tourism activity in the city and to the timing of the festival. However, it also relates to shortcomings in the city's approach to integrated tourism management.

Reproducing 'Festival Places'

The two festivals under discussion constitute examples of 'authored landscapes' where particular aspects of place are cultivated to construct a setting in which cultural production can then appear to unfold as if in a natural way (Cosgrove & Domosh, 1993). It is obvious that place has always mattered for both festivals. However, the way in which the leading architects chose to manipulate aspects of place through the festival assumed very different dimensions.

In Wexford, Walsh and his co-founders were acutely aware that place matters and determined to invent Wexford as a festival town. They adopted the popular approach of developing a festival through an association with a composer and opened the inaugural festival with an opera by Michael Balfe, the Irish composer who had once lived in Wexford. The link with Balfe was not seriously developed in subsequent years, however, and, instead, the festival organisation began to expound the extra-musical appeals of the recently invented 'festival town'. Key signifiers of this creation are the charming intimacy of the Theatre Royal, the quaint narrowness of the town's medieval streets and the warm hospitality of its people. All of these are promoted, at every opportunity, by the organisation's publicity machine. Promoting extra-musical appeals is not unique to Wexford and invites particular parallels with the Glyndebourne Opera Company in the UK (with whom Wexford has a series of historical connections). Glyndebourne's identity is intimately bound up with place and it has demonstrated that the absence of strong music-place associations do not render hosting an opera festival an impossibility. Over time, the essence of the Wexford festival has come to be encapsulated as much by the atmosphere and sociability of the town as by the quality of its operatic productions. As early as the 1960s, opera critics' accounts in British newspapers depicted local people as welcoming and friendly as well as 'benignly amused by being the centre of musical attention' (*The Observer* 30 October 1988). The definition of Wexford in terms of its quaintness, informality and friendliness is so pervasive that it informs the 'official' interpretation of the Wexford Festival Opera published in *the New Grove Dictionary of Opera* (Sadie, 1992) and the *Oxford Dictionary of Opera* (Warrack & West, 1992). The former describes Wexford as an international festival that has managed to retain its convivial atmosphere, while the latter comments on the adventurous nature of the repertory and the conviviality of the town's welcome.

The Galway festival is no less an authored landscape, although 're-inventing' Galway as a festival town was not an issue initially. Unlike Wexford, the Galway festival was not trying to position itself in a wider market of arts festivals and so had no motive for cultivating a sense of difference about its place. More fundamentally, the inspiration underpinning the festival genuinely stemmed from the artistic possibilities of the place itself and there was, therefore, no need for any invention. Building a programme around a core of locally based artists was the most obvious way in which the festival proclaimed its Galwegian status. However, in the 1990s, as the programme itself became more international, and as it sought to attract spatially dispersed audiences, the organisation seems to have placed a new emphasis on re-inventing Galway as a festival place. Its publicity material now cultivates an image of self as 'a major international arts festival with a distinctly West of Ireland atmosphere' (Galway Arts Festival, 1991).

Thus, it can be said that the essence of both festivals is rooted at least as much in their place, as it is in the arts that are produced there. Undoubtedly place still matters but the type of place in question must be qualified. Best coined the 'festival place', this is but a selected and packaged representation of the place as a whole from which it derives. It is an artificial creation, constructed on the basis of criteria designed to promote its appeal and marketability and to attract a series of inter-dependent external flows of audiences, revenue, media attention, critical acclaim and sponsorship. The components of the 'festival place' genuinely belong to the 'real' place, but what sets the former apart is the manner in which these components are constructed without any reference to the reality of the everyday lives lived out in these places. For example, considerable discussion has focused on the complex and conflicting roles and meanings that the festival holds for the heterogeneous population surveyed in Wexford. Yet, in the 'festival town' this heterogeneity is disguised in imagery that depicts a welcoming, smiling townspeople.

Conclusions

In seeking to conceptualise how tourism is implicated in influencing the meanings of place it is important to remember that tourism destinations are, in fact, places where communities of people reside. Tourism activity is 'grounded' within these places in numerous ways and, very frequently, human agents within these places play a critical role in moulding its emergence and development. This chapter has emphasised the role of agency in shaping two arts festivals cum tourist attractions. The two festivals under discussion represent excellent examples of what geographers have termed 'authored landscapes'. However, in neither case were the key figures autonomous agents. Within a local context, their actions were contextualised by the historically situated circumstances of their place and the actors themselves were shaped by the social contexts played out in Wexford and Galway. More broadly, the festival leadership acted as critical conduits, linking their place with the wider world. They were both strongly influenced by the paradigmatic cultural thinking of their day and their artistic policies and activities connected with ideals circulating internationally. Furthermore, the meanings that they tried to reproduce through the festival setting sometimes met with opposition in the local sphere, and producing strategies for securing local acquiescence has been a priority. In the case of Galway, this dimension is only recently becoming a defining part of the festival organisation's relationship with local people.

The ways in which agency is constrained by both structures and competing agency is brought sharply into focus by the workings of the tourism process. The Wexford case clearly illustrates how a small group of individuals, working on a very small scale, effectively exploited the organs of the tourism industry, to further their own aims. The local–extra-local dynamic that underpins tourism activity was, in this case, initiated and controlled by the place-based agents. The power of agency was intensified by a number of historically situated circumstances and success was predicated on the ability to control the festival's evolution as a tourist attraction. The ability to control was, in turn, promoted by a number of factors. First, tourism was moulded, as a strategy, to further an already existing set of artistic objectives. It was, in effect, construed as a means to an end. Second, the scale of tourism that evolved was relatively easy to manage. By definition, the scale and nature of tourist flows attracted by an opera festival is modest and specialist. Furthermore, the relatively modest scale of tourism activity in Wexford in general and the off-season timing of the festival were important factors. Thus, for the Wexford Festival Opera, tourism is a mechanism through which the cultural meanings produced by the festival architects can be effectively promoted because the latter are capable of manipulating the tourism process to their advantage.

If the Wexford case demonstrates how agency has the power to initiate, mediate and control, the fragility of agency, in the face of very powerful tourism forces, is illustrated by recent developments in the Galway Arts Festival. Its evolution into a tourist attraction was much less planned but it now undoubtedly faces pressure from influential gatekeepers to privilege an expansion of tourist audiences. Bord Fáilte comments, the state's selection of the festival as one of Ireland's Millenium Festivals and censure from *Irish Times* reviewers for programming local bands in an international programme represent examples of how this process manifests itself. While tourism serves identifiable purposes for the Galway festival, it fundamentally problematises the organisation's stated objectives. The local population, whose artistic needs the festival strives to meet, is showing signs of becoming distanced from the work of the festival. There seems to be a danger that tourism, now being employed as 'a means to an end', is running the risk of tarnishing that 'end'. Again control is the crucial factor, except that here it is the limited ability of the festival to control its involvement in tourism that is the issue. A key factor mitigating the situation in Galway is the question of scale. Tourism activity in Galway in July is at its peak. Furthermore, the Arts Festival's contribution to the city's significant tourism resource base is very modest. Accordingly, its ability to exert influence among the city's well-established tourism sector is limited.

Thus, the validity of construing tourism as a 'transaction process' formed through the interaction of endogenous and exogenous forces becomes clear. The critical role that individual agents can play in initiating the tourism process and in drawing, however unwittingly, external forces into the local place, has been demonstrated. That networking, effectively used to favourably connect with influential gatekeepers in all geographic spheres can strengthen tourism viability is clear. However, the power of tourism forces to overwhelm local initiatives and to constrain their ability to meet locally felt needs is also evident. It can be very difficult for local agents to withstand mounting pressures from influential gatekeepers to commodify and commercialise.

Furthermore, even when place-based agents appear to be effectively controlling the pace and form of tourism development, it cannot be assumed that the broader interests of the residential community are being advanced. The opposite can happen, as dominant meanings are strengthened by alliances that cross divisions between places. In both Wexford and Galway, the trend has been for local populations to sense themselves being adversely affected by the arrival of tourist flows. This phenomenon is very complicated and sometimes very subtle in its workings, however the outcome is that as powerful groups within the local sphere effectively connect with outside interests, wider local interests can be effectively overlooked. The privileging of visitors can be such that the structuring of the landscape can function to make outsiders feel at home, and to transform locals into the role of onlookers, 'displaced' within their own home. In the Wexford case, the élite group behind the festival found in visitors a very powerful ally. The partnership effectively strengthens the former's ability to produce a series of cultural meanings which to the world at large, appear to pass uncontested, when in fact, survey findings suggest that one-third of the local population would like to participate more fully in the festival. One of the most disturbing conclusions is that the marginalisation of local interests can occur even when the local controlling agent opposes this process. This is what is happening with the Galway Arts Festival as, increasingly, the organisation is being dictated to by forces outside its control.

As the festivals evolve away from an earlier relative autonomy to an overwhelming dependence on relationships with other places there are further implications for the nature of place itself. While a complex interplay of time, space and social and human differences conspired here to create two very different arts festivals, over time, the general indications are that that difference is diminishing. Increasingly, the places being reproduced are carefully packaged, highly mythologised, commodified places where image and marketability assume greatest significance. The move towards commodification is marked, as is the tendency to selectively represent particular dimensions of places in order to promote their commercial status.

Tourism has been an important means of reproducing place in this way. It constitutes one of the local–extra-local connections implicated in changing the meanings and experiences of place, not only for the people who live there but also for those who visit there. Currently, some of the most interesting questions about tourism places reside in this realm of local–extra-local connectedness. It is hoped that this chapter will encourage other researchers to locate some of their enquiries here.

References

Barnes, T. and Hayter, R. (1992) The little town that did: Flexible accumulation and community response in Chemainus, B.C. *Regional Studies* 26, 617–63.

Blank, U. (1989) *The Community Tourism Imperative: The Necessity, the Opportunities, its Potential.* State College Texas: Venture Publishing.

Breathnach, P. (1999) Quoted in a Galway Arts Festival special supplement in the *Irish Times* (3 July).

Chang, T.C., Milne, S., Fallon D. and Pohlmann, C. (1996) Urban heritage tourism. The global–local nexus. *Annals of Tourism Research* 23 (2), 284–305.

Cosgrove, D.E. and Domosh, M. (1993) Author and authority: Writing the new cultural geography. In J.S. Duncan and D. Ley (eds) *Place/Culture/Representation* (pp. 25–38). London: Routledge.

Envision Marketing Consultants (1994) *Galway Arts Festival.* Galway: Envision Marketing Consultants.

Farber, C. (1983) High, healthy and happy: Ontario mythology on parade. In F.E. Manning (ed.) *The Celebration of Society: Perspectives on Contemporary Cultural Performance* (pp. 33–49). Bowling Green, OH: Bowling Green Popular University Press.

Furlong, N. (1991) Wexford and Loch Garman. In I. Fox (ed.) *100 Nights at the Opera: An Anthology to Celebrate the 40th Anniversary of the Wexford Opera Festival* (pp. 53–5). Dublin: Town House and Country.

Galway Arts Festival (1991) *Submission to Arts Council.* Unpublished.

Galway Chamber of Commerce (1996) *Galway Yearbook and Diary.* Galway: Galway Chamber of Commerce.

Getz, D. (1994) Residents attitudes towards tourism. A longitudinal study in Spey Valley, Scotland. *Tourism Management* 15 (4), 247–58.

Guichard-Anguis, S. (1997) Fêtes et symboles dans les villes japonais. Paper presented at the Cultural Approaches in Cultural Geography symposium, Université de Paris IV, 8–11 December.

The Irish Press (1953) 26 October.

The Irish Times (1963) 23 October.

The Irish Independent (1962) 24 October.

Jackson, P. (1988) Street life: The politics of carnival. *Environment and Planning D: Society and Space* 6, 213–27

Jurowski, C. Uysal, M. and Williams, D.R. (1997) A theoretical analysis of host community resident reactions to tourism. *Journal of Travel Research* 36 (2), 3–11.

Lewis, C. and Pile, S. (1996) Woman, body, space: Rio carnival and the politics of performance. *Gender, Place and Culture* 3 (1), 23–41.

Manning, F.E. (1983) *The Celebration of Society: Perspectives on Contemporary Cultural Performance.* Bowling Green, OH: Bowling Green Popular University Press.

Marston, S. (1989) Public rituals and community power: St. Patrick's Day parades in Lowell, Massachusetts, 1841–1874. *Political Geography Quarterly* 8 (3), 255–69.

McGrath, F. (1997) Manager, Galway Arts Festival. Personal interview.

Milne, S.S. (1998) Tourism and sustainable development: The global–local nexus. In A.M. Hall and A.A. Lew (ed) *Sustainable Tourism: A Geographical Perspective*. Essex: Longman.

Morris, A. and Dickinson, G. (1987) Tourist development in Spain: Growth versus conservation on the Costa Brava. *Geography* 72, 16–25.

Murphy, P. (1983) Perceptions and attitudes of decision making groups in tourism centers. *Journal of Travel Research* 21 (3), 8–12.

Oakes, T. S. (1994) The cultural space of modernity: Ethnic tourism and place identity in China. *Environment and Planning C: Society and Space* 11, 47–66.

O'Hagan, J., Barrett, A. and Purdy, M. (1989) *The Economic and Social Contribution of the Wexford Opera Festival*. Dublin: Department of Economics, Trinity College.

Reed, M. (1997) Power relations and community-based tourism planning. *Annals of Tourism Research* 24 (3) 566–91.

Ryan, C. and Montgomery, D. (1994) The attitudes of Bakewell residents to tourism and issues in community responsive tourism. *Tourism Management* 15 (2), 358–69.

Sadie, S. (ed.) (1992) *The New Grove Dictionary of Music and Musicians*. London: Macmillan.

Smith, S. (1996) Bounding the Borders: Claiming space and making place in rural Scotland. *Transactions, Institute of British Geographers* 18, 291–308.

The Observer (1988) 30 October.

Warrack, J. and West, E. (1992) *The Oxford Dictionary of Opera*. London: Oxford University Press.

Wexford People (1952–1961) Various editions.

Part 2

Performing Heritage: The Globalisation of Tourist Products and Practices

Chapter 4

'The Cracked Pint Glass of the Servant': The Irish Pub, Irish Identity and the Tourist Eye[1]

MARK McGOVERN

Introduction

The 'Irish pub' is crucial to Irish tourism. In the first instance, this is due to the range of practical services that many of Ireland's more than 8000 public houses provide, ensuring that they are part and parcel of the island's tourist infrastructure (Scott, 1994). CERT (the State Tourism Training Agency) has argued that the pub in Ireland is not only important 'to the life of local communities' in small towns and villages but that in larger towns 'pubs have become central to the overall tourism product offering food, drink, entertainment and in some cases even accommodation' (CERT, 1993: 71). However, the Irish pub is more than a tourist service provider. Over the last decade the concerted drive to sell Ireland as a tourist destination has seen the 'Irish pub' emerge as a key marketing motif. In large part this is due to the place of the pub in external perceptions of Ireland and of Irish people. Many foreign visitors regard Ireland's pub culture as one of the most distinctive and attractive elements of modern Irish society. It is also tied very closely to images of Irish people themselves, who form a critical component in the appeal of the Irish pub to the tourist eye. This chapter will examine why this is so and what implications this might have for tourist development in Ireland and for its culture and people. It will argue that aspects of Irish pub culture have been objectified and commodified for the tourist experience. The form this commodification has taken has been, in large part, dependent upon tourist expectations, generated not only by tourist promotional material but also by other longer-term social and cultural processes. Ultimately, the pub has emerged as the site for a form of cultural tourism in which a socially constructed conception of Irish people

83

is consumed in a setting that also allows for tourist 'escape, hedonism and exploration' (Craik, 1997).

In the first instance, images of Irish culture and the social lives of Irish people being inextricably bound up with pubs and alcohol in the minds of many tourists needs to be put into an historical perspective. It is not a new phenomenon. Indeed, the image of 'garrulous paddy' has a long lineage and is deeply embedded in dominant representations of the Irish throughout modern history. An almost invariably alcohol-centred 'stage Irish' persona is reflected in early travel writing on Ireland from at least the late 18th century onward helping to establish a series of easily recognisable and historicised symbols and cultural reference points for contemporary external visions of Ireland. Alongside avowedly negative portrayals of 'Irishness' such images also forged a romanticised link between the 'Irish Other' and conviviality, ease of communication and an escape from 'time–work discipline'. This, it will be suggested, has been of particular significance in the attractiveness of Ireland as a site for leisure consumption.

Images of Ireland held by people elsewhere have also often depended upon their view of the Irish, and of things 'Irish', in their midst. Images associated with the marketing of Irish alcoholic export products have helped shape the preconceptions which tourists have prior to their arrival in Ireland. Similarly Irish migrant culture (and host perceptions of that culture) have also helped shape the link of the Irish with the pub. Both have proved important to the rapid spread of 'Irish theme bars' in many parts of the globe during the last decade. The rise of the Irish theme bar has paralleled the rapid expansion of tourism in Ireland and the two processes are, in many ways, interwoven. The initial impetus for the spread of the 'theme bar' was, in large part, dependent upon an opportunity identified through tourism. In turn, the increased global profile of the Irish bar that the theme pubs have given rise to has helped feed tourist expectations in a very specific way. The impact of the Irish theme bar upon tourism and upon the commodification of Irish identity must therefore be examined before the role of Irish pub culture in contemporary Irish tourism can be assessed.

Tourism is concerned with the consumption of place and the consumption of goods and services in that place. The economic context of both Irish pub culture and the Irish drinks industry is also therefore of critical importance in assessing the importance of both for tourist development. Both pubs and Irish alcohol production are important areas of economic activity and this material dimension is far from negligible in their relationship to tourist promotion. This link is further evidenced in the increasing importance of brewery and distillery visitor centres as profitable tourist attractions in their own right.

Ultimately, however, it is with the contemporary representation of the

Irish pub in the promotion of Ireland as a tourist destination and its role in the tourist experience with which this chapter in concerned. It will be argued that an essentialised notion of Irishness is in part constructed through the specific spaces, activities, sounds and symbols of the Irish bar. The cultural reproduction of such ethnicised signs represents a reification of their meaning. What is commodified and consumed in the tourist experience of the Irish pub is a notional experience encapsulated in the concept of the 'craic'.[2] Commodifying the 'craic', it will be suggested, represents a form of cultural tourism. Given the great emphasis placed upon the social actions and identity of Irish people in the commodified 'craic' there is a sense in which they, too, are being consumed by the tourist. This may have significant ramifications not only for the way that Irish people will be seen by the tourist but also for that richly diverse and almost indefinable explosion of human interaction which the concept of 'craic' attempts to encapsulate.

'Garrulous Paddy' and 'Time-Work Discipline': 19th Century Tourism, Stage Irishry and the Emergence of an Alcohol-centred Identity

From a very early date Ireland was established as a regular destination for the English tourist and one that also 'consistently impressed visitors by its foreign quality' (Hadfield & McVeagh, 1994: 134). The Irish landscape and many aspects of Irish society provided this sense of the different, the romantic and the exotic. However, it is noticeable that late 18th- and early 19th-century English travellers in Ireland regularly commented on the drinking habits of the peasantry and, indeed, of other social classes too, in large on the basis pre-conceived perceptions. Travel book representations of Irish drinking habits tended to oscillate between moral condemnation and a celebration of the exotic and primitive but seldom was an alcohol-centred identity far from the scene (Hadfield & McVeagh, 1994: 161). Indeed, such images continued to be very much to the fore through the 19th century as various social and economic changes made Ireland an ever more regular Victorian tourist destination (Grimes, 1980; Harrington, 1991).

These depictions of the drinking habits and social life of Irish peasants in early tourist writing emerged in tandem with (and were greatly fed by) the increasingly recognisable depiction of the 'comic Irishman' on the English stage (Edwards, 1994; Kiberd, 1995; Waters, 1984). Conventions for the portrayal of Irishmen and women on the popular stage were already fairly well established by the Victorian era but became even more clearly defined in this period. The Stage Irishman was a 'merry, whiskey drinking pugnacious clown' who could similarly be identified both with conversation and articulacy, as an 'outsider' who combined the romanticism of the rogue with the exotic threat of the unknown (Waters, 1984: 6).

This dual imagery of the Irish within the tourist and colonial mind (of drunken dissolution and roguish romanticism) stood at the juncture of two distinct elements of English Victorian moralism. The first was an avowed antagonism toward intoxicating drinks that was, in turn, part of a wider drive to promote 'time–work discipline' (Dingle, 1980: 8; Harrison, 1971; Shiman, 1988: 2; Thompson, 1963). Closely allied to this was a 'Eurocentric' and imperial view of colonised peoples, whose social lives and cultures were similarly seen as anti-progressive and the antithesis of modern civilisation. The 'Colonial Other' often became the symbolic mirror, the binary opposite for an emerging conception of Englishness and imperial patriotism (Memmi, 1990; Said, 1993; Samuels, 1989). In the imagery of the whiskey-loving Irish these two processes merged. In the process a pool of discursively constructed signs and symbols was established through which Irish people negotiated their relationship to the outside world for many years to come. As Terry Eagleton (1998) has recently argued the 'Celt in English eyes has meant sociability as well as savagery, the clubbable rather than the calibanesque'. This, it could be argued, has become increasingly the case for non-English eyes as well.

'Selling Beer, Selling Ireland': The Drinks Industry and Images of Irishness

That Irish drinking habits, public houses and the culture of sociability that went with them were regarded as distinctive and different abroad was not, however, solely dependent on the symbolism of 'stage Irishry'. It was also in part grounded in certain material realities. The increasing importance of the Irish brewing and distilling industries was one important factor that helped foster the image of the Irish bar and an alcohol-centred Irish identity abroad that would also have a direct bearing on future tourist development. An essentialised and reified conception of Irishness emerged as a key component of product branding by the Irish drinks industry. This process of ethnic commodification was one that has ultimately fed into the commodification of Irishness in the tourist experience of the Irish bar.

In the late 18th and early 19th century Irish breweries and distilleries tended to suffer at the hands of competition from England where mechanisation and large-scale factory production took a much earlier hold. By the end of the 19th century, however, an increasing export orientation and the trend toward an ever-greater concentration of industrial production had some dramatic results. By the start of the 20th century the production of

Irish whiskey accounted for 25% of the total UK output and the orientation of the industry was thus more and more geared toward export. At the same time as the domestic market was contracting, those abroad stimulated ever-greater production. In Ireland the impact of the temperance movement and teetotalism was reflected in the falling rate of per capita whiskey consumption in the second half of the 19th century from (an admittedly high figure by today's standards) 1.1 gallons in 1857 to 0.63 gallons by 1910 (Ó Gráda, 1995: 298). The export of Irish spirits, however, doubled in the 1860s and 1870s, and doubled again by the 1890s. In 1907 two-thirds of Irish whiskey went to markets overseas and increasingly firms such as Bushmills and Jamesons had come to dominate production (Cullen, 1972: 157–8). The relationship of spirits to the image of Ireland and the Irish was, therefore, likely to be largely immune to changes in Irish drinking habits to the external eye.

Similarly, while the number of Irish brewing firms fell from 247 in 1837 to only 24 by 1920, the output of the brewing industry increased threefold between 1850 and 1914 with as much as 40% of the total being exported by the early 20th century. Although some (such as Murphy's and Beamish) continued to cater for largely local markets the Guinness brewery had, by that time, become the largest in the world. As well as obtaining an overall dominance of the domestic market it also accounted for the overwhelming share of beer exports from Ireland; as much as 96% by the start of the 20th century. This trade was significant to the Irish economy. In 1914 beer and ale accounted for 3.2% of all Irish exports (Ó Gráda, 1995: 298). Nor did political independence substantially change this situation. In 1926 brewing accounted for 30% of net manufacturing output and was one of the very few industrial sectors to export a significant proportion of that output (Ó Gráda, 1997: 108). On the eve of the economic war with Britain in 1936 (which led Guinness to establish a brewery in London) the company exported 1.3 million barrels per year, though this dropped to 0.8 million by 1938. This is a figure that has never reached the same height again, although this is due to the fact that Guinness emerged in the post-war era as a multinational corporation with production sited around the globe, rather than its demise as a major player in the brewing business (Kennedy, 1988: 47).

Historically, then, Ireland's image abroad was always likely to be closely associated with those products that were most readily recognisable and accessible as distinctly 'Irish'. It was similarly in the interests of the Irish drinks industry to continue to foster the link between Irishness and their products. As consumption became increasingly dependent upon marketing in the latter part of the 20th century and the vogue for ethnicised consumer objects took an ever firmer hold, so the imagery of the Irish bar and of 'romantic rogue' stage Irishry constituted a language through which the seller could speak to the consumer. Marketing Irish beer and spirits abroad would increasingly provide an important part of the material basis for the imagination of the Irish bar in the outsider's mind.

The Irish drinks industry is keen to celebrate the extent to which their brands are virtually regarded as national symbols of Ireland in the wider world. In part this is because they continue to feature so prominently in Ireland's foreign trade. In 1995, for example, the phenomenal success of Baileys cream liqueur ensured that its foreign sales accounted for 1% of total Irish exports (Ó Gráda, 1997: 129). Between 1979 and 1991 export of alcoholic beverages from Ireland increased by 315% in real terms. Guinness, today one of the most recognisable brand names in the world and undoubtedly the most well-known commercial Irish symbol, continues to exemplify the link between the political economy of the Irish drinks industry and an Irish alcohol-centred identity.

It is also clear that many of those involved in the Irish drinks industry recognise the importance of images of the Irish bar and of a notional conception of Irish people for their continued high profile, particularly in recent years. The marketing campaigns of various Irish beers and stouts during the 1990s emphasised key elements of the contemporary construction of a stage Irishness. Emigration, an idiosyncratic sense of wit, spirituality and 'romanticised roguery' have all been prominent elements in the selling of Murphy's, Caffreys, Beamish and other Irish alcoholic products (McGovern, 1999). Adverts for Irish beers and spirits also parallel the tourist images of Ireland as a rural 'natural' and anti-modern place (Author's interview, 2000b). Such marketing strategies both illustrate the existence of and further reinforce pre-conceived and socially constructed images of Ireland, framing the context within which tourist expectations are constructed long before their arrival.

In addition, the drinks industry is quick to point out the link between the perception of Ireland abroad, the profile of these alcoholic products and tourism. Given that their advertising campaigns often emphasise their imagined 'Irish character', it has been argued by the lobbying organisation of the Irish brewers and distillers that they offer 'free advertising for Irish tourism' (O'Hagan & Scott, 1993: 37). The high product profile of various Irish alcoholic drinks, and of the site of their consumption, is therefore seen as having a direct impact on tourism; 'stout, Irish whiskey, cream liqueurs, and most important perhaps the Irish pub', an Irish drinks industry report concluded 'are significant in international perceptions of Ireland' (Drinks Industry Group, 1993). They also, of course, ensure that the consumption of Irish beers and spirits is closely tied to the idea of what Ireland is to the visitor (Drinks Industry Group, 1993). The pursuit of increased volume sales of beer and whiskey, outside Ireland as well as within it, has placed a premium on the promotion of an alcohol-centred Irish identity. This has also helped feed another recent development that has impacted significantly on tourist expectations of a visit to Ireland: the rise of the Irish theme bar.

'Tourism without Travel': The Emergence and Impact of the Irish Theme Bar

The Irish theme bar is a global phenomenon of the 1990s. In the last decade over 1600 'new Irish bars' have appeared everywhere from Berlin to Beijing (The Irish Pub Company, 1997). To no small degree this rapid expansion has exploited a previously untapped market first identified in relation to tourism in Ireland. With supposed 'authenticity' guiding their design, Irish theme bars construct a notion of Irishness around an anti-modern nostalgia. As Jennifer Craik (1997) has argued, it is within the original culture of the tourist that expectations of their destination are shaped. As a result, Irish theme bars may have proved important in determining tourist expectations of what their travel experience in Ireland will be like.

The rapid rise of the Irish theme bar in the last decade was, in many ways, due to the recognition of a potential market identified in the expectations of the tourist. The drinking of Guinness was already a well-established element of the tourist experience in Ireland and the company saw in this a potential untapped opportunity for future expansion. If tourists, on their return home, did not continue to drink Guinness then this was, in large part, seen as due to the absence of a suitable social setting for them to do so. Exporting the 'ambience' of the Irish bar, therefore, became the means to increase the volume consumption of Irish alcoholic products. From the early 1990s onward, Guinness' world-wide operation, therefore, worked to provide certain services and incentives to create a network of Irish bars, run almost invariably by Irish staff, that could establish the social setting seen as a necessary prerequisite for the consumption of their products (The Irish Pub Company, 1997: 2).

Often working in tandem with Guinness The Irish Pub Company, 'the largest supplier of Irish pubs in the world', is a Dublin-based design agency established in 1991. It specialises 'in the design, manufacture and installation of authentic [sic] pubs worldwide' and has developed a series of design concepts which were intended to encapsulate the 'Irish pub experience'. Three designs are supposed to reflect the 'evolution of the Irish pub', from 'country cottage', to the 'Irish pub shop' and the 'Victorian Dublin pub', emphasising the appeal of a pre-modern nostalgia and the way in which the Irish bar is, in some senses, about travelling in time as well as space. Two further design concepts, the 'Gaelic pub' and the 'Irish brewery pub', are specifically designed for markets believed to be less familiar with Irish pub culture but with an interest in Gaelicism (mainly Germany and the USA) (Author's interview, 1999d).

In the last decade the Irish Pub Company has been responsible for the design and construction of over 400 separate bars, mostly in Europe, and they are currently expanding rapidly in both America and the Far East. According to a representative for the company the choice of design is made on very specific local conditions, rather than the identification of national cultural preferences or perceptions of Irish people: 'Location', it was argued, 'is everything' (Author's interview, 2000a). Location dictates, in particular, the demographic profile of the potential consumer to be targeted, according to age, socioeconomic group, disposable income etc. At the same time the overall design concept is intended to be adaptable to create different environments to suit different groups of people (as distinct consumer markets) through the day. Indeed, when the original concept was conceived in cooperation with Guinness, the aim was to achieve potential appeal across the 'social scale'. Such a marketing logic and design characteristics have also increasingly come to inform the layout and look of pubs in Ireland itself, where The Irish Pub Company has become more and more active in recent years. The key element identified in the design of such 'Irish theme bars' is a supposed 'ambience' of 'casual and attractive sociability' where people can 'enjoy the art of conversation', 'revel in music and song' and imbibe 'satisfying and distinctive drinks' (The Irish Pub Company, 1997: 12–17). The dominant perception of the Irish pub as a 'social centre' informs the sense, too, that there is a level of 'social acceptability' for public drinking in Ireland because it is a 'part of the culture' (Author's interview, 2000a).

In almost identical vein the largest Irish theme pub chain in the UK, O'Neill's (a division of the Bass Leisure Corporation created in 1994 that now includes well over 100 outlets) suggests in its promotional material that its premises are designed to create 'an environment which encourages the rich human interaction perceived to be the key feature of traditional Irish bars' (O'Neill's, 1997). Part and parcel of the package is, therefore, the Irish people themselves. As a niche design and identity management organisation, The Irish Pub Company initially had a recruitment agency in order that they could provide Irish bar staff for their potential customers. Ironically, as the state of the Irish labour market has improved, they have ceased to provide this new variant on the 'assisted passage'. However, Irish bar workers, the company argues, provide 'vital dimensions of authenticity and ambience, in terms of accent, friendliness, professionalism, good humour and conversation'. In America, for example, they have sought to 'deconstruct the prevailing service formula' and replace it with a more informal and apparently casual approach identified as intrinsically 'Irish'. This constructed conviviality is also clearly linked to perceptions of the Irish migrant. Emigration (particularly in the last three decades) is seen as having been crucial in ensuring that the Irish are 'recognised as sociable animals [who] speak romantically about home' (Au*thor's interview, 2000a).

All in all, the design of the bars is, therefore, intended to create opportunities for informal and regular social interaction, to 'force people together' precisely because this is seen as the unique appeal of the 'craic' and the Irish. The design cues and codes employed are, therefore, intended to 'comfort and cosset people against the perils of the world outside' by representing a 'traditional view of Ireland' and reifying the experience of the 'craic' community (Author's interview, 1999d).

The link between the commodified 'craic' of the Irish theme bars and Irish tourist development are most clearly to be found in the realm of tourist expectations. This is certainly the view of those responsible for selling Ireland to tourists. One senior tourist executive saw the work of The Irish Pub Company and of the 'commodified craic' as critical (Author's interview, 1999a);

> the whole association of the pub culture thing with Ireland has influenced tourist growth in a huge way . . . I mean you go to cities like Oslo, Helsinki, Frankfurt, Dusseldorf, Lyon, Rome, Venice, they all have Irish pubs . . . they have Irish staff, they have Irish music, they have a whole catalogue of Irish musicians who they bring in and a lot of these cities and a lot of these other cultures didn't have anything like that so . . . no 'craic' and they didn't know the meaning of 'craic' and then an Irish bar opens and it's thronged . . . it's an extraordinary phenomenon and so for people that might be their only introduction to Ireland, that might be their first exposure to Ireland and the Irish and that has been very, very helpful to us . . . people feel they are meeting Irish people, that they are really getting a true Irish experience . . . people love it, that has been a great support to us. It means people are well-disposed to Ireland, they'll say, 'we'll go down to our local Irish bar and if Ireland is anything like that sure it must be great.'

There is also a sense in which the theme bars themselves represent a form of 'tourism without travel' in the ethnic bazaar of an emerging global culture. Here is a way in which the 'tourist' can 'travel' to a notional Ireland without having to go to the trouble of travelling to the 'real' one. As Chris Rojek and John Urry (1997) have argued, 'cultures travel too' and through the Irish theme bar, with its calculated design codes, its 'authentic' Irish artefacts and, most obviously, through its imported Irish people, the non-travelling tourist can have an Irish experience and the 'craic' delivered to his/her door. Clearly the non-travelling tourist is likely to be fully aware that this experience is 'inauthentic' or staged but, as various theorists have argued, this need not be a disincentive to consumption (MacCannell, 1992; Urry, 1995).

At the same time, this is a process which has resulted in the objectification of a series of social and cultural actions most readily associated with the Irish migrant. For Irish migrants themselves and, most obviously, for those who find employment in such bars, the 'craic' as a means of negotiating the potentially alienating impact of their migrant status has itself therefore become alienated in the process of commodification. Nowhere is this more evident than, for example, in the management and staff training programmes for the O'Neill's chain of Irish theme pubs in Britain, where instilling a sense of the 'craic' forms a key element (O'Neill's, 1997). There is a sense, then, in which such workers and Irish migrants more generally face the same dilemmas as those peoples whose cultural performances have been transformed by tourism, changing the very meaning of the 'craic' itself (Greenwood, 1989; Hall, 1994).

A further issue arises, however, when the potential impact that the theme bar may have on Ireland's pub culture and wider society is considered. As Rojek and Urry (1997: 10–12) go on to suggest, if there is an increasing presence of reconstructions of ethnic spaces (Mediterranean villages, Mexican saloons, Thai restaurants) in the cities of the advanced industrial world this exerts a pressure for 'ever more contrived representations of the apparent reality' of the places they are standing in for. The heavily-coded, globally present Irish theme bar may increasingly shape what it is that tourists seek when they come to Ireland itself and that may, in turn, directly affect what it is they will find. With the expansion of theme bars continuing apace, particularly (as in the largely now saturated continental European market) where received ideas about Ireland have previously been relatively weak, then they are liable to play an important part in fostering the future re-staging of 'stage Irishry'. If, as one commentator noted (Author's interview, 1999d), the image of the Irish theme bar will lead tourists to see 'Irish people as the core attraction of a visit to Ireland, the beauty [of the landscape] is relative' then this clearly may have important social implications.

'Public Drinking' in 'Safe Places': Irish Drinking and the Pub as a Tourist Site

The association of the Irish with drink, the pub and convivial sociability is therefore rooted in a longstanding, socially constructed 'stage Irish'

persona, in the identity branding of Irish products and in dominant perceptions of Irish migrant culture and the rise of the Irish theme bar. All of these
have helped to shape the prevailing expectations (and the attractiveness) of
Irish pub culture to the potential tourist. It is also clearly dependent on the
perceived role that the pub plays in modern Irish social life and the nature
of Irish drinking patterns. The particularly 'public' nature of Irish drinking
would appear to have important consequences for the way in which
foreign visitors frequent Irish bars.

Irish drinking habits have been the subject of some analysis in recent
years. A rise in the general level of consumption has been a dominant
feature through much of the last four decades. This is largely attributable to
an overall rise in living standards and disposable income, shifts in gender
relations that have resulted in a far greater rate of female consumption and
a parallel fall in the rate of total abstinence. The huge social changes that
have had a profound effect on Irish female drinking patterns have been
particularly significant in this regard, although the end of the Irish pub as a
predominantly male institution is still some way off (Drinks Industry
Group, 1993; O'Hagan & Scott, 1993; Scott, 1994). Yet, there are trends that
contradict what would, at first, appear to be a greater increase in the
amount of alcohol being consumed. In keeping with wider European
trends per capita alcohol consumption rates in Ireland have decreased in
the last two decades. In 1980 the average adult consumption of alcoholic
beverages was 10.8 litres of pure alcohol per annum. By 1990 that figure
had fallen to 9.9 and in 1997 to 9.1 (Irish Brewers Association, 1997;
O'Hagan & Scott, 1993: 12–13). The general trend would, therefore, appear
to be for more people in Ireland to take a drink but more people are
drinking less. In addition, international comparisons have shown that per
capita alcohol consumption in Ireland is, if anything, relatively low,
though it does have a higher than average rate of beer consumption. Of 20
European countries whose per capita consumption rates were compared in
1997 Ireland came 12th, far behind not only the more wine-orientated states
(such as Portugal, France and Spain) but also beer-dominated markets like
Denmark, Austria and Germany. The Irish are not, then, on average significantly bigger drinkers than others.

However, what is perhaps most distinctive about Irish drinking habits
when compared to elsewhere is its public nature (Cassidy, 1996: 16–17). A
study in 1990 showed that Ireland had an extremely low level of home consumption of beer. In Denmark 74% of total beer sales were for home
consumption, in France the figure was 65%, in The Netherlands 62% and in
Germany 60%. Even in Spain and Britain, where the figures were relatively
low they were still 25% and 20% respectively. In Ireland home beer sales
accounted for a mere 6% of the total. Whilst this picture is changing, to

some extent drinking in Ireland is still far more likely to take place in the pub than it is anywhere else or than generally happens in every other European country. In addition, Tanya Cassidy (1996) notes, Irish non-drinkers are also far more likely than their European counterparts to social-ise in public houses. The pub may, in other words, play a relatively far more important part as an arena for social interaction in Irish society than an equivalent institution would do in other parts of Europe.

It is this public nature of Irish drinking, and the culture that is seen to be associated with it, which provides an important part of the appeal of the Irish pub to the visitor. Certainly that appeal seems to be substantial. A study undertaken for the (then) Department of Tourism and Transport in 1993 showed that only shopping and heritage sites attracted a higher per-centage of overseas tourists than 'singing pubs'. Approximately 40% of tourists visited these very particular kind of public houses, about one million in total. If all pubs had been included the number would have been even higher and it seems likely that a very high percentage of all tourists to Ireland will, at one time or another, avail themselves of the facilities of an Irish pub. In similar vein, a survey of licensed premises also conducted in 1993 found that tourists accounted for over 15% of total business for more than 17% of pubs outside Dublin, and over 12% for those in the capital. Approximately 15% of all pubs also put on some form of entertainment (usually traditional music) which was specifically aimed at the tourist market (O'Hagan & Scott, 1993: 39–40). The Dublin Tourist Board recently conducted a survey of visitors to their main tourist information office asking people to indicate the images they most associated with the city: 73% said that it was 'people laughing and having a good time, the atmo-sphere of the "craic"' (Author's interview, 1999a).

In addition, large numbers of tourists go annually to the Visitors Centres attached to Ireland's most well-known breweries and distilleries. This, in itself, constitutes a particular form of heritage tourism and further evi-dences the link made between the consumption of Ireland as a tourist destination and the drinks industry. For example, in its first full year of operation, the Visitors Centre of the Old Jamesons Distillery in Dublin had over 136,000 people through its door, over 94% of whom were from abroad with over 50% coming from the UK. The Hop Store Visitor Centre at Guinness' St James's Gate Brewery is currently being substantially extended in order to cope with the increase in numbers (Author's inter-views, 1999a,b).

Whilst there remains a need for a thorough study of the social back-ground of those tourists who go into Irish bars of all descriptions there is evidence to suggest that a substantial number are middle-class 'high-yield' tourists who would not normally consider socialising in a pub in their own countries (Author's interviews, 1999a,c). Although many of those engaged in tourist promotion are at pains to suggest that it is not so much drinking itself that is important to the image of the Irish pub but the culture that goes with it, the two cannot so easily be separated. Indeed, as the volume of visitors to the distilleries and breweries illustrates, Irish drink products are themselves invested with cultural significance and heritage value. The important thing is the perception that there is little or no social stigma attached to public drinking in Ireland. As a leading marketing officer for the Dublin Tourist Board argued, 'in other countries going to a pub is perceived as a bit low-life, a very negative thing. But they have no problem doing it here because it's quite acceptable' (Author's interview, 1999a). Middle-class tourists who would rarely if ever go into bars at home avail themselves of the Irish pub because 'for a lot of these visitors one of the reasons they want to go to Irish bars is to meet Irish people'. The Irish pub, therefore, offers both a relatively safe environment and a 'novel experience'.

It is not unimportant that 'high-yield' tourists are the primary market at whom much Irish tourist promotional material is aimed (it is perhaps worth noting, too, that it is for the foreign middle-class consumer that many of the Irish theme bars are designed to cater). What therefore emerges is a pressure to manage both the tourists' perception and experience of the Irish bar so as to highlight its social acceptance and status and downplay what might be regarded as the 'less salubrious', more volatile and frenetic elements of the 'craic' culture. Middle-class tourists may want the 'native' and the 'exotic' but they want it in a way that continues to offer the shelter of safety and 'quality service'.

'The Craic and the Emotive Experience': The Tourist Experience and the Irish Pub

If the image of the 'craic' is linked to the culture of Irish migration, it is also tied to the vision of Ireland as a 'traditional society' in which certain collective actions, bonds, emotions and experiences supposedly lost to the modern world can be (albeit briefly) 'lived' by the tourist. The 'emotive experience' that is such a critical component in the selling of Ireland as a tourist destination is a product of this phenomenon. This image of Ireland as a pre-modern place must be realised in concrete social situations and specific spaces for the tourist expectation to be realised. Given the fact that this 'emotive experience' requires an opportunity for a sense of contact with Irish people themselves then the Irish pub and the 'craic' emerge as a key dimensions of the tourist visitors' 'emotive experience' of Ireland.

As Barbara O'Connor has argued, tourist images of Ireland have been dominated by the idea of the island as an 'empty place' of picturesque beauty (itself invested with metaphysical meaning) that plays host to a social order which is at least one step away from the atomised, frantic, insecure and 'inauthentic' condition of late modernity (O'Connor, 1993). The appeal of Ireland to the burgeoning market of 'post-modern' middle-class 'cultural' tourists has often been seen to lie in the retreat it appears to offer from the alienation and often seemingly meaningless nature of the advanced industrial world (Kneafsey, 1994). This image tends (in the main) to apply to the island outside of Dublin and it is not insignificant that Dublin has adopted an increasingly distinct tourist marketing strategy (aimed at the short-stay city-break market) in which it tends to be presented as a modern European capital offering a wide, 'cosmopolitan' range of cultural and leisure attractions. Even with Dublin, though, the social and cultural lives of Irish people themselves plays an important part in the city's appeal and this relates directly to perceptions of Dublin's pub culture.

However, the emphasis upon the supposedly particular nature of Irish people is even more important in the representation of the rest of the island and, most obviously, those rural areas that are primary tourist destinations (O'Connor, 1993: 72–3). This is closely linked to the construction of Ireland as a 'pre-modern' place. As O'Connor goes on to suggest, Irish people have proved to be an 'essential ingredient' in the packaging of Ireland as a tourist destination because they often appear to personify the retreat from the modern that is a key tourist goal. In such a perspective the Irish are constructed as an objectified 'other' inscribed with certain notionally 'pre-modern' and 'peasant' qualities (friendliness, honesty, naive charm). Contact with people exhibiting such traits is then regarded as an integral element of tourist expectations. As a result, an essentialised image of Irish people has been seen as critical to the 'emotional experience' of a visit to Ireland.

This has certainly been the case for Bord Fáilte. The Irish Tourist Board launched its 'Ireland – Live a Different Life' campaign in 1997. The idea of the 'emotional experience' was seen as the crucial in this marketing initiative, the 'core brand essence for Ireland tourism' (Bord Fáilte, 1997: 8). Clearly this campaign was designed to maximise the marketing potential of the particular place occupied by Ireland in the global tourist industry. This, in turn, is highly dependent on already established perceptions of Ireland abroad. A key dimension identified as framing this 'emotional experience' was the 'ease of interaction with Ireland's friendly and engaging people'. Even more significantly it was argued (based on a Visitors' Attitude Survey conducted in 1995) that 'while other destinations may boast friendly people, all visitors to Ireland have highlighted the ability to mix and interact with the Irish as being absolutely unique' (Bord Fáilte, 1995).

This 'unique' opportunity for social interaction might be achieved in a variety of locations but there is no doubt that the pub has been regarded as perhaps the most important. The Irish tourism training agency (CERT) has argued that 'visitors enjoy the informality of Irish pub life and the opportunity to mingle with local people'. 'The Irish', it was suggested, 'have a reputation for being gregarious and the type of casual acquaintances that may be struck up in pubs is an attractive facet of Irish life for visitors'. In addition, the link between the pub, the image of Irish people and pre-modernity is emphasised in the fact that 'traditional entertainment' (particularly music) whether 'planned or impromptu' was seen as 'an appealing feature of pub life for tourists, as are old style ambience and open fires' (CERT, 1993: 72). In an analysis of Irish tourist literature aimed at a continental European market, Bernadette Quinn noted that the emphasis on the rural and 'pre-modern' nature of Ireland was combined with a concentration on 'traditional pub life' as the 'night-time option' (Quinn, 1994: 69).

Rural Ireland's imagined pre-modernity and supposedly 'timeless' value system and social relationships are seen to be encapsulated and manifest through the 'craic'. 'Authentic' folk music, an atmosphere of easy conviviality, the sense of a collective, communal existence and a supposed ethnically-specific verbal dexterity and conversational skill, therefore, emerge as key motifs defining the objects of tourist consumption that can be readily accessed through the pub. Such notions owe much to the historically derived images of Irishness. For example, the emphasis upon conversational performance (the 'gift of the gab') is very much rooted in the tradition of 'stage Irishry' and is one of the most important aspects of tourist expectations on a visit to an Irish bar.

This is perhaps nowhere better illustrated than in the words of an American ethnographer (who unwittingly evidenced his own status as an 'intellectual tourist') engaged in a 'metaphorical journey' through 'global cultures' for whom the pub conversation acted as a 'metaphor' for Irishness itself. 'Irish pubs', writes Martin Gannon (1994: 192–3),

> are probably the site of the most lively conversations held in Ireland. The Irish tend to be very sociable people who generally do not believe in drinking alone ... Even more important than a good drink in a pub is a good conversation. The Irish are famous for their storytelling and it is not unusual to find an entire pub silent while one man tells an ancient folktale or what happened to him that afternoon. It is not unusual for someone to recite Shakespearean play from memory in its entirety. Besides stories, many a heated argument can erupt in a pub. The Irish seem to have a natural love of confrontation in all things.

The Irish pub conversation and the 'craic', therefore, emerge as the constructed antithesis to the tense, atomised and insecure condition of modernity and, as a result, essential to the experience of the cultural tourist to Ireland who is in retreat from the same.

This process also, of course, places a heavy burden of expectation and constructed meaning upon the moment of interaction with Irish people themselves which can, in turn, have great implications for the very culture that is the object of tourist consumption. The potential for tourism to directly affect and alter a pre-existent culture has been a major concern for many analysts. Certainly this has been so for a number of critical commentators on the trajectory of Irish tourist development, particularly in rural areas of the West. The 'staged authenticity' of heritage sites and tourist attractions has been identified as already having impacted upon not only the landscape of the West but also upon the 'thought worlds' of its inhabitants (Byrne *et al.*, 1993). As Irish pub culture and its attendant social activities become increasingly subjected to the presence and gaze of the tourist, it is highly unlikely to remain unaffected. Change should not, of course, in and of itself be regarded as a bad thing. However, given the role the pub and the 'craic' have played in the social world of rural communities then the result may be the loss of an environment in which a distinctive collective experience was lived. The objectification of the self that such a process can also bring in its wake may also be seen as having potentially dramatic social and psychological consequences.

In addition, the commodification of the 'craic' and the changing cultural context within which it operates ensures that the Irish pub has itself become an arena for 'staged authenticity' (MacCannell, 1973: 1249–58). Studies of cultural performances that have moved away from their original function within the local community to form part of the tourist product have shown that the social and cultural implications of such a shift can be far-reaching (Greenwood, 1989; Hall, 1994). In terms of Irish pub culture, the nature of the music 'session' may be undergoing a similar process (at least in certain areas and contexts) as the players and musicians become less the bearers of an indigenous, distinct and living culture than cultural workers in the tourist industry. The social relations of the session in tourist pubs and areas are increasingly defined by a performer–audience divide that equates directly to that of producer and consumer and which is at odds with the more collective experience of the session in its original setting. Similarly, the very content of the session can be altered as the space for difference and musical experimentation gives way to the need to perform that which is congruent with what the visitor expects Irish music to be. In either case there is no doubt that the culture itself can be significantly affected by the demands of the tourist eye and ear.

In many ways, it is the immediacy and ease of access to an apparently 'authentic' aspect of Ireland's culture that is the key element of the appeal of the Irish bar to the tourist. The Irish pub is a place of relatively easy and causal social interaction that can be entered into with a limited sense of intrusion and in which can be found a specific series of cultural practices. As such, the Irish pub links directly to the primary role of various forms of 'cultural tourism' to Irish tourist development. There is little doubt that Ireland has been heavily marketed as a destination that will attract the 'cultural tourist'. The emphasis upon Ireland's supposed 'difference', the importance of the island's history and culture in tourist literature and the notion of the 'emotional experience' as the 'core brand essence' for Irish tourism would all suggest as much. Cultural tourism has been identified as one of the key areas for government investment during the last decade (O'Donnchadha & O'Connor, 1996).

For a number of analysts, the concept 'cultural tourism' has two distinct elements: 'heritage tourism' and 'experiential tourism' (Zeppel & Hall, 1991: 87). The numerous recently established heritage centres (including those based on brewery themes), well-visited sites of historic interest and the general prominence given to Ireland's (in particular literary) past in tourist promotion all evidence the importance of the former to Ireland's tourist appeal. 'Experiential tourism', in contrast, is based on 'being involved in and stimulated by the performing arts, visual arts and festivals'. Whilst there have been attempts to devise cultural events in a range of venues and formats the forms of cultural performance and patterns of social interaction that take place in many Irish pubs ensures that the tourist experience of the Irish pub could be understood as such 'experiential tourism'. In addition, it has been suggested that whilst there are 'cultural tourists' whose primary focus is upon 'self-improvement, education [and] discovery', there is a wider constituency of 'culturally-inspired' or 'casual cultural tourists' for whom the consumption of culture is a part, but by no means necessarily an all-consuming aspect of the tourist experience (Author's interview, 1999a). People want to 'experience' culture but they do not necessarily want to have to work too hard at it or take it too seriously. They may also want to satisfy other less edifying, more hedonistic but nevertheless key tourist desires, goals and expectations.

A broad definition of what constitutes 'cultural tourism' that includes the pub has been evident in the thinking of those charged with promoting Irish tourism:

> When we sell cultural tourism we're selling it in the broadest sense. We're selling it as everything from just sitting in a pub drinking a pint and just listening to the banter around you, to buskers on the street, art

exhibitions around the Green to more 'upmarket' culture with the traditional museums, a lot of the national cultural institutions. But the
pub scene we have always used as something quite unique, that it's not
the same type of culture that you would get in other countries
(Author's interview, 1999a)

The pub can, therefore, offer itself as a site for what might be termed
'encultured hedonism'. The archetypal tourist can have a 'good time',
enjoying (at least the representation of) the 'craic' and still feel that they are
gaining an insight into a unique, and therefore 'worthy', cultural experience. Thus, whether the visitor to Ireland is considered to be in search of the
'authentic' (gaining a glimpse at the 'back region' of an indigenous social
experience) or playing the ironic, semiotic games of the 'post-tourist', the
pub may prove to be of primary importance as a site for the materialisation,
performance and consumption of a rarefied and essentialised conception
of Irish culture that also proves to be 'good craic'.

Conclusion: 'A New Stage Irishry'? Tourism, the Irish Pub and the Tourist Escape from 'Time–Work Discipline'

There are, then, a number of factors that have ensured that the Irish pub
is a central element of tourist expectations and experience of a visit to
Ireland. The practical and material contribution of Ireland's public houses
to the island's tourist infrastructure matter but of perhaps greater importance is the cultural construction of the pub as a quintessentially Irish
institution that offers an ideal opportunity to 'consume' Irish culture and
people. Such expectations, often generated in the visitors' own culture
through a variety of media-derived, historically-inherited and / or product-
orientated images, construct Irishness as (in part at least) an alcohol-
centred identity associated with the 'pre-modern' values of sociability and
witty conviviality. Images of the Irish developed first in those societies that
saw a significant influx of Irish migrants and over the last 150 years have
since become almost globally recognisable. To no small degree this has
been directly linked to the recent commodification of aspects of that culture
in the form of the Irish theme bar. Such perceptions have subsequently
been critical in shaping what it is tourists expect to find when they arrive in
Ireland and (increasingly perhaps) what it is that they are subsequently
offered. In addition, the Irish pub offers a relatively accessible arena in
which the 'casual cultural tourist' can satisfy his/her desire take in a
unique cultural experience with the less elevated (but perhaps more immediately satisfying) goal of imbibing the best that Ireland has to offer.

Perhaps tourist representations and perceptions of Irish pub culture
may be seen to rest upon a new variant of 'stage Irishry' that has translated

the 'anti-time–work discipline' ethos associated with the pre-industrial 19th century Irish into an object of desire for the contemporary tourist fleeing their post-industrial condition. In the realm of tourism as a leisure pursuit a people long seen as having a peculiar gift for pleasure-seeking, wit and conversation may find themselves elevated from the status of the work-shy to a model of the right living. Significantly, of course, the essentialised construction of such a people may be vogueishly re-interpreted but it is still left ultimately intact. The 'romantic rogue' imagery of the 19th century Irish has, in other words, found a new updated niche for itself in the tourist eye that (as Declan Kiberd (1995) discussed in relation to its historical antecedents) also offers itself as a series of symbols and signifi-ers through which many Irish people will themselves construct, negotiate and contest their sense of self. It is in perceptions and consumption of Irish pub culture that much of this construction, negotiation and contestation takes place. Looking through the 'cracked pint glass of the servant' the casual cultural (and pleasure-seeking) tourist is invited to briefly escape the regulated and fractious condition of his/her everyday life and enter a land of conversation, song and slightly risqué (but ultimately relatively safe) new 'romantic roguery'.

Notes

1. In the first chapter of *Ulysses* James Joyce employs the image of the 'cracked looking glass of the servant' to portray the difficult and complex relationship between the idea of 'Irishness' and Irish culture given the pervasive influence of the external, colonial eye.
2. The term the 'craic' (pronounced and sometimes written 'crack') is a bowdlerised Irish word of disputed etymological origin that has a variety of uses but is generally taken to refer to having a good time!

References

Author's interview with Senior Marketing Officer, Dublin Tourism 1999a.

Author's interview with representative of Old Jameson's Distillery Visitor Centre. August 1999b.

Author's interview with Spokesperson for Temple Bar Properties Ltd. August 1999c

Author's interview with Senior Marketing Manager, The Irish Pub Company. August 1999d.

Author's interview with Senior Marketing Manager, The Irish Pub Company. January 2000a.

Author's interview with Senior Marketing Manager, The Irish Pub Company. February 2000b.

Bord Fáilte (1995) *Visitors Attitude Survey*. Dublin: Bord Fáilte.

Bord Fáilte (1997) *The Fáilte Business: Tourism's Role in Economic Growth*. Dublin: Bord Fáilte.

Byrne, A., Edmondson, R. and Fahy, K. (1993) Rural tourism and cultural identity in the West. In B. O'Connor and M. Cronin (eds) *Tourism in Ireland: A Critical Analysis*. Cork: Cork University Press.

Cassidy, T. (1996) Irish drinking worlds: A socio-cultural reinterpretation of ambivalence. *International Journal of Sociology and Social Policy* 16 (5/6), 5–25.

CERT (1993) *Tourism and Travel in Ireland*. Dublin: CERT.

Craik, J. (1997) The culture of tourism. In C. Rojek and J. Urry (eds) *Touring Cultures: Transformations of Travel and Theory*. London: Routledge.

Cullen, L. (1972) *An Economic History of Ireland Since 1660*. London: B.T. Batsford.

Department of Tourism and Transport (1993) *Operational Programme for Tourism, 1989–1993*. Dublin: DTT.

Dingle, A.E. (1980) *The Campaign for Prohibition in Victorian England: The United Kingdom Alliance*. London: Croom Helm.

Drinks Industry Group (1993) *Drinks Industry Group Statistical Handbook*. Dublin: Drinks Industry Group.

Eagleton, T. (1998) *Crazy John and the Bishop, and Other Essays on Irish Culture*. Cork: Cork University Press.

Edwards, O.D. (1994) The stage Irish. In P. O'Sullivan (ed.) *The Irish Worldwide: History, Heritage, Identity. Vol. 3. The Creative Migrant*. Leicester: Leicester University Press.

Gannon, M. (1994) *Understanding Global Cultures: Metaphorical Journeys through 17 Countries*. London: Sage.

Greenwood, D.J. (1989) Culture by the pound: an anthropological perspective on tourism as cultural commoditization. In V. Smith (ed.) *Hosts and Guests: The Anthropology of Tourism*. Philadelphia: University of Pennsylvania Press.

Grimes, S. (1980) *Ireland in 1804: A Contemporary Account*. Dublin: Four Courts Press.

Hadfield, A. and McVeagh, J. (eds) (1994) *Strangers to that Land: British Perceptions of Ireland from the Reformation to the Famine*. Gerrards Cross: Colin Smythe.

Hall, C.M. (1994) *Tourism and Politics: Policy, Power and Place*. Chichester: John Wiley and Sons.

Harrington, J.P. (1991) *The English Travel Writer in Ireland: Accounts of Ireland and the Irish through Five Centuries*. Dublin: Wolfhound Press.

Harrison, B. (1971) *Drink and the Victorians: The Temperance Question in England*. Pittsburgh: University of Pittsburgh Press

Irish Brewers Association (1997) *Brewing Industry Fast Facts*. Dublin: IBA.

Kennedy, K. (1988) *The Economic Development of Ireland in the 20th Century*. London: Routledge.

Kiberd, D. (1995) *Inventing Ireland: The Literature of the Modern Nation*. London: Jonathan Cape.

Kneafsey, M. (1994) The cultural tourist: Patron saint of Ireland? In U. Kockel (ed.) *Culture, Tourism and Development: The Case of Ireland*. Liverpool: Liverpool University Press.

MacCannell, D. (1973) Staged authenticity: Arrangements of social space in tourist settings. *American Journal of Sociology* 79 (3), 589–603.

MacCannell, D. (1992) *Empty Meeting Grounds: The Tourist Papers*. London: Routledge.

McGovern, M. (1999) The Craic market: Irish theme bars and the commodification of Irishness in contemporary Britain. Paper delivered to the Sociological Association of Ireland, Annual Conference, Belfast.

Memmi, A. (1990) *The Coloniser and the Colonised*. London: Earthscan.

O'Connor, B. (1993) Myths and mirrors: Tourist images and national identity. In B. O'Connor and M. Cronin (eds) *Tourism in Ireland: A Critical Analysis*. Cork: Cork University Press.

O'Donnchadha, G. and O'Connor, B. (1996) Cultural tourism in Ireland. In G. Richards (ed.) *Cultural Tourism in Europe*. Wallingford: CAB International.

Ó Gráda, C. (1995) *Ireland: A New Economic History, 1780–1939*. Oxford: Clarendon Press.

Ó Gráda, C. (1997) *A Rocky Road: The Irish Economy Since the 1920s*. Manchester: Manchester University Press.

O'Hagan, J.W. and Scott, Y. (1993) *The Economic Importance of the Drinks Industry in Ireland*. Dublin: Drinks Industry Group.

O'Neill's (1997) *O'Neills: A More Considered Irish Bar*. London: O'Neill's Promotional Material.

Quinn, B. (1994) Images of Ireland in Europe: A tourism perspective. In U. Kockel (ed.) *Culture, Tourism and Development*. Liverpool: Institute of Irish Studies.

Rojek, C. and Urry, J. (1997) Transformations of travel and theory. In C. Rojek and J. Urry (eds) *Touring Cultures*. London: Routledge.

Said, E. (1993) *Culture and Imperialism*. London: Chatto and Windus.

Samuels, R. (ed.) (1989) *Patriotism: The Making and Unmaking of British National Identities*. London: Routledge.

Scott, Y. (1994) *A Study of Licensed Premises: A Report Commissioned by the Drinks Industry Group*. Dublin: DIG.

Shiman, L.L. (1988) *Crusade Against Drink in England*. London: Macmillan Press.

The Irish Pub Company (1997) *The Irish Pub: A Remarkable Business Opportunity*. Dublin: Irish Pub Company Promotional Literature.

Thompson, E.P. (1963) *The Making of the English Working Class*. Harmondsworth: Penguin.

Urry, J. (1995) *Consuming Places*. London. Routledge.

Waters, M. (1984) *The Comic Irishman*. Albany: State University of New York Press.

Zeppel, H and Hall, C.M. (1991) Selling art and history: Cultural heritage and tourism. *Journal of Tourism Studies* 2 (1), 29–45.

Chapter 5

Constructing an Exotic 'Stroll' through Irish Heritage: The Aran Islands Heritage Centre

EAMONN SLATER

Introduction

On the 13 November 2000, the Minister for Arts, Heritage, Gaeltacht and the Islands announced details of a £100 million expenditure plan for Irish heritage projects (*The Irish Times*, 13 November 2000). Such a large investment suggests that Irish heritage has become a crucial component in the Irish tourism industry. In the 1980s and early 1990s, it seemed that every local community was attempting to develop heritage 'attractions' such as historical houses and castles, wildlife parks, historical monuments and heritage gardens. However, many of these local initiatives in the heritage industry revolved around the provision of a visitor/heritage centre by these communities. Why the centre became the lynch-pin of these initiatives is that tourists demanded an immediate confrontation with the past (Sheerin, 1998: 46). To respond to this demand, the centre had to 'visualise' its past so that it could be easily consumed by their visitors. And in attempting to visualise the past, heritage had to move from being 'locked' into written texts and local folklore to be 'imaged' in a display performance in the new heritage centre. One consequence of the emergence of this visualisation of local heritage is the privileging of space over time in the presentation of the past (Johnson, 1999: 187).

In this chapter, I want to suggest that the dominance of the visual imagery (visual narrative) over chronology (written narrative) in the presentation of heritage in these centres is the key to understanding how knowledge is constructed. The reason for this is that these centres are essentially about providing pleasure to the visitor. The consequence of this is that the visit to the centre is 'constructed' as a 'stroll' through a reconstructed landscape made up of 'exotic' visual imagery. I want to conclude that such a flaneur's stroll can only concentrate on the visually exotic, where space dominates over time. In order to arrive at this end point, we need to enter a heritage centre, the one I have chosen is on Inis Mor, the largest of the three Aran Islands. And before we begin our sojourn into the epistemological structures of this particular centre, I want to assert that this analysis of mine is about an attempt to understand how knowledge is structured in this location. It is not about how an audience may interpret that epistemological structure.

The Aran Islands of Western Ireland have become a 'Mecca' for those interested in Irish culture. This is not a new phenomenon. It has been going on for the last two centuries. Writers, artists, scientists and movie and TV producers have visited Aran and according to J.C. Messenger, the anthropologist, many of their works have 'served to familiarise the world with the unique and picturesque way of life of the islanders' (Messenger, 1967: 15). In doing so they have successfully signposted these islands as an exotic location for tourists to visit. On 5 August 1995, it was reported that the residing population of the islands (3000) had swelled to 13,000 people (*The Irish Independent*, 14 June 1996). Accordingly, it is an important example of how diverse cultural signposting can impact on a local community and its economy, through encouraging an interest in a place. But now, it has a new cultural signpost, in its heritage centre. In order to discover the type of culture being presented to these growing masses of tourists we need to get inside this centre. The centre was opened to the public in 1992 and is situated just outside the village of Kilronan, in the old coast-guard station.

The Visual as Exotic

As you pay you are handed an introductory leaflet.[1] Under its title and subtitle it states: 'Aran's Heritage, where your visit to Aran begins . . . ' and it continues, 'Aran's Heritage Centre will not only introduce you to the landscape and traditions of the Aran Islands, but also to a culture that once spread over much of Western Europe. The history and present day lifestyle of the people of Aran are highlighted in the centre by the use of informative charts, photographs and maps'. So the opening line of this leaflet states emphatically the main thrust of the centre's ambition and establishes its own sense of self.

On entering the exhibit area you pass through a curtain rather than a door. This curtain is closed and only opened by the centre's cashier/usher to allow you in. The curtain and its theatrical opening heightens one's excitement, as it suggests the fact that one is leaving mundane reality and entering a world of performance. Having passed through this dramatic threshold prop, the first object encountered is a display panel, which is a

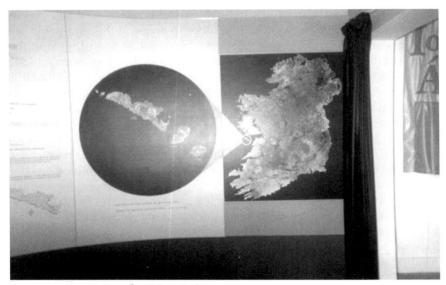

Figure 5.1 Locating the Islands from outer space

panoramic outer-space photograph of Ireland, in which the location of the Aran Islands is circled (see Figure 5.1). These circled islands are blown up in the next panel, with the following caption, first in Irish with an English translation underneath: 'Athenry was, Galway is, and Aran will be [Aran saying]'. Even in this first encounter between the visitor and the Centre's display, we can detect the style of presentation. First, the display is presented within a panel and a number of these panels make up a gallery. Second, each gallery is concerned with a specific topic or subject matter. Third, this style of presentation presupposes a walking tour, which creates the way in which the exhibits are to be viewed and read. And fourth, the design of the panel has created its own structured order of interpreting, so that you encounter the panel initially as a complete visual entity, where the visual representations are intermingled with the spaces given over to the written narratives. And since the visual image is bigger than the written caption, your attention is attracted to the visual and then to the verbal. The written narrative is framed within the visual structure. In this context, the display narrative is not a 'book on the wall'. The display panel operates in the realm between the visual and the verbal but with written text acting merely as an appendage to the visual. In this context, we can observe two contrasting narratives – the written and the visual – coexisting and impacting on each other. However, the structure of the presentation of the information within the centre is not being determined by a linear logic within the written narrative but by the appearance of an object or an image of an object on the display panel. The written narrative responds to the visual narrative in order to make sense of the presence of the image or the artefact within the gallery.

Since the size of the display panel within the gallery is physically designed only to allow a single person (or a couple) to view and read in comfort, the experience of the Centre is to be of an individual nature. This structuring by the architectural design of the panels in this Centre is no different from the old type in the museums. The visitor is borne along and directed only one way – forward (Brett, 1993: 188) and in silent solitude rather than in a guided group. This silent sojourn around the centre replicates one of the essential characteristics of museum visiting in the 19th century, and this is the sense of aura, which accompanied such visiting. This insight comes from the work of Walter Benjamin (1973: 216). Benjamin has suggested that the architecture of museums and the ways in which works were displayed (the viewer is not allowed to touch them) created an atmosphere of church-like reverence which alienated the viewer from the objects displayed. Upon entering the majestic doorways of the museum, the viewer felt compelled to contemplate the works displayed in hushed silence, always maintaining a respectful distance from them. Benjamin conceptualised this mood as aura. An aura which is now maintained not by one object alone but by respect for the collective representations of a culture. This feature of the museum seems to continue into modernity and specifically into these centres. With no facility for guided tours or no physical room to guide herds of enthusiasts around the centre.

As you can see the next gallery is made up a number of panels (see Figure 5.2[2]) which deal with a general view of the physical landscape – the geological formation of the islands, the types of rocks on the island, the formation of limestone and how the fossils become trapped in the stone. Again, the panels tend to be grouped around a specific theme – the geological structure. However, what is interesting is that each gallery is physically highlighted by the presence of a real object/artefact in the gallery display. In this case, the real artefact is a granite erratic resting on a bed of limestone.[3] Here we see the crucial difference between the museum and the heritage centre in that the centre is essentially made up of images of artefacts, rather than real artefacts. And unlike the museum artefacts, these objects have no documented history to them (no date given when they were found or by whom). They are in the centre because they fit into the overall structure of the display by exhibiting the necessary visual characteristics. But the essential difference from the museum displays is that here there are

Figure 5.2 The exotic granite erratic

many more representations of objects than there are real artefacts. As a consequence of this, the actual display of real artefacts becomes the exotic aspect of the centre, as they stand out from the visual representations. Examples of such exotic artefacts include a curragh, a kelp creel, a butter churn and a Galway hooker filled with turf, etc. These real artefacts seem unreal in two senses. First, these mundane objects of the real world appear out of context in an exhibit. Their very mundaneness becomes the exotic in this artificial image landscape. Second, the artificial light directed upon these objects pushes them beyond the reality of everyday life into objects of performance.

The tug-of-war rope (see Figure 5.3) is a good example of an object performance. The rope is displayed lying in a pile on the floor. It has not fallen from a hook. There is no place to hang it on the wall. The haphazardness of its position on the floor highlights an attempt to transform the mundane into the exotic. This rope and other newly created exotic objects are crucial in focusing the attention of the viewers as they pass from one gallery to the next. They function not only as attention grabbers but also they focalise the panels around them. As the exotic centrepieces of the centre they create the order of viewing the displays. Since there is neither

Figure 5.3 The tug-of-war rope

an obvious chronological ordering nor thematic order to the centre, each gallery centres on its own exotic subject matter and subsequently creates its own self-contained explanatory order. There is no thematic link between the galleries and consequently no established order in which to view them. Because of the discrete nature of the galleries, they are likely to be experienced by the viewer as a series of items, of the same weight and significance. No one gallery dominates the centre, as a way of a conclusion to the experience, or as an attempt to tie up the themes within the various galleries. Consequently, the physical structure of the design panels does not allow for the possibility of a comprehensive survey of the islands' economy or culture. Discreteness reigns in the centre, the discreteness of the visually exotic.

Therefore, it is likely that the visitor is borne along from one gallery to the next by first locating the visual curiosity of the real artefact in the gallery and then moving on to the surrounding display panels and finally on to the written captions. It is the visual, which is the key to understanding how knowledge is constructed in the centre.

The 'Exotic' Within the Written Narrative

But, since artefacts and their images 'cannot speak for themselves', they need written captions and labels to give them meaning (Jones, 1992: 915). These are taken from direct quotations from visiting writers or from the pen of the anonymous author of the master narrative. The first writer quoted is Roderic O'Flaherty [1648], under a display panel entitled the 'Rock Garden'.

THE ROCK GARDEN

"The soil is almost paved over with stones, so as, in places nothing to be seen but large stones with wide openings between them, where cattle break their legs. Among these stones is very sweet pasture so that, beef, veal, mutton are better and earlier in season here than elsewhere".

The first thing to notice about this quotation is that it highlights the exotic nature of the Aran landscape and a sense of otherness. Exotic in the sense that there seems to be a reversal of the normal relationship between soil and rock, in that here on Aran the rock seems to cover the soil rather than the other way round. Aran from the O'Flaherty quotation is constructed as a unique location, beyond the mundane mainland, with bountiful natural forces, except, of course, for those, which break the legs of the cattle.

The exoticism of nature on Aran is further reinforced in another display panel on the weather, two captions are used, one quoted from a published source, the other from the master narrative:

The Weather

The Weather in the islands is drier than that on the mainland because rain generally does not form until moist air from the sea reaches the mountains of Connemara.

"The meteorological aspirations of the Aran farmers are for rain, diametrically the opposite of what their brethren on the mainland desire".

Oliver J. Burke, 1887

This idea of otherness is again highlighted in the most dramatic gallery of the centre – the cliff gallery. Here, for obvious reasons, the real artefact of a cliff does not appear but its imagery does which is captured in photographs and in line drawings. Again, this is a crucial point to make. The ability of the heritage centre to include pictorial representations allows it to provide a more comprehensive survey of the island's artefacts, especially the non-moveable ones, than a museum. By presenting these images or views, it allows the anonymous narrator of the centre the power to classify real artefacts in the real landscape as if they were actually in the centre rather than just pictorially displayed in a panel. Therefore, the power to include the representations of physical phenomena seems only to be limited to their visibility. In this respect, the heritage centre is much more powerful in classifying than the museums, which were themselves limited to the display of real and authentically documented artefacts. Above the central panel of the cliff gallery is a panel containing a drawing of a storm beach. But, like all the natural features highlighted on the island, this is no normal storm beach:

> *Storm Beach*
>
> Most beaches are of pebbles or sand worn smoothly by the sea. But the huge storm beaches on the Cliffs of Aran are on a scale with the full power of the Atlantic Ocean.
>
> Storm waves have ripped huge boulders from the edge of the cliffs and gradually forced them inland into a gigantic cluster. Some of these storm beaches have piled up on Cliffs up to 100 feet above sea level.

The focus of the verbal/written narratives in addition to the visual concerning the physical aspects of the island is to emphasise the exotic aspects of these features.

Compositional Techniques of the Visual

In this cliff gallery, there are two line drawings depicting fishing from the cliff top and the activity of hunting birds on the cliffs. These drawings allow the panel designer to depict images beyond either the historical time of the camera or the scope of the camera, i.e. a drawing showing a cliffman crawling along a ledge of the cliff face in the middle of the night in the 19th century. The second line drawing depicts the thatching of a roof (see Figure 5.4).

The original illustration of this thatching scene was drawn by Jack B. Yeats for Synge's *The Aran Islands*, published in 1907. The image shown is a close-up representation of work being done. But by 'cartooning' this representation, the harshness and the dullness of this type of work is excluded (Barrell, 1980: 149; Jones, 1992). In a sense, the particular type of mediation used in this panel, anaesthetises the reality of an island work practice, as it represents it. Accordingly, we need to address not only the content of the centre's representations – its message – but also the style in which that content is expressed – the medium. I would claim the medium is as important as the message, if not more so. For example, with regard to the use of

Figure 5.4 A line drawing of work being done

paintings (reproductions) in the centre. On a side panel of the cliff gallery, there is a reproduction of George Petrie's 'atmospheric view of Dun Aengus'. Petrie has himself described this fort as 'probably one of the most barbaric monuments in the West of Europe' (De Courcy & Maher, 1985: 47). In painting the fort in a particular style, Petrie has 'framed' it into a sublime landscape, by exaggerating the overhanging cliffs and the turbulent seas below. Here, the compositional techniques of the Claudian picturesque are used to create an 'atmosphere' for the fort.[4] Therefore, the real artefact of the fort has been mediated in two ways. First, the fort is visualised as a reproduced image in the panel and second, this image has become 'aestheticised' through the compositional techniques of the picturesque. And in aesthetising the image of the fort, the image has become more visually exotic.

The compositional techniques can make not only the style of representation exotic but also make the representation of time exotic. An example of this is from the panel shown in Figure 5.5. Here, we have a series of black and white photographs depicting scenes of island people with animals. I want to suggest that there is something rather odd about this series. In using the medium of black and white photographs, the concept of time has nearly been collapsed. In the first photo, a woman as indicated by her garb is of the 19th century, feeding her ducks and hens. She is probably part of the 1890s' egg economy of the West of Ireland. However, a problem emerges with the other two photographs. On close inspection, their clothes and shoes suggest that they are children of the 1970s, i.e. the shoes of the kid, holding the kid-goat and the bell-bottoms of the donkey drover. These last two representations would normally be taken through the medium of

Figure 5.5 Time emptied through photography

colour photography but here they have been made ageless, through the use of black and white. Here, we have an example of how time has been compressed by the way the final reproduction of the images in the display panel suppressed the difference of their original reproduction (black and white, and colour). This highlights the power of the display designer to manipulate the past to suit contemporary demands of presentation.

The Exotic as Unsolved Mysteries

Another way in which the exotic is constructed is by the creation of a sense of mystery and intrigue around the images presented. Again, the cliff gallery provides an example of such an endeavour. Below the panel showing a panoramic view of the Dun Aengus is a caption from Tim Robinson's *Stones of Aran*: 'Dun Aonghasa, heavy with centuries, dreams upon a pinnacle of another world'. The mystical and mysterious tone of the narrative is continued in the next written caption:

Dun Aonghasa

Named after the mythical hero Aonghas. Dun Aonghasa has all the appearance of a military fort, but there is no fresh water inside so how could defenders hope to survive for long? And who could live here during a violent storm? Some experts say it was a ceremonial theatre and . . . some say it would be more suitable for the worship of storms.

What do you think?

In asking the last question a number of issues are raised. First of all, by asking the individual spectator for their opinions, the master narrative is attempting to engage the reader in reflexive thought (Giddens, 1990: 88). Second, how can we as mere spectators 'think' in this situation and provide an answer to the question (see Figure 5.6).

The only way I suggest we can attempt to provide an answer is by looking back at the photograph of the fort and coming to some sort of opinion based upon our visual surveillance. This again highlights the dominant principle of visuality in the structuring of knowledge in the centre. However, before we leave this image, I want to point out another feature of this representation. In that this is no ordinary or mundane photograph of this artefact in the landscape. It is a panoramic view, shot from an

Figure 5.6 The mystery of Dun Aengus from the air

exotic angle that is from the air and over the sea. The average tourist would not be in such a position to take this photograph.

But another consequence of asking the question is the adding of a greater sense of mystery to this artefact of Dun Aonghasa. In that it is not the physical presence of the artefact in the landscape, that is doubted but the attempted immersion of that artefact into a societal setting. It is the people of Aran who made the fort that have become the mystery as we attempt to discover the rationale behind their construction. This is highlighted in the caption under another special aerial photograph of the Black Fort: ' . . . Was the Fort built by a warlike people who needed massive defence against a strong enemy – or is the entire site simply an elaborate display of power? Archaeologists are still arguing.' This mysterious aspect of the Aran Islander's character spans the centuries. As is revealed in the glass cabinet display of a model wearing traditional garb. The accompanying caption is from the pen of the Irish 19th century novelist – Mary Banin:

> "Many of the women looked strangely like their own Eastern ancestresses: the sandalled feet, Venetian red petticoat, and, with many of them, bawneen or white flannel jacket worn, covering the head, forehead and body in truly Eastern style".

Mary Banin, The Aran Isles, 1896

Here we see the exotic nature of the islander's appearance is attributed to their eastern origins. But how have the people on the furthest fringe of Western Europe end up looking like their 'own eastern ancestresses'? The mystery is left unanswered. In the opposite cabinet stands a male model in his stockings, shoeless in order to draw attention to his footwear – his pampooties. The captions read as follows:

> "The fisherman of Aran has sure feet. He wears a rough sandal of untanned cowhide, without heels, open at the arch, and tied with rawhide laces".

James Joyce 1912

> Pampooties – ideal for climbing over rocks and working in boats. To keep them soft, the men had to wet them constantly by walking into the sea or soaking them overnight in a pot of water.

The unusual treatment of these 'shoes' reveals how the people of Aran have oriented their garb and themselves to their exotic landscape. And in doing so, they themselves have taken on the characteristic of being – exotic. This exotic relationship between the natural and the human aspects of Aran reaches its dramatic climax in the artefact of the land itself:

The Land of Arainn

Many of the fields of Arainn are man-made. There was probably a time when the limestone rock of Arainn was covered with a thin but fertile soil held loosely in place by plants and tree-roots. When the first farmers came to the island, they cut down the trees to plant their crops.

But as soon as the protective tree-cover was removed the fragile soil began to be eroded by wind and rain. Soon a bare limestone desert was created.

Ever since the people of Arainn have had to make their own land from sand, seaweed and handfuls of soil gathered from between the rocks. This is particularly so in the extreme west of the island at Bun Gabhla where most of the land has been made by hand.

The truthfulness of the 'master narrative' in this panel is taken for granted as it is displayed like all the other vignettes of information in the centre but in actual fact it hides the controversies over what the original landscape of Aran looked like and the how and when the fields were made. Opposing points of view which do not get mentioned suggest that it is mere speculation to propose that once Aran was covered with fertile soil. Second, most of the artificial soil of Aran has been created since the 1920s, when the appearance of the parasitic 'eel worm' necessitated land fallowing. The soil manufacturing activity was spurred on by government subsidy (Robinson, 1986: 66). Therefore, not only are the people of Aran depicted as mythical, but also the depicting narrative itself ends up as myth.

Constructing a Stroll for the Modern Flaneur

It could be argued that the heritage centre is like the museum, in that the centre still creates the illusion of adequate representation of a world by taking objects and images of objects out of their real specific contexts and displaying them in a recontextualised environment (Giddens, 1990: 88). But there is a crucial difference – unlike the museum the heritage centre tends to display more images of artefacts than real objects. And because of this, the centre has a greater power to appropriate exotic things. Therefore, the heritage centre because of the technologies associated with the paint-brush and the camera can achieve greater mastery over its surrounds by being able to impose its classification procedures on immovable artefacts in the landscape. For example, Dun Aengus is represented through three dif-fering types of media – as a plastic model, as a painting and as a photograph. The more media are used, the more comprehensive a survey can be presented in the centre.

As we have seen the visualisation process in the Aran heritage centre operates on a number of different levels. First of all, we have discovered that the layout of the exhibits is determined by the visibility of the exotic real artefact, leading the viewer from one gallery to another. Within the gallery structure itself the visual dominates over the verbal as the visitor's attention moves in sequence from the real artefact to the images of other artefacts, and then onto the verbal captions. If one was to use a television metaphor, the design of the centre with regard to the dominance of the visual over the verbal is like a subtitled programme. The sequence of attention moves from the action to the subtitles. Second, the most important aspect of the visualisation process is the ability of the centre to capture images of real artefacts in photographs (both moving and still) and in pictorial representations. In doing so it allows these media to 'aestheticise' their subject matter according to their respective methods of composition. For example, the camera can take panoramic shots, black and white or colour, in order to create visual sensations. The panoramic perspective in the centre's photography and landscape painting can thrill the viewer by giving an all encompassing perspective. This perspective not only thrills but also provides a commanding view (Smith, 1989). The consequence of creating these exotic perspectives is that there is a distancing of the viewer from the grim appearance of everyday life and reality.

In extracting the exotic from the complex reality of the island life, the Centre's narrative, both visual and verbal, has created a dichotomy between us, the viewers, and them –those who are viewed and 'captioned' in the display panels. The 'not-us', those others have always to be 'out there', to be recorded, interpreted and explained.[5] But, in establishing this difference, which is a logical consequence of attempting to discover the uniqueness of a locale or the exotic nature of a landscape and its inhabitants, the master narrative must speak in place of the represented – the other. The represented other can never speak on its own behalf, as this would undermine the carefully constructed exoticism, by overcoming the created distance between them and us. In speaking directly to us and sounding normal, they would no longer seem exotic or mysterious. Therefore, the depicted people of Aran have to remain mute in order to maintain their supposedly unique exotic nature.

Therefore, the medium is the main mechanism for creating the exotic – the visually exotic. For example, landscape painting can use the compositional techniques of the picturesque in creating opposing images of the beautiful and the sublime. The technical means of the visualisation of the artefacts in the centre creates the material structures for the emergence of the aestheticisation process. Therefore, real artefacts of the landscape are mediated in three ways. First, they are reproduced as images on the panels, and second, these objects become visualised and finally they become aestheticised through the various compositional techniques available.

At this point in our analysis, we can assert that the construction of the 'exotic' in the centre has a tendency to mould the viewer into becoming a flaneur. The flaneur can be seen as an actor in modernity and even post-modernity, according to certain cultural theorists. These have attempted to use the work of Baudelaire, Benjamin and Simmel to account for the new experiences of modernity in the big cities of Europe. Charles Beaudelaire focused on Paris of the 1840s and 1850s. Later Benjamin and Simmel focused on Berlin and in particular on the emerging consumer society. The modern city was seen as a site for experiencing the intoxication of the dream worlds associated with modern consumerism – a world full of a constantly changing flow of commodities and their exotic images in shops, department stores. And crucially, these new forms of experiences of modernity were to be discovered through walking through the boulevards and streets of these cities. But, it was not just through walking that one enjoyed the visual sensations of modernity but significantly through a particular style of walking – strolling.

Therefore, the stroller or flaneur has come to hold a considerable fascination for the cultural theorists of modernity. The stroll is now being associated with the way a person experiences and enjoys the delights of modern consumer society. In this cultural framework, differing ways of walking are directly connected to differing ways of understanding and interpreting one's immediate surrounds.

According to Game, strolling or wandering is to move away from the straight and narrow and to be led astray by what takes one's fancy (Game, 1991: 38). I may add this fancy is a visual fancy. In contrast, non-strolling or purposefully walking is concerned with arriving at a particular destination and usually within a particular time period. Walking to work would be an example of the latter. Strolling has none of these constraining considerations with regard to space and time. The stroll has no concern with arriving at a particular end or destination; it is merely interested in distraction and the attraction of the visually exotic. In following one's sense of curiosity one is lead along an uncharted path within the dreamworld of sensational consumer images.

I now want to suggest that this urban stroller of modernity has actually been created by the physical layout of the centre and the social constructions of the image representations in the centre. In our discussion of the architectural design of the panels and the galleries, we discovered that the experience of the centre was structured to be a walking tour – a sojourn of silent solitude. Also, with regard to the processes of visualisation and crucially asthetisation, the heritage flaneur or stroller is led through this labyrinth of sensational visual images. According to de Cauter (1993), the magnificent dreamworlds of the flaneur wherever they are located, including now the heritage centre, all fit into the cult of distraction. In the centre, the flaneur is not on a purposeful walk, the stroll has no concern with a purposeful end, it is merely interested in distraction and the attraction of the exotic. In following one's sense of curiosity one is led along an uncharted path. All the differing ways of walking are directly related to different ways of understanding our immediate surrounds and are about moving through space and time. In the heritage centre the construction of space is determined by the representation of other spaces through the images presented to be consumed. Therefore, the experience of space is twofold. First there is one's own physical movement through the centre and second there is the observation of space in the displays. Both experiences are similar to sightseeing and everyday strolling. The crucial difference is that the latter experience is artificially constructed by the centre. For example, the images of the forts are displayed in a few square feet of each other while in reality they are located a number of miles away from each other. Consequently, space and time are compressed in the representation of island spaces (both old and new). Their history and culture have become a compressed artificial landscape, in which the modern heritage flaneur is guided through. And because of the way they have been represented here: 'Their time is not Our time, and Their space is not Our space' (Peace, 1989: 94).

Notes

1. However, there is a problem with this so called introductory leaflet, and that is its length. It takes about five minutes to read it, which can only be done by standing in a public passageway. I want to suggest that because of time needed to read it, it performs another function or functions, rather than its stated intention as an introductory text to the centre. Essentially, I see it as a political statement, as it attempts to lessen the fears of the native islanders, who are also engaged in tourism, that the centre will not deflect the tourists away from the other tourist services in the island. This is a real fear on account of the vicissitudes of the Irish weather and the impression given that the centre can show all that is to be seen on the island, without the inconvenience of physical travel and its expense. Therefore, the leaflet attempts to represent the centre as a guide to the island and islands. Also, as it is taken away by the tourist, it probably becomes more of a summary and a memory of the experience, when the tourist finds time to read it.

2. As you turn away from the first panel, you get a glimpse of the real artefacts also on display. Immediately, you get the impression that you have entered a museum. The original intention behind the establishment of museums was that they should remove artefacts from the context of private ownership and

use, and insert them into a new environment with public access. Within these museums, the collections of artefacts on display were not arbitrarily arranged but were organised according to systematic principles and a recognisable scheme of classification. These classificationary procedures were being determined outside the museum walls, by archaeologists and antiquarians, who in their writings were attempting to apply evolutionary categories of species and chronological time, as was occurring in Natural History under the influence of Darwin. Therefore, the development of museums in the 19th century was governed by the principle that it was possible to give a total representation of human reality and history, by an ordered display of selected artefacts reflecting this reality.

3. A granite erratic is a rock which has been transported by a glacier during the last ice age and dropped on the limestone rock structures of the Burren and the Aran islands.

4. The Claudian dualism of the beautiful and the sublime in painting has had a profound effect on landscape painting in the 18th and 19th centuries (Le Bris, 1981) *Romantics and Romanticism*, pp. 28–30.

5. According to James Clifford (1985) the word 'appropriate' comes from Latin meaning to make one's own – one's own property.

References

Barrell, J. (1980) *The Dark Side of the Landscape: The Rural Poor in English Paintings 1730–1840*. Cambridge: Cambridge University Press.

Benjamin, W. (1973) The work of art in the age of mechanical reproduction. In Hannah Arendt (ed.) *Illuminations*. London: Fontana.

Brett, D. (1993) The construction of heritage. In B. O'Connor and M. Cronin (eds) *Tourism in Ireland: A Critical Analysis*. Cork: Cork University Press.

Clifford, J. (1985) Objects and selves – an afterword. In G. Stocking (ed) *Objects and Others, Essays on Museums and Material Culture*.

de Cauter, L. (1993) The panoramic ecstasy: On world exhibitions and the disintegration of experience. *Theory, Culture & Society* 10, 1–23.

De Courcy, C. and Maher, A. (1985) *Fifty Views of Ireland*. Dublin: National Gallery of Ireland.

Game, A. (1991) *Undoing the Social: Towards a Deconstructive Sociology*. Milton Keynes: Open University Press.

Giddens, A. (1990) *The Consequences of Modernity*. Oxford: Polity Press..

Johnson, N.C. (1999) Framing the past: time, space and politics of heritage tourism in Ireland. *Political Geography* 18, 187–207.

Jones, P. (1992) Museums and the 'meanings of their contents'. *New Literary History* 23, 911–23.

Le Bris, M. (1981) *Romantics and Romanticism* (pp. 28–30). Geneva: Skira.

Messenger, J.C. (1967) Man of Aran revisited: An anthropological critique. *University Review* 3 (9), 13–47.

Peace, A. (1989) From Arcadia to anomie: Critical notes on the constitution of Irish society as an Anthropological object. *Critique of Anthropology* 9 (1), 89–111.

Robinson, T. (1986) *Stones of Aran: Pilgrimage*. Dublin: Lilliput.

Sheerin, E. (1998) Heritage centres. In M. Peillon and E. Slater (eds) *Encounters with Modern Ireland: A Sociological Chronicle, 1995–1996* (pp. 39–48). Dublin: Institute of Public Administration.

Smith, C.S. (1989) Museums, artefacts and meanings. In P. Vergo (ed.) *The New Museology*. London: Reaktion.

The Irish Independent (1996) Paradise lost. 14 June.

The Irish Times (2000) 13 November.

Chapter 6

'Come and Daunce with Me in Irlande': Tourism, Dance and Globalisation

BARBARA O'CONNOR

The title of this chapter 'Come and Daunce with Me in Irlande', is a line from a 14th-century anonymous Irish poem and popularised more recently by president-elect Mary Robinson in her inaugural speech of 1990. It neatly encapsulates the long association between tourism and dance in Irish culture. In following the trajectory of this invitation we might want to sketch in some key moments. We could include how dance became a marker of ethnic/national identity for the Irish diaspora, (see Cullinane, 1997) and how their descendants returned to Ireland as tourists and performers in the World championships decades and generations later. We might also want to point to the professional theatrical performances of Irish dance for tourists such as those of Siamsa Tíre and the dance acts in hotel shows and cabarets over the last decades. In a contemporary context, we might want to depict the increasing popularity of dance generally (both performance and participative) as part of a selection of 'fun' things to see and do in a 'festival culture' (see Peillon, 2000). With reference to 'traditional' dance specifically, we might explore the role played by summer schools and weekend set-dance workshops catering for tourists. And we might want to highlight the way in which the success of *Riverdance* has enhanced the visibility of step-dance as a marker of Irish culture for tourists and has resulted in an increased provision of dance for tourist entertainment.

It is easy to understand why dance has been central to both tourist imagery and practice. Dance fits easily into the 'tourist package' since it is regarded as a traditional and unique expression of the host culture, facilitating relaxation and fun (and learning new skills in a fun way in the case of participative dance), and providing an opportunity for involvement, however fleeting, with local culture. The increasing popularity of 'traditional' dance as part of the tourist experience is not peculiar to Ireland and can be seen as part of a wider process of the globalisation of ethnic dance cultures. Just as *Riverdance* initially attained a global reach through the Eurovision Song Contest, flamenco reached a worldwide audience during the opening ceremony of the 1992 Barcelona Olympics and subsequently led to an increased interest on the part of tourists in experiencing this aspect of Spanish culture (see Malefyt, 1998).The purpose of this chapter is to address some issues in the relationship which has developed between tourism, dance and globalisation through empirical research on a dance show catering for tourists in Dublin city.

Dance, Tourism, and Globalisation

Current debates on cultural performance and change are centrally informed by the related concepts of 'globalisation' and 'authenticity'. These debates are complex and extensive and here I merely want to draw attention to the general thrust of the arguments. To caricature slightly, at one end of a continuum are those who welcome the mixing and interchange of 'traditional' cultural forms and practices. They see cultural hybridity as a genuine attempt to further the development of multiculturalism. Others welcome cultural hybridity as a form of consumer pluralism. At the other end of the continuum are those who adopt a negative approach to mixing cultural forms and practices because they argue that global capitalism controls cultural production, that local and indigenous cultures are transformed for dissemination in the global marketplace and that these cultural products and performances are impoverished or eroded in the process. Concepts such as McDonaldisation, McDisneyisation and wall-to-wall Dallas have become catch-phrases for the standardisation which is perceived to be a consequence of cultural flows – a standardisation which is regarded as a prerequisite for success on the global market. The latter type of position is generally associated with Marxist and neo-Marxist schools of thought and with critiques of culture in late capitalism. These are powerful but partial arguments.

While acknowledging that the critical approach to globalisation sketched here exhibits diversity, I would like to raise three problems with it. The distinction drawn between the local and the global as hermetically sealed units is over-emphasised (an argument which is also made in this volume by Kneafsey, and Quinn). The claims regarding cultural impoverishment are usually made on the basis of an analysis of the political economy of production often emphasising the aspects of ownership/control. All too often cultural production is treated in mechanistic terms and does not take into account the crucial element of human agency in the production of a cultural performance.

And, finally, the concept of culture is regarded for the most part as content rather than process-based. In relation to the latter point, I find Friedman's (1995) work on globalisation instructive in that he argues, convincingly, in my view, that to adequately understand globalising processes we must approach the concept of culture not as a vessel in an essentialist way but as a process in which social actors are forging new patterns and identification within the 'space of modernity'. Indeed in the following extract he uses the hypothetical example of dance cultures to illustrate the problems which arise when culture is perceived in an essentialist way:

> If Brooklyn-born Polynesian dancers represent the Hawaiian Hula to tourists by putting on a Tahitian fire dance on a Waikiki stage (though this no longer occurs in today's world of monitored authenticity), this need not be understood as postmodern chaos. On the contrary, it is surely one of the constants of global cultural history. It is only chaotic for the culture expert whose identification of origins is disturbed by the global processes of changing identities, a disturbance that is, consequently, translated into a de-authentification of other people's 'actually existing' cultures. The problem can only arise on the basis of the notion of culture as essence or substance. (Friedman, 1995: 85)

Research on tourist dance tends to reflect the general positions on globalisation as outlined here. For example, Malefyt (1998) in his analysis of Spanish flamenco, argues that performances for tourists have concentrated on display and objective commodification for its publics and he sees it as contrasting with the tradition of 'private' flamenco clubs where a more authentic version is performed. He supports his arguments with similar findings from other sources who claim that commercialised flamenco has become more spectacular, in line with tourist entertainment expectations, and less rooted in the meanings of the local community. A similar point is made by Travelou (2000) in the context of tourist entertainment in nighttime Athens. She argues that the dance performances are based on and include spectacular elements for tourist entertainment rather than being part of any authentic dance tradition. Parallel arguments are advanced in relation to touring objects/commodities. Sherlock (1999: 205), for instance, in analysing *Riverdance: The Show*, cautions against the effects of commodification:

> While audiences may be responding to resonances of homeland and nostalgic memories of community, the feeling of cultural belonging can provide sinister as well as positive connotations. These can be

related to both faces of nationalistic belonging. Riverdance may be shown to provide a sense of a new cultural identity for Ireland, but it should not be forgotten that as a cultural commodity it is serving the interests of capitalist profit-making.

However, other writers take an opposite view. For example O'Toole (1997) regards *Riverdance* as the exemplar of the liberation of Irish dance. He sees it as a unique expression of a national sense of self-confidence and pride which enables us to play with traditional cultural forms and re-assemble them in innovative and imaginative ways. He contrasts the spectacular and exciting new style of Irish dance favourably with the competitive dancing of the era of the 'feiseanna'[1] which had preceded it and which was characterised, in O'Toole's view, by a rigidity and lack of imagination emanating from a cultural climate of narrow nationalism and puritanism.

While the critical comment on dance tourism tends to emphasise either the positive or negative end of the globalisation continuum, some writers acknowledge the complexities involved in specific cultural milieu. Each case, therefore, must be judged on its own merits and any understanding of globalisation should be a matter for empirical investigation rather than a foregone conclusion. As Malefyt (1998: 71) notes in this regard:

> [T]ourism can act negatively to co-opt local festivals of their historic meaning and 'commoditize' them for general consumption (Green-wood 1972, 1989) . . . and it can also raise local self-consciousness by bringing to the community the idea of otherness, creating a new conception of community (Nogues Pedregal, 1996). In these varied ways tourism can be viewed as destructive or as invigorating the local cultural system.

Tourism, Dance and Authenticity

The concepts of globalisation and authenticity have generally been intertwined in cultural debates to the extent that a binary opposition is often constructed between local/traditional cultures which are seen to be authentic and global cultures which are seen to be dis-embedded from the local and consequently inauthentic.

The concept of authenticity has been germane to debates on cultural tourism. MacCannell (1976, 1989), one of the first writers to theorise the concept in relation to tourism, has claimed that authenticity is the corner-stone for understanding contemporary tourism since the primary motivation for tourism in western societies is precisely a search for the authentic in an increasingly inauthentic world. This quest is usually pursued by seeking out 'simple' places and people and 'traditional' ways of life. However, according to MacCannell, while people seek they do not often find. He utilises Goffman's distinction between 'frontstage' and 'backstage' regions to develop the idea of 'staged authenticity' by which he means that what is usually on offer to tourists is a 'frontstage' (inauthentic) disguised to look like a 'backstage' (authentic).

While MacCannell's foundational work on authenticity has contributed much to debates on tourism, it has been critiqued on a number of counts. Of interest in the current context is the critique of his historicist and object-oriented approach to the concept. Wang (1999: 9) pinpoints the problems with such a perspective as follows:

> Traditionally 'authenticity' from a historicist perspective, it is usually assumed that authentiticy is equated to an origin in time. This then implies that subsequent alteration, creativity, transformation and emerging attributes are inauthentic in terms of this origin. However, the problem is that there is no absolute point of origin, nor is anything static; rather change is constant.

Wang suggests that we should re-evaluate authenticity as it relates to tourism and goes on to offer the concept of 'experiential authenticity' which she sees as operating in the following way:

> tourism involves a bodily experience of personal authenticity. In tourism, sensual pleasure, feelings and other bodily impulses are to a relatively large extent released and consumed and the bodily desires (for natural amenities, sexual freedom, and spontaneity are gratified intensively). In short, all these aspects of tourism constitute an ontological manifesto for personal authenticity.

Given the importance of the body in 'experiential authenticity', one common way in which it can be experienced is through participating in dance performance.

The importance of the body in tourism generally, and of dance in particular, is also addressed by Jokinen and Veijola (1994: 133), in the context of their plea for embodying studies of tourism, and in their related critique of the 'tourist gaze':

> Isn't it rather the tourist body that breaks with established routines and practices? We do gaze at dance performances and museums at home don't we? But instead, hardly ever engage ourselves in singing and dancing together; very rarely at home do we share the feeling of being together in this big, wild incomprehensible world, whose words and

gestures don't say anything. Here we know it in our conscious bodies that are temporarily united in an utterly physical ritual.

While Wang (1999) and Jokinen and Veijola (1997) bring the body back into the equation, their emphasis is on the experience of the tourist. Of particular interest in the current context is the way in which this sense of bodily engagement is further developed by Daniel (1996) to include the dialectical relationship between the experiences of the tourists who participate in the dance and the dancers themselves. Based on her ethno-choreological work in Cuba and Haiti she (Daniel, 1996: 789) refers to the ways in which dance can transform the tourists' world by temporarily enabling them to escape the quotidian:

> As performing dancers, tourists access the magical world of liminality which offers spiritual and aesthetic nourishment. Tourism in moments of dance performance, opens the door to a liminal world that gives relief from day-to-day, ordinary tensions, and, for Cuban dancers and dancing tourists particularly, permits indulgence in near-ecstatic experiences.

It is worth noting that these ecstatic experiences are linked to tourists participation in the dance rather than being simply spectators. I will return to this point later in the discussion.
While acknowledging that dance performances are to some extent commodified like other cultural and artistic forms and products, Daniel (1996: 782) claims that they are also unique in that

> [D]espite shifts in scale and context, dance performance for tourists remains 'authentic' and creative. Possible explanations for this include the manner in which 'authentic' and 'creative' are defined, the unique properties of dance as expressive behavior, and the particular politico-economic situation of differing tourism settings.

She goes on to develop a definition of 'authenticity' as follows:

> Authenticity prevails when the individual is affected / touched so that she/he feels that the 'real' world and the 'real' self are consonant. It is here that touristic dance performance runs parallel to living history projects in that it relies heavily on the desire for 'authentic' experiences of the performer to satisfy the tourist's desire for 'the authentic' (Daniel, 1996: 783).

She argues for both authenticity and creativity on the part of the performers themselves. 'What happens to the performer is often deemed critical in determining "authenticity"' (p. 785). And to ascertain whether it is an authentic performance one must turn attention to the performer:

> the performer is often the critical item, the indicator of authenticity. What happens to the performer in the process of or as a result of a performance is often deemed critical in determining 'authenticity'. In fact both within or outside of the tourism setting, authenticity that is located within the performer's dancing is a critical criterion in judging and evaluating dance performance. Beyond this setting, on the concert stage, this criterion is noted by critics in terms of 'the performer's commitment to the dance', in terms of the 'transformation' that occurs in performance, or in terms of the effect experienced by the audience due to the intensity of the dance. (pp. 785–6)

The foregrounding of the dancers' experience which was called for in previous discussions of globalisation and authenticity, is also reflected in other writings in performance and tourism studies. In the context of the former, Schieffelin (1998: 198) claims that 'the burden of success or failure in a cultural performance is usually laid on the central actors, but the real location of this problem (and of the meaning of the terms 'actor', 'spectator', 'participant' is the relationship between the central performers and others in the situation'. He continues, to suggest that 'it is important to make the relationship between the participants and other in performative events a central subject of ethnographic investigation'(p. 204). Brown (1996: 44) makes a similar argument in relation to tourism research and suggests that the proper focus of study is not the tourist, nor indeed the host but the relation between them. While the current research does not include the response of tourists in this setting, it goes some way to achieving these objectives by concentrating on the dancers experience and the meanings of the dance for them, including their relationship with their audience.

Performance and Authenticity in the Irish Context

It is to this relationship that I now turn. I chose to examine dance performance in Fitzsimon's pub in the Temple Bar area of Dublin city. The show which had been running for approximately five years, at the time of the research took place on week nights, Monday through Thursday, on Saturday and Sunday afternoon, and on Sunday evening. I interviewed a number of the regular dancers about their experience of dancing in this venue. The research took place during the months of July and August (high tourist season) of 2000 and the discussion here is based predominantly on interviews and group discussions with eight dancers, seven female and one male aged between 16 and 23 years.[2] I also observed the performances and spent time in the 'backstage' region where performers met before the show and to which they retired during their break. I had a number of informal discussions with the entertainment manager for the dancers and also with other dancers and one of the musicians. The formal interviews included questions on: the trajectory of the dancers' career; comparison of performance contexts, motivations for dancing in Fitzsimons, dance repertoire and basis of selection; favourite and least liked parts of the dance routine; and perceptions of, and interaction with, audience.

Performance and Identity

Comparing performance settings

I was curious about how the dancers experienced the performance setting of Fitzsimons as compared with others. One of the most immediately obvious things to emerge from the interviews was the dancers' enthusiasm about performing in the pub context. Generally, they compared the current context to the competitive context of the 'feiseanna'. Although all of them had been centrally involved in 'feiseanna' (and some still are), in their estimation, the latter compared unfavourably with dancing in Fitzsimons. The former appeared to be a source of considerable stress and anxiety, whereas the latter performance environment was perceived to be conducive to their own enjoyment which included audience appreciation as the following accounts testify:

> There used to be only competitions. At 'feises'[3] you are being judged, people waiting for you to make a mistake. (Cathy)

> There's a rush . . . exhilarating . . . I thrive on it. It has helped so much in confidence . . . It's completely different from 'feiseanna' where you are judged. Here you are being complimented. (Jill)

> The 'feises 'are full of politics and the adjudicators have their favourites, whereas [dancing in Fitzsimons] is a great bit of 'craic'.[4] (Rachel)

Empowerment, confidence and pride

I tried to get a sense of how dancers felt during the performance[5] and found that performing helped to give them a very positive sense of self. They have all been dancing from a very early age (3–4 years in most cases) and are all highly skilled. This means that they do not have to concentrate on the steps but even if they do make a mistake it will go unnoticed by the audience. In addition, part of the pleasure of performing is the knowledge that they have a skill which is relatively rare and which cannot be easily acquired. Indeed, it appeared that part of their sense of pride came from this distinction between themselves and the audience. As Nathalie commented 'they [the audience] can't do it'. Cathy said that because Irish dancing takes years of practice you can always differentiate between Irish dancers and modern dancers who have learned some Irish dances for a particular show. Jill talked about the current craze for 'Riverdancing' classes in America and how Americans think they can gain proficiency very quickly because it looks so effortless in *Riverdance: The Show*. With some pride she also recounted an anecdote of a tourist who happened to be a professional dancer and who asked Jill to show her some foot/ankle movement at the interval. The dancer thought that she would be able to pick it up very quickly. After 20 minutes trying, she still could not do it. Mark thought that some people don't realise that Irish dancing takes so much time and practice and when parents do not see any great improvements, they take their children out of classes. These comments make it clear that the dancers were fully aware of the time, effort and discipline that their levels of skill entail and consequently they feel that there is a greater appreciation on the part of the audience.

Dancers talked about how an appreciative audience imbues them with a sense of enthusiasm, confidence and pride:

> When the crowd are really into it I get a great buzz. You might be tired starting but once you start dancing you get into the buzz. (Cathy)

> I feel proud, really positive . . . even more so when doing it as a group . . . It's a team effort . . . they break up [i.e. do individual steps] and then all four together . . . The timing is perfect. There's an adrenalin rush. (Jill)

> When you get a good crowd you dance well. You go home feeling good. (Nathalie)

> All those people are watching you and it makes you feel special. If the crowd has energy it gives you more energy and the show is more enjoyable. It is great to see them enjoying it. (Mark)

> The audience has a lot to do with the way you feel. (Jill)

> How you feel depends on the crowd. If you get a good response you dance well. (Rachel)

Jill, in talking about evenings when she was present at the show but not dancing, said that she could feel a knot in her stomach because she wanted 'to be on that stage'. She indicated that this was a common feeling among 'the girls'. Nathalie said that on nights when she is not dancing but watching the show, she feels really proud of the other dancers.

It is clear from the dancers' comments that the audience played a major role in affecting the mood of the performance. My initial assumption had been that since the audience members do not participate in the dancing that there would not be such a synergy between them. However, this does not appear to be the case and seems to contradict the suggestion that physical participation in the dance is a prerequisite for a feeling of 'existential authenticity'. Indeed, it could well be that the relative physical restraint required by the audience enhances rather than quenches the desire for movement.[6]

The dancers were keenly aware of their audience and adept at differentiating between 'good' and 'bad' audiences. They thought that audiences were generally appreciative regardless of ethnic origin or prior knowledge of Irish dance. They estimated that many of the tourists are American but there are also tourists from Britain, Japan and mainland Europe. The Americans were perceived to be most interested in Irish dance as judged by the way they approached the dancers to ask questions after the performance. Nathalie said that they were the most interested in learning about Irish dance because many of them were here tracing their Irish roots. While they assumed that many of these visitors would have seen *Riverdance* or its equivalent, they felt that they would not need an intimate knowledge of Irish dance to enjoy it. Indeed, the lack of knowledge on the audiences' part, as we saw earlier, was a source of pleasure for the dancers.

The unappreciative or 'dead crowds' were mainly visitors for stag weekends and football fans. The dancers make a distinction between the afternoon gigs on Saturday and Sunday where one was most likely to get the 'dead' crowd' and the night-time slots when they were most likely to get the 'good crowd'.[7] In addition to the type of audience which the night performances attracted, Jill drew attention to another factor which made dancing at night more enjoyable: 'The evening has more energy, when it gets darker, then the lights go up. It becomes more of a show. Maybe its a power thing', she mused.

The spatial geography of the pub also seemed to assist in generating a good rapport with the audience. The stage, though elevated from floor level, was small and gave the impression of intimacy. The space in front of the stage was uncluttered with furniture and allowed people to stand close to it so that there was a physical proximity between performers and audience. Jill gave some idea of the way in which this setting created a chemistry between performers and audience by comparing it favourably to her experience of dancing in a pub in Montreal. In Fitzsimons, because the audience members nearest to the stage were standing rather than sitting, they appeared to be more enthusiastic. She also claimed that the elevated stage allowed more people to see the footwork. And dancing to live music, she felt, added considerably to the atmosphere of energy and excitement.

It is clear from the dancers' comments that dancing was a really enjoyable experience and that they were both committed to the dance and were transformed within it. This high level of experiential authenticity during performances was intrinsically connected to the enthusiastic audience response. It was also apparent that the pleasures of performing were not guaranteed but could vary according to context. Indeed, the fragility of 'experiential authenticity' was borne out by the dancers recounting of neutral or negative responses to their performance. They all stressed that these are the exception rather than the rule but they were very conscious of them when they did occur. Of interest in this context are the strategies the dancers used to regain this sense of 'experiential authenticity', both for themselves and the audience. While there were about 15 dances in their repertoire, they discussed the up-coming number at the end of each dance and could choose which one to perform next. They claimed to know which dances the audience liked best and least. Jill said that the crowd responded more to the hard shoe reels.[8] Nathalie, in commenting on her favourite parts of the dance routine, said she liked what she thought the audience liked best: 'The acapella dancing and the set where you are doing a swing. The crowd likes a quick beat. It's better when the crowd like it.' Alternatively, if they thought the crowd was 'really dead', they would not do a hornpipe because it was 'too slow'. And in the same situation they would probably include two set-dances rather than one because it was lively, fast and involved swinging with other dancers.

Spectacle, Power and Gender

The power of the 'male gaze' has been a central theme in discussions of women and public space generally and in relation to women and dance specifically (e.g. see Thomas, 1993). Mindful of this literature I had anticipated prior to fieldwork that the dance situation might lend itself to a sexual objectification of the female dancers in particular. In such a situation I estimated that 'experiential authenticity' in terms of a consonance between the 'real world' and the 'real self' would be compromised. This did not appear to be the case. While the dancers recognised an element of voyeurism (Jill said that 'when you are dancing you think the men are looking at your footwork but when you sit down after the dance they are still looking!') they are not unduly troubled by it and said that 'You don't let it get to you'. Gillian remarked that this kind of male attention is commonplace – 'You get the same thing on the street or in your car'. The dancers were not disturbed by this and appeared to handle these situations with a mixture of good sense and humour. Indeed, the incidents about troublesome or voyeuristic men were recounted to me as comic anecdotes and seemed to have become part of the repertoire of shared memories and mythic stories, functioning to create a sense of security and belonging among the group. Anne, the dance manager, said that she looks out for the girls and that the bouncers also look out for 'trouble-makers in the audience'. Though not incident free, overall, one got the impression of a safe environment in which any potential objectification or harrassment of dancers was quickly defused.

I had also anticipated that experiential authenticity could be compromised by gender stereotyping within the dance performance. For instance, I have argued elsewhere (O'Connor, 1998) that *Riverdance: The Show* accentuated 'traditional' masculinity and femininity by various means. And, here again, I was curious as to the possibility of this gendering in terms of visual style and in terms of choreography. At the time of my research the dancers were predominantly young women but during the research period a male dancer joined the troupe. Sartorially, the style could be described as 'subdued *Riverdance*' in that the female dancers wore short black dresses in soft material (though any kind of black dress would suffice) and black tights. This certainly had the effect of emphasising both body contours and leg length. Mark, the male dancer, wore a plain black trousers and black shirt but was definitely not into what he referred to as 'macho image of the leather trousers and tight muscly tops' of the male dancers in *Riverdance*. It seemed to me that visually, the female dancers were more sexualised than the male.

However, in choreographic terms gendering was not in evidence. From observation it was clear that the stage was too small to allow for the expansive movements and gestures of a lead / 'star' dancer. Both male and female dancers did the same steps and routines. Mark corroborated these observations and elaborated when I asked whether being the sole male made a difference in this respect. He thought that while it is theoretically possible for the male to take the lead, that in practice it did not happen. He talked about dancing in another pub where he had the lead in one dance. But in other dances the female dancers would have had the lead. In Fitzsimons, however, they did more or less the same steps so there was no question of the male dancer dominating.

The *Riverdance* Factor

There is no doubt that the Fitzsimons show is heavily influenced by the spectacular global extravaganzas, *Riverdance* and *Lord of the Dance*. According to Anne, the dance manager, the initial idea for the show itself was generated because of the success of *Riverdance* when she realised that all kinds of people could find Irish dance entertaining. It was also evident that the influence of the 'big shows' was also present in choreographic elements such as the acapella dancing and in aspects of the visual style. Yet these features were not slavishly copied and it was evident that the pub context provided scope for individual improvisation and negotiation of personal styles and identities.

The dancers were conscious of the influence of *Riverdance* on their per-formance and saw this influence as positive overall. They commented on the fact that the new shows provided them with an opportunity for dancing which they would not otherwise have had, since the majority had given up competing in 'feiseanna' at 15 or 16 years of age and would not have had another expressive outlet since then. Jill, for example, said that she had quit Irish dancing when she was 16 but returned three years later because of the influence of *Riverdance*. She was attracted by the increased visibility of Irish dance and by the possibility of doing shows. Cathy, who had also stopped enjoying dancing and going to dance classes, decided to return again when she started dancing in Fitzsimons. Mark pointed to the fact that *Riverdance* has generated more shows so that it was now possible to have a career in dance and to travel. He regarded it as a reward after all the years of hard work. Many of the other dancers also mentioned the opportunity to travel which the globalisation of Irish dance presents and some expressed an ambition to join one of the well-known travelling shows.

In addition to increasing the popularity of Irish step dancing, *Riverdance* was also seen to alter its cultural status and trendiness. A number of dancers mentioned that, wheras previously they would have been reluc-tant to tell their school mates that they were Irish dancers for fear of being perceived as 'untrendy', they were now relaxed about doing so. As an example, Cathy said that in her school music class she now helped class-mates to differentiate jig-time from reel-time by dancing the beat for them.

However, while the overall response to *Riverdance* was approving and enthusiastic the dancers were also critical of some developments which they associated with the 'big shows'. For instance, they contrasted their own relatively relaxed dance environment with the treatment of dancers and their responses in the latter. Nathalie reckoned the dancers were treated like a 'herd of cattle'. She spoke of her own experience of participat-ing in a workshop for one of the shows, and of how the auditioning dancers were required to stand in line with number tags, and of how there were pools of water running down the walls due to condensation and gathering on the floor because of the lack of proper ventilation, and of how the overall experience was 'so degrading'. They told of how they had heard stories from friends who worked in the 'big shows' of extremely hard work with endless hours of rehearsal and problems of dehydration, blisters, sprained and broken bones and limbs. There were also stories of dancers being kicked out for using cocaine, and of the increasing problem of anorexia and bulemia among dancers.

Conclusions

This chapter is an attempt to address the relationship between tourism and dance in the context of the increase in step-dance entertainment for tourists visiting Ireland. The concepts of globalisation and authenticity were used to address these issues. My general predisposition towards the tourist dance shows prior to conducting the research was towards a 'negative globalisation' interpretation given the proliferation of the 'Riverdance' style in a number of entertainment venues. I had anticipated that I would find a substantially commodifed, and standardised situation which worked to objectify the performers and some of the research questions (such as the presence of the 'male gaze') were constructed on the basis of my expectations. During the research process, however, what struck me most forcibly was the sheer vibrancy, excitement and energy of the show. My 'conversion' was due to the time spent observing and talking to the dancers and confirmed the importance of attempting to understand the meanings of the situation from the point of view of the dancers themselves.

But what exactly does this perspective based on the empirical research tell us about the relationship between tourism, dance and the issues of globalisation and 'authenticity' which I set out to address? With reference to globalisation, it was apparent from the research that the show was strongly influenced by Riverdance and Lord of the Dance in terms of style and choreographic elements but this did not seem to lead to a blanket standardisation or commodification. And while dancers welcomed the advent of the celebrity shows because they offered them a new status and opportunities, they were critical of the commodification of dancers which they saw as a feature of those shows.

As regards authenticity, if we return to the two models of authenticity outlined earlier, it is clear that the Fitzsimons show is authentic in terms of the 'experiential' model but is not in terms of the 'object-oriented / historical' model. The findings clearly indicate that 'commitment to the dance' and 'transformation' on the part of the performers were present in the performance context. Dancing in Fitzsimons was a joyful and pleasurable experience providing an important expressive outlet and promoting a sense of self-confidence and pride. The dancers worked to build a good rapport with the audience and the audiences' response was a pre-requisite to their enjoyment. However, if I had adopted an exclusively object-oriented and historicist view of authenticity, the performance would have to be deemed inauthentic because it was obvious that many aspects of the step-dancing performance style have changed and evolved over the years (see Brennan, 1994; Hall, 1997).

The picture emerging from the Fitzsimons case is that of the everyday context in which the dancers perform and the ways in which they constructed meanings around the performance. This approach enables us to see the dancers' performance in terms of identity construction and to see cultural performance in terms of social agency. To return to Friedman's (1995) terminology, we might see the dancers as ' forging new patterns of identification within the 'space of modernity'. The meanings associated with dance for them included, expressivity and performativity, freedom, travel, self-confidence, skill, pride, discipline – traits, accomplishments and activities which are positively valued within contemporary society. While the meanings and experience as identified by the dancers gave priority to the positive aspects, it is also possible, even plausible, to suggest that other, less positive, but commonplace, meanings were experienced by dancers but not manifest because they are less amenable to articulation either because they might not have been perceived as socially acceptable (e.g. narcissism) or were unconscious.

It is also important to acknowledge that the cultural meanings of the performance for the dancers themselves are not the only ones available and I would concur with Ward (1997: 14) when he states that 'a dance's meaning might be quite different to the feelings a dancer is experiencing'. Indeed, one might suggest that other meanings associated with the dance shows include: the valorisation of youth and beauty, ambition, competitiveness, success and desire for celebrity status – meanings which may be seen as either positive or negative.

To highlight the necessity of addressing experiential authenticity does not, in my view, obviate the need to retain an 'object-oriented' or historicist account. It is also important to ask questions about the specific ways in which the increasing popularity of theatrical / commercial shows are influencing Irish step-dance. For instance, if tourists prefer hard-shoe dances associated with rhythm, will it lead to a decline in the performance of soft-shoe dances? Or, similarly, if tourists prefer fast-tempo dances will it lead to a decrease in the slower?

Any comprehensive assessment of dance in tourist settings would entail an integration of the research presented here with work on the political economy of dance in tourist settings, with structural analysis of the dance, and with the experiences of the tourists themselves. What I have been arguing in this chapter is that attempts to understand cultural performances in the context of global cultural flows of commodities and people in the form of tourists, must take into account the role of the performers and, more specifically, the meanings which the dancers attach to their performance. It is this aspect which has been the most neglected in discussions of tourist dance and globalisation to date.

Acknowledgements

I would like to thank the staff and management of Fitzsimons for allowing me to loiter with intent. I am especially grateful to Anne, the dance manager, and the dancers – Caroline, Cathy, Gillian, Jill, Leanne, Mark, Nathalie and Rachel for taking the time and effort to talk to me during their busy schedule. Without their generosity this project would not have been possible. And thanks to my colleague, Bill Dorris, for his encouragement and support.

Notes

1. Feiseanna is the name for the competitions which had been the dominant form of institutionalised exhibition of Irish step-dancing from the 1930s.
2. Since the dancers to whom I spoke were self-selecting it is necessary to bear in mind the possibility that those who were most willing to participate in the interview were the most enthusiastic about their experience.
3. Although the plural of the Irish word 'feis' is 'feiseanna', the word 'feises' is commonly used in English and the dancers themselves generally used the latter term.
4. The word 'craic' is generally used in the context of having fun in a convivial group atmosphere.
5. Some dancers found it difficult to have an extended conversation on this aspect of their performance: a difficulty commonly experienced in trying to communicate bodily feelings verbally.
6. It might be useful to think of this situation as analagous to the Lacanian 'mirror stage' of development in which the child thinks that his/her motor skills are more developed than they actually are thereby creating an illusion of perfect power.
7. They do not perform on either Friday or Saturday nights as the pub runs a disco on these nights.
8. All the numbers are hard-shoe dances apart from one soft-shoe reel. This is probably due to the influence of *Riverdance*.

References

Brennan, H. (1994) Reinventing tradition: The boundaries of Irish dance. *History Ireland* (Summer), 22–4.
Brown, D.(1996) Genuine fakes. In T. Selwyn (ed.) *The Tourist Image: Myths and Myth Making in Tourism* (pp. 33–47). Chichester: Wiley.
Cullinane, J.(1997*)* Irish dance world-wide: Irish migrants and the shaping of traditional Irish dance. In P.O'Sullivan (ed.) *The Creative Migrant, Vol.3. The Irish World-Wide: History, Heritage, Identity Series.* Leicester: Leicester University Press.
Daniel, Y. (1996)Tourism dance performances: Authenticity and creativity. *Annals of Tourism Research* 23 (4), 780–97.

Friedman, J. (1995) Global system, globalization and the parameters of modernity. In M. Featherstone, S. Lash and R. Robertson (eds) *Global Modernities*. London: Sage.

Hall. F. (1997) Not Irish/now Irish: Contradictions of nation and experience in expressive body movement. Paper presented to The Scattering Conference, Cork.

Jokinen, E. and Veijola, S. (1997) The disoriented tourist: The figuration of tourism in contemporary cultural critique. In C. Rojek and J. Urry (eds) *Touring Cultures: Transformations of Travel and Theory*. London: Routledge.

MacCannell, D. (1976) *The Tourist: A New Theory of the Leisure Class*. New York: Schoken..

Malefyt, T. (1998) 'Inside' and 'outside' Spanish flamenco: Gender constructions in Andalusian concepts of flamenco tradition. *Anthropological Quarterly* 71 (2), 63–73.

O'Connor, B. (1998) Riverdance. In M. Peillon and E. Slater (eds) *Encounters with Modern Ireland*. Dublin: Institute of Public Administration.

O'Toole, F. (1997) 'Unsuitables from a distance': The politics of Riverdance. In *Ex-Isle of Erin: Images of a Global Ireland*. Dublin: New Island Books.

Peillon, M. (2000) Carnival Ireland. In E. Slater and M. Peillon (eds) *Memories of the Present: A Sociological Chronicle of Ireland, 1997–1998*. Dublin: Institute of Public Administration.

Schieffelin, E. (1998) Problematizing performance. In F. Hughes-Freeland (ed.) *Ritual, Media, Performance*. London: Routledge.

Sherlock, J. (1999) Globalisation, western culture and Riverdance. In A. Brah, M. Hickman and M. Mac Ghaill (eds) *Thinking Identities: Ethnicity, Racism and Culture*. Basingstoke: Macmillan.

Thomas, H. (1993) An-Other voice: Young women dancing and talking. In H.Thomas (ed.) *Dance, Gender and Culture*. London: Macmillan.

Travelou, P.(2000) 'Athens by night' or how a tourist became Zorbas the Greek. Paper presented at the Third International Crossroads in Cultural Studies Conference, 21–25 June, Birmingham, UK.

Wang, Ning, (1999) Rethinking authenticity in tourism experience. *Annals of Tourism Research* 26 (2), 349–70.

Ward, A. (1997) Dance around meaning (and the meaning around dance). In H. Thomas (ed.) *Dance in the City*. London: Macmillan.

Part 3

The Power of the Gaze: Negotiating Tourist and Native Identities

Chapter 7

Power, Knowledge and Tourguiding: The Construction of Irish Identity on Board County Wicklow Tour Buses

ANNETTE JORGENSEN

Tourism industries construct and communicate images of the cultural, ethnic and national identities of host populations, images which are repro-duced in brochures, guidebooks and in the language of tour guides. Such representations are attempts at attracting foreign visitors to holiday desti-nations by portraying these as exotic, mysterious or in other ways different from the every-day lives of potential travellers. In doing this, however, tourism imagery may also creates a sense of 'otherness', of difference between the intended audience, the tourists and the people and culture of the destination country (see, for example, O'Barr, 1994). Irish tourism imagery can be seen as a discourse on Ireland and Irish identity, which it constructs by selectively representing certain features of Irish culture, while dismissing others. Whereas media researchers have long acknowl-edged the need to examine audience readings of messages found in mass media, no attention has so far been paid to how Irishness is understood by foreign visitors during their holiday in the country. This chapter seeks to address the lack of attention to tourist interpretations by offering a prelimi-nary exploration of how Irish identity is constructed on one-day tours to Glendalough in County Wicklow, not only by the tour guides, but also by the tourists themselves.[1]

The Tourist(ic) Gaze

Urry has illustrated how the Foucauldian notion of a constructive, powerful gaze can be applied to the tourist experience. He argues that such a tourist gaze stems from expectations of (visual) pleasure and experiences out of the ordinary, which are constructed and 'endlessly reproduced' through various mass media and objectified in the tourism imagery (Urry,

1990: 3). Yet Cheong and Miller (2000) feel that Urry attributes too much of the construction of the gaze to the tourists themselves. In an elaboration of Urry's work they argue instead that a *touristic* gaze is constructed and controlled by powerful professionals in the tourism industry such as brokers, guides, hotel employees and writers of guide-books. These, according to Cheong and Miller, are the agents of power, who are able to select which aspects of the holiday destination are to be submitted to the gaze. Both these perspectives see the gaze as created by imagery, by touristic representations. In other words, the gaze is sustained by touristic discourses.

The Touristic Discourse

International tourism creates a world to be gazed upon by transporting people thousands of miles to gaze upon it, and it constructs this world by interpreting and explaining it to us. The information given by guides and guidebooks can be seen as part of a wider touristic discourse, in Hall's (1997a: 44) words a 'group of statements which provide a language for talking about – a way of representing knowledge about – a particular topic', which is shaped by a particular historical context. Foucault (1972: 6) suggests that the discipline of history has been characterised by an attempt to reveal an underlying continuity between our past and our present. Like history, the touristic discourse seeks to create an uncomplicated past (and present) to be gazed upon, and it presents consistencies in its subject matter, the destination, rather than contradictions. And like historical discourses, the touristic discourse lends speech to artefacts, which 'in themselves, are often not verbal, or which say in silence something other than what they actually say' (Foucault, 1972: 7). Thus, the touristic discourse gives speech to the destination by translating it to foreign travellers, enables the place to say more than what it says 'in silence' that is, uninterpreted. A foreign country, experienced in a 'raw' state, as a jumble of sounds, sights, smells and tastes, cannot be 'understood' that is, given coherence and narrative, without some form of mediating, of interpretation by tourist guides or guidebooks.

Power, Knowledge and Tourism

This raises the question of the relationship between knowledge and power in tourism. Here, again, we may draw upon the work of Cheong and Miller (2000). They argue that although tourists are most often potential targets of the power of agents and guides, in Foucauldian terms, power is everywhere in tourism. The authors thereby highlight the omnipresence of power in tourist relations. Foucault does not see power in static terms, it is not something that is acquired and held. On the contrary, power is 'produced from one moment to the next, at every point, or rather in every relation from one to another' (Foucault, 1980: 93). We must not think of power as running in a straight line from oppressors to oppressed. Instead, we must start by considering the 'local centres' of power, the micro relations of the discourse in question. We must consider how these relations make particular statements possible and, in turn, how the discourses support the power relations. Foucault (1980: 98) suggests that, for instance, the specific relationship between confessor and priest led to a certain type of discourse on sexuality, which again reinforced the relations between these agents. With regard to the touristic discourse, the most 'local centres' of power might be the relations between tourist and tour guide. The guide possesses professional expertise, which gives him or her the power to construct what he or she is interpreting. The tourists are strangers to the place they visit, whereas the guide is a local, one who revisits it and re-interprets its meaning again and again. In addition, as the tourists are out of their own culture (Crick, 1989), they are dependent upon the explanations of the guide. So, if they are to 'understand' the destination, they must accept the guide's expertise. Implicit in the touristic discourse lies the claim that the local culture, history or landscape can only be 'understood' from the point of view of the guide. The locals are constructed as 'other', to be gazed upon. Therefore, for a tourist, it is the guide, the person who 'speaks one's own language' – culturally as well as linguistically – that one must turn to in order to comprehend them. Thus it appears to be the tour guide who has the power to speak, not the tourists and not the locals.

Encoding and Decoding Touristic Messages

If tour guides construct 'Ireland' through discursive practises, the tourists on the Glendalough bus can be seen as their audiences. How they interpret what they are presented with – how they 'read' Irish identity – may therefore be similar to the ways in which other audiences have been found to interpret the messages of the mass media. In order to examine whether the tour guide holds any measure of power to influence tourists' interpretations, Hall's (1980) model of encoding and decoding may prove useful. This model has successfully been applied to other discourses on cultural identity, such as interpretations made by museum visitors (Dicks, 2000; Fyfe & Ross, 1996). According to Hall (1980), meaning is produced at both the production and consumption stages of communication, at the moment of encoding and that of decoding, as well as in the text itself. Hall argues that meanings are imposed on audiences in the form of a dominant or preferred meaning, yet cultural texts are polysemic, and audiences actively decode such texts, thus the resulting reading cannot be guaranteed. To understand how meaning is constructed at different moments within such a 'circuit of communication' (Hall, 1980) of tourism, the micro power relations on the Glendalough tour, one must become a passenger on the bus. On this tour the bus driver takes on the role of guide and engages in constant narration. This 'text' can be seen as containing encoded messages. The guiding, therefore, is the first moment to be examined. The following discussion is based on findings collected through participant observation and interviews during and immediately after four one-day tours to Glendalough. The four guides are referred to as guides A to D. The passengers on all tours were of European or North American nationality, the majority were female, and apart from four Austrian students in their early twenties, all were aged between 38 and 64. Full details are given below for each respondent quoted. In addition to the observations, a total of eight tourists and two tour guides were interviewed at length.

Directing the Gaze

As the bus carries us through Wicklow towards Glendalough, the driver – who is also our guide – provides explanations and information, which shape our perception of the world outside. Ireland is presented to us, all we have to do is remain in our seats, lean back and watch as it unfolds outside the windows, as if in a cinema. Each scene in this 'film' is brought to our attention as we approach it. The guide will inform us that, for example, 'on the left you see . . . ', and, as if he[2] had physically pulled strings attached to our heads, we all move and turn to the left so as not to miss this aspect of Ireland. We 'zoom in' on what he has mentioned, focus our attention on it. At this specific point of the tour, then, the windows on the left-hand side of the bus make up the screen in this Cinema of Ireland. Whatever might be on the right-hand side ceases to exist as it is not part of this particular scene. An actual film shown in the visitor centre at Glendalough is a continuation of the form of presentation on the bus rather than a break with it. Our understanding of what Ireland is, therefore, includes only carefully selected tourist markers towards which our gaze is directed by the guide's narration. It is a fractured text we are presented with, consisting of many discursive elements, including the guiding, the landscape, the monastic ruins at Glendalough, items for sale in tourist shops, the interiors of a pub in which we have lunch, as well as tapes of traditional music played on board the bus. Each object or each word spoken can be understood as a sign with a signified meaning, a message for the tourists to decode. All of these signs can be read for ideological messages regarding Irish identity. The messages sometimes seem to contradict each other and visitors are confronted with multiple 'Irelands' throughout the tour. There are, however, certain themes, certain dominant meanings, of Ireland and Irishness that can be identified on all the tour buses I joined.

Themes

First of all, Ireland is presented as a place of unspoilt natural beauty. The selected route follows the South Dublin coast, then continues through the Wicklow mountains and is chosen to encompass the most beautiful parts of the area. In addition, the guide's narrative focuses our attention on particularly scenic aspects of the Ireland we pass through and what is pointed out to us includes trees, lakes, hills and valleys. The guide facilitates us to read what we see as picturesque – he points out the 'neat little villages', the 'nice scenery and lovely greens' – and informs us that when we get to Glendalough we will be able to 'feel the stillness, no matter how busy it is' (guide B). Throughout most of the tour, Ireland also remains old-fashioned and traditional. The focus in much of the guiding is on historical elements rather than on the Ireland of the present, the items selected for us to admire are medieval castles, churches and towers. In Glendalough we are transported back in time as we walk through the old gateway to the monastic city. The narrative of the guide allows us to imagine life in the tenth century but we also get a sensory experience thereof by walking through the place, in the footsteps of medieval monks, and by entering the darkness of the church called 'St Kevin's Kitchen' and breathing in the cold, damp air inside. In the guide's narrative, a hollow in a stone wall becomes a holy water fountain and he encourages us to touch it, to feel the marks left by centuries of fingernails. Thus, at Glendalough, we not only gaze at Ireland's past. We smell, taste and touch medieval Ireland. In this way, much of the tour presents Ireland as an escape from modernity, to a place, like the Wicklow boglands through which we pass, where 'nothing has changed since the ice age' (guide C) and where 'the bog only grows one foot every thousand years' (guide A). Other messages concern the Irish people who appear friendly, entertaining and talkative. The guides claim to be 'cuddly' (guide A) and loveable, offering hugs and friendly advice. However, other aspects of the Irish stereotype also emerge, as Irish people are shown, through jokes and anecdotes, to be superstitious beings, drinkers of whiskey and stout. The Irish may be fun but they cannot be trusted: at the beginning of the tour, guide C promises us: 'I'll tell you lots of lies'. This image of the Irish(man) as a loveable but untrustworthy rogue mirrors what Rolston (1995) has called the paternalistic racism towards the Irish, often found in tourism literature on the country.

On this tour, modern-day Irish life is also mentioned, although less frequently. The Celtic Tiger now seems to have become a tourist marker, with references to the economic boom and the low unemployment. The tour guide, therefore, unavoidably touches on political issues. However, comments regarding such are infrequent, and they tend to be downplayed. For example, after briefly criticising the government for not acting on the housing crisis, guide C quickly adds, 'I won't go into politics' and moves on to talk about a bird sanctuary we are passing. Political aspects of Irish history are also downplayed, frequently by the use of humour. Medieval tribal wars are referred to as 'these two squabbled a lot' (guide B), and the most horrifying example of warfare we encounter is 'two men pulling at each other's beards' in the film at Glendalough. Although invasions are addressed by the guides, and indeed Irish history sometimes is constructed as one long occupation ('then after the Vikings came Oliver Cromwell' guide D informs us), any mentioning of such issues is transient and always decontextualised. Ireland's largest minority ethnic group, the travelling community, receives little attention, despite the fact that their halting sites are passed several times on the tour. When referred to, the issues involved are depoliticised – we are told that the travellers refuse social housing and jokes are made about their 'expensive new cars' (guide B) – of which I see none. Thus the guide selects aspects of Irish history and culture and physical objects in the Irish landscape and gives them significance through narration. Tourist interpretations are aided by the guiding and by the film at the Glendalough visitor centre, which helpfully informs us that 'small stone churches and round towers' have become 'symbols of Irish culture'. That is, they have become signs signifying Irishness. What can be read from them is most often the international stereotypical myth of 'Ireland as Emerald Isle': natural beauty, old-fashioned and traditional, inhabited by friendly rogues, decontextualised historically and politically.

Frameworks

Therefore, the presentation draws on broader, international touristic discourses. All the messages – the guiding, the film, the selected signs – can be understood as discursive elements part of a larger narrative about Ireland. It is this narrative which is reproduced by the tour guides rather than the guides constructing their own version of Ireland. Although the guides appear to make the discursive choices – they are given free hands by the companies[3] – most often they choose to point out aspects of the country which are already part of the wider touristic discourse on Ireland. For instance, while passing through Ashford, they will point out Mount Usher Gardens and comment, 'This is what the village is famous for' (guide B). In other words, this is how the village is constructed through national and international touristic discourses, all other aspects of it remain invisible, to the guide as well as to the tourists. When I (a Scandinavian) asked him in an interview why certain features are selected, guide B answered: 'Eddie Irvine, Daemon Hill, Bono, people all around the world would know about them. Van Morrison, I'm not sure, do you know him?'; thus at the same time assessing whether his presentation (which includes pointing out alleged homes of these celebrities) is consistent with the international image of Ireland.

The touristic discourse not only gives messages about Ireland as a tourist destination, it also claims to explain historical facts about the country. On this particular tour, the discourse alleges to interpret the ruins of the Glendalough monastic site for us. It gives voice to the early medieval buildings and monuments, and it is related to what Slater (1993) calls the 'oral framework' of the 19th century local Glendalough guides, who offered tourists interpretations of the place based on folklore and tales. The discourse of the driver-guide who leads us through the site tends to be at variance with the more academically informed discourse of the audio-visual show and exhibition at the Glendalough visitor centre, which the tourists are given the opportunity to visit. Both discourses present histori-cal information about the ruins upon which we gaze and both highlight the same buildings and sites within the monastic city but, depending on the framework, the physical space which we interpret as Glendalough is con-structed differently. In the narrative of the visitor centre, the ruins become archaeological discoveries, examples of the craftsmanship and monastic culture of tenth century Ireland, as the film explains the materials and skills needed to build them. Whereas that of the visitor centre is a formal, scien-tific discourse, which appears informed by archaeology and history, the discursive choices made by the driver-guides seem to be based on the entertainment value of the anecdotes through which the place is inter-preted, such as stories about the life of St Kevin, the founder of the monastery. This is a narrative based on myths and legends about Glenda-lough. Perhaps this construction of Glendalough as a supernatural place facilitates the touristic messages about Ireland as a place out of the ordinary, unlike the world from which the tourists have come, a romantic and mythical land. However, neither of the two narratives exists in pure form. The driver-guide draws upon both as sources for his narration of the place, weaving together fact and fiction. Even the formal audio-visual show at the visitor centre includes items of humour, which gives a sense of entertainment and pleasure, facilitating a more light-hearted reading of Glendalough. Finally, the guides also draw on other sources of information for their presentation, although less frequently than the two mentioned earlier. They might comment on inflation and add 'so I hear on the radio' (guide D) and sometimes personal frameworks seem to emerge. Most obvious an example is guide C's comment on Temple Bar, which does not seem tailor-made for his audience: 'Dublin people don't really go there, cos it's full of tourists'. Such statements are relatively rare but they can perhaps be seen as examples of an 'authentic' local voice.

Touristic Readings

If the dominant meaning of the messages on board the tour buses, as we saw earlier, can be said to communicate the international touristic discourse on Ireland as Emerald Isle, then significant evidence can be found of this reading being accepted by the intended audience. At first glance it would appear that most of the participants do not challenge the touristic discourse of the guides but take on subject positions required for the discourse to make sense. They take on identities outside traditional, beautiful Ireland, in modernity, and place themselves in the exclusive tourist world which, according to Boniface (1998), is neither destination nor home, from which they can gaze at the Irish people as a friendly 'other'. They seem to accept the expertise of the guides and the information presented. When tourists are asked in interviews what they will remember from the tour, they describe Ireland as a place of scenic beauty, it is 'quiet', 'serene', 'green' and 'beautiful'. It is seen as empty space. Or when commenting on what they think is typically Irish, they mention the 'quaint little villages' encountered on the tour. Historical elements are also dominant and the Irish people are very much described in terms of their stereotypical qualities. In the words of the tourists, they are 'friendly', 'lovely', 'charming' or 'accommodating'. They 'like their drink' and 'there is a mystical thing attached to them'. In other words, the tourists reproduce the language of the guides and of the touristic discourse.

Interviews with passengers reveal that although they recognise the guiding as constructed, that the guide is 'just doing his job' (passenger H: American female, age 48, 'half Asian',[4] controller of corporate travel agency, first visit to Ireland), they still accept the information and advice he gives and they see his 'entertainment' style of presentation as a reflection of his friendly Irish nature, rather than evidence of tourism as a staged event. 'He was very proud of his background, his Irish roots, and the history and what Ireland has to offer', the same passenger comments. What is interpreted as the guide's sincerity is not contrasted with his showmanship or what another passenger calls his 'theatric' performance; on the contrary they are seen as one and the same. A similar view is expressed by other passengers in a conversation I overheard during the tour:

K: I love the Irish, they're so, *echt*, what they say they mean it . . .

J: Yes, so sincere.

K: Sincere, yes. [The guide] is very good, he is like an actor.

          (Passenger K: German female, age 59, retired accountant, second
          visit. Passenger J: American female, age 44, occupation unknown,
          first visit.)

Being entertaining, therefore, is accepted as an integral part of the Irish
identity, deception as a sign of sincerity.

Critical Interpretations

However, it seems that not every tourist simply accepts all given information nor all suggested connotations. On the bus some forms of
oppositional readings are also made. These may take the form of a refusal
to play along or deconstructing the touristic discourse of the guides. At the
Upper Glendalough Lake, guide C announces: 'It's lucky to take a pebble
and bring it home'. This comment draws upon the touristic discourse of
Ireland as mystical, of the Irish as superstitious and of Glendalough as
supernatural. The guide takes on the role of expert and, as gatekeeper,
enables us to take part in the magic and bring with us a token of enchanted
Ireland. Some people take a stone but passenger G (an English female
midwife, age 42, on her first visit to Ireland) comments instead to the guide:
'You must be very lucky, if you come here all the time'. Throughout the
tour her attitude is clearly ironic, a feature of what sociologists have called
post-tourism (see, for example, Lash & Urry, 1994). She reveals the underlying assumptions of the touristic discourse, of the guide sincerely sharing
the magic of Ireland with passive, accepting visitors and she 'reads' not
messages about the Emerald Isle but instead focuses on the logic of the
guide's presentation. This does not mean a dismissal of his skills, in a later
interview she praises them ('He is very good, very funny'). The guide's narrative is appreciated for its style rather than its content, it is recognised as
an art form, as a constructed media discourse rather than a source of information about an objective Irish reality.

Other passengers are more directly critical of the guiding. When one
guide points out the house belonging to Eddie Irvine (the Formula One
driver), a passenger turns to me and asks, plainly, 'Is that true?'. After
another tour, an American 40-year-old male accountant (passenger L, on
his first visit) mentions to me that he thought the guide's reference to
unemployment – in passenger L's words that 'they used to export people
but now they can't get enough' – was 'a funny comment', then asks me to
verify it. It therefore seems that, rather than passively accepting the preferred meanings of the guide's narrative, some of the tourists seek out
other sources of information with which to compare it. Perhaps such

critical comments can be more effectively understood by returning to the Foucauldian concept of power. According to Foucault (1980), discourse can be both an instrument of power, as we saw earlier, but also a point of resistance, a starting point for an opposing strategy. The new discourse may, in this case, be a post-touristic one, through which pleasure is gained from reading and analysing the strategies employed by the guide rather than from the touristic messages about Ireland which he seeks to communicate.

However, this alternative, ironic touristic reading of Ireland seems to be applied to isolated events, rather than to the tourist experience as a whole.

> Last night we went to a pub in the city centre to listen to traditional Irish music. [laughs] It's not very authentic. It's a mix of Irish music and 60s and 70s English music done in an Irish way, isn't it. But I suppose that's what you would expect to find in Dublin, it's not like a pub in the country, is it? (Passenger B: English male, age 39, mature student, first visit)

This comment could, perhaps, at first be understood as an oppositional reading of the touristic discourse, recognising the staged nature of tourism in Dublin. However, there is at the same time an unwillingness to let go of the touristic image of Ireland, even when it is not found. There remains the belief in such an authentic, traditional Ireland, albeit physically located elsewhere, beyond reach.

Indeed, most touristic decodings of the guide's messages seem to be negotiated and whereas they may accept the overall construction of Ireland as Emerald Isle, passengers will negotiate meanings of specific signs in specific situations as exceptions to the rule (Hall, 1980). Some passengers on the buses are actively engaging in the construction of Ireland through their own discourse, through talking and thinking about it. Some seem to have their own agenda, their own narrative, which they confirm to one another, such as discussing the houses the bus passes. At other occasions, tourists seem to listen to what is said by the guide but give it their own meaning, they may giggle at comments which do not seem amusing to others or turn the factual information given into a joke:

Guide: Dublin is a corruption of an old Irish word.
E (to me, seated next to her):   The Irish are all corrupt aren't they, they're like the English [laughs].

> (Passenger E: English female, age 58, occupation unknown, first visit)

Here, pleasure is gained from engaging playfully with the subject matter and creatively attributing alternative meanings to it, yet without necessarily challenging those intended by the guide.

Tourists' Cultural Resources

In their reading of Ireland and Irish identity, the tourists do not only draw upon the messages in the discourse of the guide. When interviewed after the tour, they combine the narratives encountered with other discourses, their own cultural resources. Some draw upon experiences as tourists elsewhere. Thus, Ireland as a tourist destination is compared to others, such as when passenger H (details given earlier) mentions to me at Glendalough that 'the stones here remind me of Macchu Pichu'.[5] However, more often Ireland is found to be somehow inferior, friendlier but less grand, as when Glendalough is contrasted with Rome: 'The ruins were less, what shall I say, impressive, than Roman ruins, they're more bare, they look just so much older. Em, somehow I think I expected more' (passenger M; Italian-American female, age 62, first visit). Readings of Ireland and Irish identity are also facilitated by drawing upon other cultural resources from tourists' personal background or life experiences. Many of the American passengers had attended Catholic schools where they had come in contact with Irish Americans, and all are familiar with Saint Patrick's Day celebrations, which they read as signifiers of Irishness. Tourists' own ethnicity may also influence how they engage with the question of Irish identity. When discussing what it means to be Irish, passenger M, a second-generation Italian-American woman discusses Irishness in terms of Irish-Americans whom, she believes, 'are Irish in their own way', relating their position in society to her own life experience: 'Americans think I am Italian and Italians think I am American'. It would, therefore, seem that although tourists at times objectify and stereotype the native Irish, at other occasions tourism cannot be said to lead to 'othering' of the host population. Rather, tourists draw on their own cultural resources to relate to the Irish in various ways. Passengers H (details given earlier) and I (American female, age 42, homemaker, first visit), discuss the economic situation in the country with reference to that of their own. They compare the situation of Irish civil servants (mentioned by the guide) to that of teachers in their own state and recognise them as similar. In the same interview they discuss Irish lifestyle with reference to their experience in restaurants, where they were surprised to encounter smoking. This creates a certain distance and they conclude that the Irish are less healthy than their own kind. However, this is not interpreted as a specific trait of the Irish people, rather as a result of socioeconomic structures of Irish society, considered inferior to their own:

'We have more choices in California, it's a healthy and wealthy state' (passenger I).

Other frameworks frequently drawn on are those of mass media representations of Ireland and the Irish people. Fictional accounts such as Hollywood images of the country are mentioned by passenger L (details given earlier) as influencing his understanding of the Irish past and present:

> My picture of Ireland is almost like, you know, from the media I've always understood that there are certain countries that people have always wanted to get out of. And Ireland, you know that movie that Tom Cruise made,[6] I mean, he basically had the picture of beauty, living on a mountainside with the sea, and they couldn't wait to get out. So I think that's the history, at least that's what I understand about Ireland.

Passenger L's image of Ireland as a place of natural beauty and emigration does not appear to have been changed or elaborated by the actual encounter with the country or by the presentation of the tour guide. Other passengers frequently refer to discourses of international news media, which represent Ireland as a place of political violence. Many of the tourists express the view of Ireland as a country touched by terrorist acts or civil war and their vision of the country appears to involve the IRA in a prominent place. They are unlikely to have had such a view consolidated by their stay in Dublin[7] and certainly there is nothing on the tour which brings this aspect of Ireland to mind. Indeed, the audio-visual show at the visitor centre at Glendalough involves a direct attempt at disassociation from violence. It mentions the 'ascetic streak' in the Irish, and explains how medieval Irish monks chose to 'do battle with the devil rather than with other human beings'. Yet, for many the idea of Ireland as a place of violence remains unchallenged by the visit.

Thus, many of the passengers on board the tour buses seem to maintain an understanding of Ireland which is based, at least in part, on their expectations and pre-tour conceptions – informed by various other media – rather than on the information they are given by the guide or the events they experience. Therefore, their decoding of Irish identity must be understood not only in the context of the tour but also their holiday as a whole and indeed that of their general lives. A final example from interviews carried out with passengers after the tour may serve to illustrate how tourists discuss and actively negotiate the meaning(s) of Irishness. They draw upon multiple frameworks for arriving at an understanding, and these include the guiding and the tour.

Int.:   Is Ireland the way you imagined it would be before you came here?

I: Yeah, green and [laughs] rainy.

H: Yeah, definitely, it's very green, that really was not a shock to me.

I: Like today, when we were out looking in the countryside and stuff like that . . .

H: It's just so green, more, more, more, it's just impossible. And now we know why, it's like [guide's first name] says, it's like, what did he say, six months of rain and the rest is wet, six months of being wet.

I: Or the T-shirt that says 'four seasons in one day', that's definitely totally true, and the other thing that strikes me too, is you won't see too many cosmopolitan . . .

H: Yeah, it's a very white race. That's the first thing, I'm half Asian, the first thing I notice when I go to see a different country is the ethnic . . .

I: I've been to different parts of Europe, you see a little more . . .

H: I don't know, maybe because it's an island, kind of isolated, the first stop is London, and they remain there.

I: You do see a few pockets here and there.

H: But if you go to San Francisco you see Chinese, walking out of your house, you know, so it's no big deal.

(Passengers H and I; details given earlier)

In this example the two American tourists draw upon the following frameworks: pre-existing understandings based on international touristic discourse ('green and rainy'); visual signs during the tour ('what we saw today'); verbal signs in the guiding ('like [guide] said'); visual signs in tourist shops ('the T-shirt'); own experience as member of an ethnic minority ('I'm half Asian'); touristic experience elsewhere ('different parts of Europe'); geographical knowledge ('it's an island'); own experience of Ireland outside tourist world ('you do see a few'); own experience of life in the United States ('if you go to San Francisco' where the respondent lives). Thus, unlike the touristic discourse of the tour guide, in which – despite some contradictions – a preferred or dominant reading could be detected, in the active and continuing negotiating of meaning of Irishness which can be found in the discourse of the tourists, Irish identity remains fragmented, ever changing, made up of multiple signs, and no final or fixed definition arises. As Hall (1997b) argues, we continually define and redefine identity through discursive practice, it is never constant or complete.

Discussion: Power and Knowledge in Tourism

So, what can be concluded about the power to construct knowledge about a touristic destination? In the present exploration it has seemed that the situation is more complex than what Cheong and Miller (2000) have described as 'power-ful guides' and 'power-bound tourists'. The guide does hold a powerful position as professional expert and does control much of what is gazed upon and what is dismissed and, therefore, is able to mediate much of the tourists' encounter with the place they visit. However, his or her power to influence tourists' interpretations of this place and its people is less obvious. As we have seen, when examined closely, both messages and readings have proven less than straightforward. In the presentation of the guide, we found several different frameworks, different Irish 'voices' competing, although the touristic discourse tended to be the strongest. This is due to the nature of discourse, its intertextuality. According to Fairclough (1992: 56), texts are always shaped by other texts and utterances that have gone before. The guide must rely on pre-existing cultural frameworks to construct Ireland, because, as Hall (1997a) states, culture depends on the exchange of shared meaning. Therefore, the meaning of Irishness relies not on the material things used to symbolise it but on how people have agreed to interpret them. Our notions of what being Irish can or cannot mean, therefore, depend on how Irishness has been represented before, in other discourses, such as the international touristic discourse which informs so much of the guiding on the Glendalough tour.

The tourists' narratives, too, are intertextual and contradictive, as they draw upon the cultural resources available to them to interpret both the messages sent by the guide and the Ireland they encounter outside the tour. Although the tourists often view the Irish as 'other', most interviewees were unwilling to make definite statements based only on the tour or on their short stay in the country. They seemed aware of their lack of cultural knowledge to interpret Irishness conclusively. Although when asked what they believed was 'typically Irish' most answered in terms of the touristic discourse, this may simply illustrate their knowledge of and ability to express and engage with this discourse. By no means is this necessarily their only interpretation. Tourists may be removed from their own culture but this does not restrain their cultural abilities, and they still have resources to draw upon in interpreting cultural meaning. In the case of the tour-bus passengers I spoke to, these resources included touristic discourses on Ireland and elsewhere, fiction and news media discourses on Ireland as a place of violence or emigration, Irish friends and acquaintances, as well as their own autobiographies. The tourists turn to these when creating a narrative on Ireland and Irish identity, which existed parallel, and sometimes in contrast, to the interpretation offered by the guide.

In these micro relations of tourism between coach passengers and their guide, power to construct the destination therefore is indeed omnipresent, flowing between points rather than remaining fixed or stable, and extending to the tourists themselves. The position of the guide, powerful as it is, can never be considered permanently fixed, and neither can the touristic discourse be expected to be reproduced unchanged forever. The guide must keep in mind the audience whom he or she addresses, and 'try to find out what sort of people are on the bus, what they like, if they want a lot of information or a laugh' (guide A). It is up to the guide to 'read' the audience and decide which discursive elements will provoke the least resistance. According to Foucault (1980), power is productive rather than repressive. Through a touristic discourse it produces subject positions from which we can understand the meaning of Irishness. But, in addition, the omnipresence of power, the resistance and active negotiation which takes place in and over this touristic discourse produce new ways of reading and interpreting Irishness and will continue to do so. Neither tourists nor guide can be said to hold exclusively the power to construct Ireland and neither are completely free to choose discursive elements in their narrative on Irishness. Due to the intertextual nature of representation, both will base their version of Irish identity on the symbols that have been used to represent Ireland before in the various discourses – touristic or otherwise – which deal with this complex and ever-changing issue. Finally, the degree to which tourists display resistance to the touristic discourse and construct their own interpretations of Irish identity may be greatly influenced by their sociocultural position and hence their access to cultural resources. Yet this study suggests that even tourists who seem to uncritically accept the messages in the guiding do, at other times, draw on alternative discourses. It seems unlikely that tourists take on a specific, stable position on a continuum between the touristic gaze, negotiated readings and post-touristic irony. They cannot be said to apply any one such lens consistently, rather they seem to incorporate various interpretations when actively negotiating the meanings of Irishness, which is recognised as more complex and contradictory than the friendly people and a green unspoilt land offered by the guides. Further research is needed to examine how different tourists engage with various touristic texts on Irish identity. It is likely, however, that they will all display some sort of power and resistance to the discourses they encounter and that all will be found, at least to a certain degree, to actively negotiate their understandings of Ireland and Irishness.

Acknowledgements

I am grateful to the two tour operators who allowed me permission to carry out the research on board the buses. I wish to thank Gary O'Neill, Mary Kelly and Sara O'Sullivan, and the editors of this volume for helpful comments and encouragement. A postgraduate essay prize was kindly awarded by the Social Science Research Council for an earlier version of this chapter.

Notes

1. The data presented in this chapter were collected on bus tours on four dates in Winter 1999 and Spring 2000. Although the tours were arranged by two different tour operators they followed similar routes, collecting passengers at various points in Dublin's city centre, then following the coast south of the city, into the Wicklow Mountains to Glendalough, where passengers were given a guided tour of the monastic city and the opportunity to visit the exhibition. All tours lasted between seven and eight hours.
2. On all the tours attended the driver-guides were male.
3. According to interviews with two of the guides. One comments on his employer: 'He doesn't know anything about that end of it . . . if I tell him something he believes it.'
4. Ethnicity given when and as stated by respondents.
5. City of the Incas, a popular tourist destination in Peru.
6. *Far and Away*, the 1992 Hollywood film starring Cruise in the role of an Irish emigrant.
7. Throughout the period of fieldwork for this paper the Northern Ireland peace process was ongoing and no major incidents of violence were reported in the media.

References

Boniface, P. (1998) Tourism culture. *Annals of Tourism Research* 25 (3), 746–9.
Cheong, S. and Miller, M.L. (2000) Power and tourism: A Foucauldian observation. *Annals of Tourism Research* 27 (2), 371–90.
Crick, M. (1989) Representation of international tourism in the social sciences: Sun, sex, sights, savings and servility. *Annual Review of Anthropology* 18, 307–44.
Dicks, B. (2000) Encoding and decoding the people: Circuits of communication at a local heritage museum. *European Journal of Communication* 15 (5), 61–78.
Fairclough, N. (1992) *Discourse and Social Change*. Cambridge: Polity Press.
Foucault, M. (1972) *The Archaeology of Knowledge*. London: Tavistock.
Foucault, M. (1980) *The History of Sexuality* (vol. 1). New York: Vintage Press.
Fyfe, G. and Ross, M. (1996) Decoding the visitor's gaze: Rethinking museum visiting. In S. Macdonald and G. Fyfe (eds) *Theorizing Museums* (pp.127–52). Oxford: Blackwell.
Hall, S. (1980) Encoding/decoding. In S. Hall, D. Hobson, A. Lowe and P. Willis (eds) *Culture, Media, Language* (pp. 128–38). London: Routledge.
Hall, S. (1997a) The work of representation. In S. Hall (ed.) *Representation* (pp. 13–64). London: Sage.
Hall, S. (1997b) Cultural identity and diaspora. In K. Woodward (ed.) *Identity and Difference* (pp. 51–9). London: Sage.

Lash, S. and Urry, J. (1994) *Economies of Signs and Space*. London: Sage.

O'Barr, W. (1994) *Culture and the Ad: Exploring Otherness in the World of Advertising*. Oxford: Westview Press.

Rolston, B. (1995) Selling tourism in a country at war. *Race & Class* 37 (1), 23–40.

Slater, E. (1993) Contested terrain: Differing interpretations of Co. Wicklow's landscape. *Irish Journal of Sociology* 3, 23–55.

Urry, J. (1990) *The Tourist Gaze: Leisure and Tourism in Contemporary Societies*. London: Sage.

Chapter 8

The Native Gaze: Literary Perceptions of Tourists in the West Kerry Gaeltacht

MÁIRÍN NIC EOIN

Sociologist Barbara O'Connor, in an article on tourist images and national identity in the volume *Tourism in Ireland: A Critical Analysis* (O'Connor, 1993: 68–85), alludes to the dearth of empirical research on the social relationship between natives and tourists in Ireland. In seeking to identify issues which have emerged from research in this area in other countries, however, she draws attention to a number of questions which may be of relevance to tourism studies in an Irish context, questions such as 'feelings of insecurity, servility and resentment on the part of locals', the native 'desire to please tourists', and the manner in which that desire may translate into deference or resentment, anxious self-criticism or outright antipathy to the outsider (O'Connor, 1993: 79–81).

What I intend to do in this chapter is to present an example of the kind of evidence literary works can provide in relation to questions such as these, by examining the depiction of tourists in the work of four male Irish-language authors from the West Kerry (or Corca Dhuibhne) Gaeltacht and in the letters of a Blasket Island woman. Though the example is a specific – and in many ways an exceptional – one, it is of value in so far as the works cited provide a remarkably honest inside account of individual and community experiences of tourist activity in a region which has since the turn of the 20th century become one of the most popular Irish tourist destinations (Convery *et al.*, 1994: 82). As will become apparent, these accounts turn on its head the notion that natives are passive objects of tourist attention, a notion which can become prevalent when there is a critical overemphasis on the nature and power of the tourist gaze (Urry, 1990, 1995). What I will argue here is that if Jonathan Culler (1981: 127) was correct in his characterisation of tourists as those 'unsung armies of semioticians', then such a description could also be applied to the perceptive native whose own reading of tourist culture often includes a self-critical analysis of native behaviour.

Tomás Ó Criomhthain (1856–1937), the first author to be discussed here, is most famous for his autobiographical work *An tOileánach* (translated by Robin Flower as *The Islandman* (1951)). He was also author of numerous essays published in newspapers and journals (Ó Criomhthain, 1997) and of another extended prose work *Allagar na hInise* (1928) (translated by Tim Enright as *Island Cross-talk* (1986)), a series of dramatised sketches based on his own observations of his neighbours on the Great Blasket Island in the years 1919–22. Much could be said about Tomás Ó Criomhthain and his local and national importance. Certainly when the history of tourism in the West Kerry Gaeltacht is written, Ó Criomhthain will emerge as a central figure in that narrative. His home on the Great Blasket became a destination for such renowned cultural tourists as the English Celtic scholars Robin Flower and Kenneth Jackson, the Scandinavian professors Carl von Sydow and Carl Marstrander, not to mention the native Irish language scholars and cultural nationalists such as the enigmatic Brian Ó Ceallaigh from Killarney who encouraged Ó Criomhthain to write his life story or Pádraig Ó Siochfhradha (An Seabhac) who was responsible for editing the first edition of *An tOileánach* (Ó Lúing, 1989; Ó Glaisne, 1989; Mac Conghail, 1989, 1998; Ó Coileáin, 1992; 1998; Dew, 1998; Foster, 1998). One could argue that Ó Criomhthain's work – and that of Blasket Island authors Peig Sayers and Muiris Ó Súilleabháin – was as much the outcome of cultural encounters with tourists as it was of native genius. That work, in turn, provided an impetus for younger generations of scholars, university and secondary school students to descend on the region and by being translated into English and other European languages and vigorously marketed locally, the books have become part and parcel of the tourist experience.

Tomás's son, Seán Ó Criomhthain (1898–1975), was born and raised on the Great Blasket but moved to the village of Muiríoch on the mainland in 1942 when his eldest child Niamh was approaching school-going age. The population of the island was well and truly on the decline at that stage – from a population of 121 in 1930, it had fallen to 106 by 1938, dropping to 50 by 1947 and 22 by 1953 (Stagles & Stagles, 1980: 131) – and the island school had been closed due to lack of pupils. Seán Ó Criomhthain wrote one book and several essays. The book *Lá dár Saol* (1969) (translated by Tim Enright as *A Day in Our Life* (1992)) is an account of the final days of the island community – the last of the islanders were evacuated in 1953 and provided with local authority houses in the mainland village of Dún Chaoin – and the adjustment to mainland life. His wife, Eibhlís Ní Shúilleabháin, was a second cousin of Blasket Island author Muiris Ó Súilleabháin (1904–50). A selection of excerpts from her correspondence with an English visitor George Chambers has been edited (n.d.) and provides an interesting female perspective on traditional island life and the interaction between the islanders and tourists.

The fourth author to be discussed will be Tomás Ó Criomhthain's grandson Pádraig Ua Maoileoin (1913-2000), born in An Com, Dún Chaoin, and author of five novels, a memoir and many essays, including the collection entitled *Na hAird Ó Thuaidh* (1960). The discussion of tourism in this collection and the depiction of outsiders and of touristic activities in his satirical novel *Ó Thuaidh!* will be examined. Ua Maoileoin left Dún Chaoin as a young man to join the Garda Síochána and has spent most of his life in Dublin, working in his later years as an editor and lexicographer with An Gúm (Government Publications). My final example is a work by a writer of a younger generation. Pádraig Ó Cíobháin (1951–) of An Ghráig, Dún Chaoin, has published three novels and three collections of short stories. I will refer briefly to his first novel, the autobiographical *An Gealas i Lár na Léithe* (1992).

When Tomás Ó Criomhthain was writing *Allagar na hInise* in the years 1919–22, the island (and the Dingle peninsula in general, of course) was becoming a popular tourist destination. The most common feature for the Blasket Islanders was the holiday or Sunday daytripper and it is in the context of native reaction to the arrival of such daytrippers that Ó Criomhthain alludes to them regularly throughout the book. The main source of preoccupation is the cost to the islanders of the hospitality shown free of charge to these visitors:

> Lá saoire is ea é. Ní radharc go dtí ar naomhóga é ag teacht as gach aird faoi dhéin an Bhlascaeid. Ba dhóigh leat gur piastaí mara ag gluaiseacht iad, ó seisear go hochtar i ngach ceann acu. Ní bhíonn imeacht gan a ndinnéar orthu. Dúirt duine éigin gur dhóigh le duine gur díolta ón Rialtas a bhí an tOileán ach a bheith ag ullmhú tae dóibh gach Domhnach agus lá saoire . . .
>
> 'A Mhuire mháthair,' arsa Micheál, 'nach mór an cion atá acusan go léir ar an áit seo.' 'Dhera, go mbeire an diabhal uait iadsan,' arsa Seán. Ná fuil an áit seo creachta acusan ar an gcuma sin le fada de bhlianta.'(p. 91)

> [It's a holiday. There's nothing to be seen but *naomhógs* making for the island from every direction. They move like sea monsters, each of them carrying six or eight people. They don't leave either without their dinner. Someone said that you'd think the islanders were paid by the Government to prepare tea for them every Sunday and holiday . . .
>
> 'A Mhuire mháthair', says Micheál, 'Don't they have a great liking

altogether for this place'.
'*Dhera*, may the devil take them away from us', says Seán. 'For many's the year now they've been plundering this island'.]¹

Lá Domhnaigh. Lá aoibhinn. Nuair a bhí na daoine ina stad i dteannta a chéile:

'Is dócha,' arsa Micheál, 'go mbeidh a oiread ag déanamh faoin oileán seo inniu agus a bhí an lá saoire.'

'Ná caithfear an cháin a dhíol ar chuma éigin,' arsa Seán, 'le muintir Dhún Chaoin, agus dar Muire, b'fhusa dúinn an cháin ríthiúil a dhíol ná a bheith ag cur citeal síos dóibh seo gach uile nóimeat den ló.'

'Ná caith caint air,' arsa Micheál, 'ach má leanaid ar an bhfuadar atá fúthu go gcuirfid gach uile dhuine atá istigh ann amach as,' ar seisean.

'Go rabhairse imithe an chéad Domhnach eile rompu,' arsa Micil, 'murab ort féin atá an scanradh rompu, a thincéirín gorta, chun a bheith á admháil poiblí don dúthaigh go gcuirfeadh sclogóg tae a thabharfá do do chomharsain ón dtigh thú,' ar seisean.

'Ach, dar Muire,' arsa Seán, 'tá earraí daor dochraideach sa tsaol seo ar dhaoine bochta, agus ambaiste féin, aon tithe a bhfuil siad siúd tugtha do bheith ag teacht iontu go bhfuil cíos a ndóthain orthu go n-imí an bhliain,' ar seisean.

'Dhera, mo chroí thú,' arsa Micheál, 'bhainfeá ceart éigin do na fir ach na pacairí ban a bhíonn in éineacht leo, agus na práisléadaí agus an ornáid a bhíonn ina dtimpeall gur dhóigh leat gur le rí nó le ridire gach duine acu,' ar seisean. (p. 93)

[It's a Sunday. A glorious day. A day when everyone can take a rest:

'I suppose there will be as many making for the island today as there was on the holiday', says Micheál.

'Don't we have to pay our debts to the people of Dún Chaoin by some manner or means', says Seán, 'and by God it would be easier for us to pay the king's tax itself than to be putting down the kettle all day long for that crowd.'

'Don't be talking', says Micheál, ''cause if they continue at this rate it won't be long till they'll have evicted everyone of us from the island'.

'May you be gone when they arrive next Sunday', says Micil, 'aren't you the one that's scared by them, you stingy good for nothing, announcing to the world that the sup of tea you'd give to your neighbour is going to put you out of house and home'.

'But, for sure', says Seán, 'things are getting expensive these days for poor people, and the truth is that any house that attracts those will have enough expenses for the rest of the year'.

'You're dead right', says Micheál, 'and you might get some satisfaction from the men, but the sorts of women they bring with them, with their bracelets and their ornaments. You'd think each one of them belonged to a king or a knight'.]

The main point being made, not by Ó Criomhthain but by his neighbours, is that the island's resources are being depleted by these visitors. What is presented as the islanders' natural hospitality and friendliness towards strangers is now being questioned and put to the test by the scale of the intrusion. The resentment expressed by some of the characters is due to a sharp perception of class difference and the debate in *Allagar na hInise* focuses on the tension between the native desire to please the visitor and a need to preserve a sense of self-worth in the face of the social and economic privilege represented by the visitors (pp. 108–9).

Some of the references reflect the islanders' astonishment that so many people would want to visit the island. The fact that the islanders are seeking to outdo each other in hospitality is a cause of concern and the huge social divide between natives and visitors is articulated in terms of freedom to travel and the different expectations of consumers and producers (which is put very succinctly in the Irish):

> 'Nach mór an obair', arsa sean-Eoghan, 'a rá nach féidir le haon duine anseo aon tamall a chaitheamh ar a laethanta saoire?'
> 'Mhuise, don diabhal go bhfuil siad go sponcúil agat,' arsa Micil. 'Ní mar a chéile lucht airgid a chaitheamh agus lucht a bhailithe!'(p. 114)

> ['Isn't it a wonder', says the old man Eoghan, 'that nobody here can take any time off to go on holidays?'
> '*Mhuise*, you've put your finger on it', says Micil. 'There's a big difference between those who spend money and those who earn it'.]

References to the tightfistedness of tourists (the fact that they do not bring sweets to the children or tobacco to the adults) indicates that the islanders expected something (however small) in return for their hospitality (p. 116). Irish-speaking visitors to Dingle are also tourists in the eyes of the islanders. I say this because, to this day, many Irish-speaking visitors to Gaeltacht areas assume that they have a special (more intimate) social relationship with the native population. Allusions to them in the work of these authors question such assumptions. One passage in *Allagar na hInise*, for example, presents Irish-speaking visitors in Dingle in terms of the uneven distribution of tourism-generated income and the general effect of tourists on prices in the town and its hinterland:

> 'Dar Muire!' arsa Micil, 'is dócha gur mó an díobháil atá á dhéanamh acu ná de mhaitheas.

Tá an baile mór ite acu agus nithe daor dá ndeasca,' ar seisean.

'Tá daoine buíoch díobh agus daoine ná fuil,' arsa Pádraig. 'Táid siad ag díol lucht an ósta go maith agus iad ag déanamh maitheasa do dhaoine atá ag díol nithe sa bhaile mór.'

'Fág sin,' arsa Micil, 'ach ná fuil nithe daor ar lucht na tuaithe dá ndeasca. Mórán daoine ag lorg sa bhaile mór, deineann sin nithe daor i ngach áit.'(p. 118)

['By God!', says Micil, 'they seem to be doing more harm than good. They have all that's in the town eaten and prices are going up as a result'.

'There are people that are thankful to them, and people that aren't', says Pádraig. 'They're paying the hoteliers well and they're benefiting those who have goods to sell in the town'.

'Never mind that', says Micil, 'aren't the same goods more expensive for the country people as a result. Great demand in the town, that makes things dear everywhere'.]

Ó Criomhthain himself avoids value judgements or critical comments such as this. Instead, he tends to report and leave the commentary to others.

This is in marked contrast to his son Seán who, in *Lá Dár Saol*, articulates an attitude towards tourists which lacks the sympathy with which Tomás presents his own views and those of his neighbours. For Seán, encounters between tourists and natives are presented as being exploitative and often as being unsatisfactory for both parties. Not only does he focus on the unreasonable demands made by tourists but he also makes no attempt to hide the acquisitive and selfish motives of natives who are happy to milk the gullible visitors dry. The opening section of the book deals with the desertion of the Great Blasket. During his own youth there, visitors were still arriving, now armed with his father's books, but many of the houses which formerly provided accommodation for visitors were gradually being deserted:

Bhí stróinséirí ar dalladh ag teacht chughainn anois, *an tOileánach* agus *an tAllagar* ar bharr a mboise acu, agus sinn curtha ó cháitheadh an phóir acu isteach agus amach chughainn go bhfeicfidís an tigh inar saolaíodh an gaiscíoch. Bliain ar bhliain lean an gotha san.

Ach tháinig an lá gur imigh an mhuintir a choimeádadh na stróinséirí, agus ná raibh ar an mbaile ach aon tigh amháin a bhí oiriúnach dóibh. (p. 5)

[Strangers were coming in their droves to us, with *The Islandman* and *Island Cross-talk* in their hands, and we were constantly being interrupted as they came in on top of us so that they could see the house where the hero was born. That went on year after year.

But the day came when those who used to keep the visitors left, and there was only one house left in the village which was suitable for them.]

Seán Ó Criomhthain's book documents what is a classic case of the expansion of tourism coinciding with the erosion of the native lifestyle which provided part of the attraction for the tourist in the first place. One must ask if Tomás Ó Criomhthain was aware when he wrote his famous line 'The likes of us will never be seen again' how his book would feed the curiosity of generations of tourists. Eibhlís Ní Shúilleabháin, in one of her letters to George Chambers, provides an amusing account of an encounter she had with a tourist to the island who had read her cousin's book *Fiche blian ag fás* (1933) (translated by Moya Llewelyn Davies and George Thomson as *Twenty Years A-growing* (O'Sullivan, 1933)) but who had never heard of her father-in-law Tomás:

> We talked during her meal and she had read *Twenty Years A-growing* but did not know anything of *The Islandman*, so we showed her the book, and Tomás too, and she was delighted about meeting us then. She brought in her husband and Martin – the brightest boyeen I ever met – and her two lovely daughters before they went. She was a very lovely wife and she sent Tomás four plugs of tobacco from Killarney. A few weeks ago I received a letter from her and she has *The Islandman* read and was delighted to have seen and met us that day and was very interested in the Island . . . 13.12.36 (n.d., p. 52)

Eibhlís's accounts of native encounters with tourists are full of the wonder and enthusiasm of youth. Before she marries, it is her dream to have 'a nice house and . . . lodgers in summer' (p. 16) but with the decline of the island community she comes to the realisation that they can no longer endure the hardships of living there. She comes to terms with her settlement on the mainland by reconstructing the island in her imagination as a place of recreation, a place to which she can return in the summer and recall the pleasures of her youth by becoming herself a holidaymaker there.

Whatever he felt about being evicted from his father's house on the island while visitors tramp through the Islandman's natural habitat, Seán Ó Criomhthain has no time for those students of Irish (nuns as it happens) who come to him in his mainland home, armed with his father's book (*An tOileánach*) and looking to him as an authoritative source of information. His curt reply to one of them is that when he is paid as well as the college professors who are employed to teach them Irish that only then will he be prepared to help them overcome their linguistic difficulties (pp. 24–5). He then goes on to criticise those students of Irish, especially nuns, religious brothers and priests, who though they like to come to the Gaeltacht to meet 'native speakers' will only do so if there is an Irish college willing to accommodate them. These colleges, according to Seán, are often organised independently of the native inhabitants who, in turn, benefit little from their presence.

On other occasions he relates particular events. He tells us, for example, how two young men from Dublin – both fluent Irish speakers – arrive at his doorstep looking for accommodation. After he has found lodgings for them, they ask him to be their guide that night as they try out the local hostelries. These are young fellows who have been around the area before, and who need no initiation into Gaeltacht pub culture. Ó Criomhthain's only regret is that he cannot keep up with them for the five nights they stayed in the area (p. 41). If this is a clear example of the kind of mutually satisfactory relationship which may develop between urban Irish speakers and their Gaeltacht hosts, it is not the only one represented in the book. Ó Criomhthain also describes the cultural impact of large groups of university students when they descend in force on the area. The behaviour and attire of both male and female visitors of this class are commented on. Though they can drink and converse freely with notables such as Seán Ó Criomhthain, for example, their linguistic competence is not enough to surmount the huge social barrier between them and the local young men:

> Stróinséirí timpeall fós. Buachaillí agus cailíní ó Ollscoil Chorcaí. Nílid dall ar an nGaelainn. Ná ní lú ná atá ar aon ní eile. Ólann siad smeathán, fireann agus baineann mar a chéile. Is cuma cén sórt dí é, ón seilp is sia suas go dtí an mbairille ar an urlár. Féasóga agus meigill fhada ar chuid acu, agus cuid eile acu chomh glanbhearrtha leis an easpag. Cuid des na mná fáiscthe go maith. Cuid eile acu agus iad nochttha go hard a dtóna. Tá gach sampla fén spéir á thaispeáin acu do mhuintir an cheantair. Ligfeadh cuid acu ar an sine thú, agus raghadh beirt nó triúr acu féin ar an sine dá mbeadh sé le fáil acu. Rud ná fuil, mórán, anso.
>
> Má tá Gaelainn agat scaoil chúchu í, is í atá uathu. Ach maidir le buachaillí óga na háite dhe, ní mór de bharra na Gaelainne a bheidh ós na cailíní acu, ach fear mar gharda ar gach ceann acu chomh luath agus a thitfidh an oíche orthu. (pp. 43–4)

[Strangers around still. Boys and girls from University College Cork. They're not ignorant of the Irish. Nor or anything else for that matter. Both the males and the females among them can take a drink. And it doesn't matter what drink it is, from the stuff on the highest shelves to the contents of the barrel on the floor. Some of them have long hairy beards, and others are as cleanshaven as a bishop. Some of the women are well-dressed. Others are exposed up to their backsides. They're showing every example under the sun to the local people. Some of them would stand you a drink (lit. would let you on the teat) and some of themselves would accept drink (lit. would go on the teat themselves) if offered it. But that doesn't happen much here.

If you have the Irish, give it to them. That's what they want. But as for the local young lads getting anything in return for their Irish from the girls, they've little chance when they each have a man standing guard over them as soon as night falls.]

Pádraig Ua Maoileoin's *Na hAird ó Thuaidh* (1960) originated as a series of radio talks, in which he describes his native region in terms of a journey in time back to the Dún Chaoin of his youth. Much of the account focuses on the question of social and cultural change and one is aware throughout that he is now interpreting his own native culture from the perspective of someone who is no longer an insider. He devotes a full chapter to the question of tourism and begins by classifying the types of tourist he saw coming to the area when he was a boy. He identifies three main types, all of whom had an interest in the Irish language. The first of these are the 'Laethanta Breátha', the daytrippers who would come for the day during the summer months, meet the locals and be gone again in the evening. The second group are those Irish speakers or students of the language who would come and stay in the ordinary houses of the people for the purpose of improving their Irish and with whom the native population built up a steady bond of friendship. Ua Maoileoin looks on these as having a very positive influence on the self-perception of native Irish speakers as a cultural group (p. 132). The third group he mentions are the internationally renowned scholars who came to this Gaeltacht region because they saw in it a repository of what was richest and purest in Gaelic culture. He refers specifically to Robin Flower, Carl Marstrander, Kenneth Jackson, Marie-Louise Sjoestedt, and comments on the warm affection in which they were held in the hearts and minds of the local people. The main point he makes about these visitors is that their relationship with the locals was one of mutual respect and love: 'Do dheimhnigh na daoine galánta so dhuinn gur thuigeadar sinn agus gur thuigeadar duinn. Chun é seo a dhéanamh, do thánadar ar aon leibhéal linn féin'(pp. 134–5) ['These gentle folk made it clear to us that they understood us and that they understood our predicament. To be able to do this, they approached us at our own level.'] He recounts examples of how they went native, eating the flesh of seabirds directly off the tongs just as they did themselves (p. 135). The main outcome of these three forms of tourist encounter, according to

Ua Maoileoin, was that the local people saw that their cultural tradition – so long under threat – was valued and valuable.

Ua Maoileoin then goes on to relate how tourism in the region was to change since his boyhood. The Irish speakers continue to arrive but they are now outnumbered by English speakers who come with no understanding of the cultural specificity of the region and whose influence on the locals is a detrimental one. The book was published in 1960, so he is referring to the 1950s, before the advent of mass tourism to the Dingle peninsula and well before the development of the tourist services with which the peninsula is now provided:

> Béarlóirí críochnaithe iad so ná fuil uathu ach Béarla, agus nach aon mhairg leo an loitiméireacht atá á dhéanamh acu. Tagann siad ann ó Bhaile Átha Cliath comh maith le Sasana, agus gan aon fhuadar fúthu ach, mar a déarfá, intellectual slumming, rud nach féidir dóibh a dhéanamh i nDún Chaoin ná i mBaile an Fhirtéaraigh ná i mBaile na nGall, dá dtuigfidís féin, ná an dream a thugann ann iad, i gceart iad féin . . .
>
> 'Tair i measc na n-asal ar feadh tamaill go bhfeicfidh tú á n-iomlasc féin i smúit an mhóinteáin iad; tair go gcloisfidh tú an patois teangan atá fágtha ag na natives. Sea, tair go Corca Dhuibhne agus tabharfaimídne Béarla dhuit a chabhróidh leat chun an phictiúra a bhreith abhaile in iomlán leat . . . ' (pp. 135–6)

> [These are monoglot English-speakers, and all they want is English and in the process they are unconcerned about the destruction they are wreaking. They come from Dublin as well as England, and all they want is to engage in what you'd call 'intellectual slumming', something which is difficult for them to do, mind you, in Dún Chaoin or in Baile an Fhirtéaraigh or in Baile na nGall, if the truth were known to them, or to those who bring them there.
>
> 'Come down amongst the donkeys for a while, and see them wallowing in the filth of the bog; come and listen to the 'patois' spoken by the 'natives'. Yes, come to Corca Dhuibhne and we will give you the kind of English that will help you bring the full picture home with you . . . ']

He claims at one stage that the natives are a step ahead of these naive travellers in pursuit of local colour, though the visitors themselves may never be aware of that. He acknowledges the sense of superiority of those natives who, like himself, presumably, know that the tourist cannot decode native speech or native behaviour.

What irks Ua Maoileoin, however, is the knowledge that certain natives are only too willing to play the part which is expected of them by the tourist, to speak to them in broken English and send them off with another humorous anecdote which can later be recounted at the expense of the native population in general. Though Ua Maoileoin is critical of the uncultured tourist, his outrage is directed most pointedly at his own people:

> Is é an chuid is measa dhe so, comh fada lenár muintir féin de, go bhfuil giollaí agus scraistí aimhleasta ina measc a dheineann tláithínteacht leis na stróinséirí seo sa teangain iasachta, agus gan í sin acu ach go breallach, rud a thugann blas den local colour dom dhuine agus gur fiú leis nóta a dhéanamh ina dhialainn de.(136)

> [The worst thing, as far as our own people are concerned, is that there are gillies and good-for-nothings amongst them who flatter the tourists in the foreign language, when they themselves can barely speak it, and that, of course gives your man a sample of 'local colour' which is worth recording in his journal.]

When reading accounts such as this, one is forced to question the relevance, in a bilingual cultural context, of Dean MacCannell's' (1973, 1976) concept of 'staged authenticity. What we seem to have in the examples cited so far is a differentiation between possibilities for authentic encounters (which may, of course, be highly staged) between tourists and natives, and the acceptance that authentic communication between visitor and tourist (based on mutually satisfactory expectations) is often impossible. As is obvious from both Seán Ó Criomhthain's and Pádraig Ua Maoileoin's accounts, the native's response to Irish-speaking visitors is directly related to those visitors' linguistic competence and understanding of social codes. The fact that it is not simply a case of language proficiency is illustrated by the fact that Ó Criomhthain can relate quite easily to the two young men who bring him out on a 'tear', while nuns with their copies of *An tOileánach* are merely a source of annoyance.

Pádraig Ua Maoileoin's analysis of tourist encounters in his native region informs his depiction of social relations in his satirical novel *Ó Thuaidh!* (1983). This book is a farcical account of how a newcomer to the area, an American who bears the nickname Bod–Bod (literarily Penis–Penis, but probably more accurately translated as Big Prick), attempts to turn Oileán Ban (The Great Blasket Island) into a sex-holiday camp called Paradise Island. The ex-islanders, now living on the mainland, are only too willing to sell their island and its heritage to the highest bidder but the scheme is eventually thwarted by language revivalists (from Cork) and Mícheál the Poet, son of Peig Sayers (who appears anachronistically – she died in 1958 – under the name of Meig in the book). This book is extremely

interesting as an illustration of a Gaeltacht writer's perception of his own
people's response to the annual influx of tourists. It was published in 1983
when the Dingle peninsula was well and truly established as a tourist destination. Also worth noting is the fact that some of the ex-islanders did
actually sell their holdings on the island to an American around that time. It
was as a result of anxiety about private development of the island felt by
certain locals and by those Irish speakers from Cork and elsewhere who
were interested in the area and its cultural heritage (some of them having
built holiday / second homes there) that Fondúireacht an Bhlascaoid (The
Blasket Island Foundation) was established in 1987. The Foundation was
responsible for the opening of the Blasket Island Centre in Dún Chaoin in
1993 and its ultimate aim is that the Great Blasket Island become a National
Park, and be developed as a heritage site under state protection. The constitutionality of aspects of the Blascaod Mór National Historic Parks Act
passed in 1989, however, was successfully challenged subsequently in the
High Court, rendering the Foundation's aspirations in this respect increasingly problematic.[2]

In Ua Maoileoin's novel, the region is depicted throughout as a resource
to be exploited not so much by the tourist but by the natives who have now
lost any sense of their own cultural self-worth. If outsiders such as Bod–Bod
are merely highly exaggerated comic depictions of the worst kind of non-
native exploitation of peripheral regions, the real force of Ua Maoileoin's
satire is directed not at him and his ilk but at the native population who col-
laborate in implementing his outlandish scheme. One of the chapters opens
up with a description of the arrival of the annual batch of tourists:

Bolg an tsamhraidh anois ann agus blás ceart ar fuaid Chorca Chaoin.
Cuairteoirí ina gcéadta agus gach aon tigh aíochta lán gan leaba le fáil.
Na mílte ag teacht isteach ann gach Aoine go Domhnach, cuid mhór
acu ar thuras lae agus na tránna ag brúchtadh leo. Bhí gach aon teanga
san Eoraip mar ritheann le clos ar thaobh na mbóithre ann. Gach aon
déantús cairr ó Oirthear Áise go hIarthar Eorpa, agus fiú amháin
Meiriceá féin, ag snámhacáil leo i ndiaidh a chéile agus ag teacht sa tslí
ar a chéile agus ná feadair aon cheann acu cá raibh a triall ná a ceann
cúrsa. Gan aon duine ag dul in aon áit ná ag teacht as aon áit ach ag
tiomáint leo d'iarraidh an lá a mheilt idir gach aon dá bhéile. Daoine
eile sínte bolg le gréin ag teitheadh uathu siúd – gach aon duine ina shlí
féin ag seachaint an dara duine nó go dtiocfadh an oíche.
Ansin Tobar na Croise agus an dioscó; nó, b'fhéidir i measc na
gcaipíní, aon chuid acu a raibh caitheamh i ndiaidh an tsuaitheantais
aige, ceamaraí ag splancaíl agus pictiúrí den scoth á dtabhairt abhaile
le taispeáint do chairde ná raibh riamh san áit shuaithinseach seo.

Agus, i measc daoine suaithinseacha, cuimhnigh air, seanchaithe, veidhleadóirí, rabhcánaithe, lucht cleas is cordaí. Ach daoine breátha, an bhfuil a fhios agat? Bhíodar chomh deas linn, chomh muinteartha. Gan dabht, sheasamar cúpla deoch dóibh, ach ní dóigh linn gur ar a son sin a bhíodar chomh lách. A, ní hea, ní chreidim é. Daoine bochta simplí, tá a fhios agat. Gaeilgeoirí. Cuid acu ná raibh ar scoil riamh. Agus scríbhneoirí agus filí, cad déarfá leis sin? (pp. 67–8)

[The height of the summer has arrived and all over Corca Chaoin people are in great form. Visitors arriving in their hundreds and not a bed to be got in any of the guesthouses. Thousands coming in each weekend, some of them daytrippers headed for the beaches which are packed out with them. Every language in Europe is to be heard on the roads. Every kind of car from eastern Asia to western Europe, and even America, crawling after each other and getting in each other's way and nobody knowing where the other was heading. Nobody going anywhere or coming from anywhere in particular, but driving on trying to kill the time between each meal. People stretched out sunbathing, trying to escape from the others – everyone in his own way trying to avoid the next person, until night-time.

Then Tobar na Croise (the pub) and the disco. Maybe down with the peaked caps, any of them who are looking for something exotic, cameras clicking and brilliant pictures being taken which can be brought home and exhibited to friends who were never in this exceptional place. And in the company of remarkable people, remember, storytellers, fiddlers, balladeers, three card tricksters. But fine people, you know? They were so nice to us, so sociable. Of course, we stood them a few drinks, but I don't think that's why they were so friendly. Not at all, I don't believe that. Ordinary simple people, you know. Irish speakers. Some of them were never at school even. And writers and poets among them, what do you say to that?]

Ua Maoileoin retains this sardonic tone throughout most of the book. Though he certainly understands the tourist mindset – the desire to make contact with the exotic, to capture the scene on film for reproduction and interpretation at a future date – his main concern is with the performance of the natives. If not depicting them as spongers willing to entertain the tourist in return for drink, he shows them with their binoculars zooming in from their fishing boats on the naked sunbathers on the island beach. One of them, Tadhg, becomes Bod–Bod's local agent, organising daytrips to the island and bookings for the holiday homes and tents now being rented out on the island to tourists. However, certain natives in the book are so worried about the social changes they are witnessing that they broach the issue with the local priest who condones the direct action taken by a small group of them.

From where is Ua Maoileoin's negative depiction of the social effects of tourist activity derived? I think the answer is to be found in his own ambivalent status within his native community. No longer an existential insider – having spent more than 60 years of his life outside his native region – it is as a visitor that he has himself for a long time now been experiencing the social changes in the West Kerry Gaeltacht. Ironically, his critique of his own people can be interpreted as being merely the flipside of that idealisation of the native (as less corrupt, less materialistic, less worldly than himself) which often informs tourist perceptions and expectations. Scottish Gaelic writer Iain Crichton Smith (1986: 16–17) compares the exiled Gaelic-speaking islander to the tourist in the following terms:

> The islander who is living in the city is like the tourist in that he does not want to acknowledge change either, he wants the islands to belong to the world which he too has created, one of happy boyhood, perpetual summers, nice, kind people, lack of ambition and adult emotions. He too wishes to return to a place where doors were never locked, where crime was unimaginable, where real sorrow was not to be found, from which death had been banished. He too returns in summer, and when he sees television sets in the houses, regrets their presence as if the islanders had somehow let him down. Why, the islands are just like the city. How could the islanders have betrayed him so profoundly, so cheated him of his dream?

I think it is also no coincidence then that Ua Maoileoin empathises in this book with those Irish-speaking visitors who, due to the expansion of tourist activities throughout the peninsula, no longer have an opportunity to interact socially with the native population. In one exchange in the book, one of the characters alludes to the nebulous position of such a person whose 'special visitor' status will be acknowledged by the native outside the tourist season, but as soon as the throngs arrive is treated as just another 'Lá breá' (p. 85).

Observations such as these raise fundamental questions for those organisations, local or national, who wish to promote the concept of cultural tourism as a benign form of tourism, while failing to take into account fully the actual linguistic implications of their initiatives (see Convery *et al.*, 1994; Ó Sé, 1992; Champetier, 1992; Jones, 1992). Could the more personal mode and the more intimate scale of social contact encouraged by the proponents of cultural tourism ultimately have a more direct linguistic effect on native populations than the more impersonal and functional interactions associated with mass tourism? If Irish-speaking visitors are a minority group among cultural tourists to Gaeltacht regions, how can native services respond adequately to their cultural expectations? One must also consider the circumstances in which non-local initiatives will be tolerated while native enterprise will be criticised as avaricious and exploitative. Interestingly, another Gaeltacht island author, Seán 'Ac Fhionnlaoich (1910–82) of Gola off the Donegal coast (deserted in 1969), is more tolerant of the outsiders who purchased abandoned houses on the island as holiday homes than of those (presumably Irish-speaking) main-landers who sought to exploit the depopulated island's resources for commercial purposes ('Ac Fhionnlaoich, 1975: 170–1). In this instance the outsiders attracted to Gola were seen as rejecting 'conventional urban ideas of a good holiday' (Aalen & Brody, 1969: 117) in favour of the peace and simplicity of island life. Linguistic factors are not alluded to at all as a matter of concern for those who wish to maintain the island's cultural integrity:

Tháinig an coimhthíoch agus cheannaigh sé teach agus feirm ar chomhartha. Bhí sé ar lorg an tsuaimhnis agus fuair sé é. Tháinig siad as Sasana agus as Albain, as Béal Feirste agus Baile Átha Cliath, b'fhurasta dóibh gabháltas a fháil ar shaorchonradh agus in am ghairid bhí scaifte acu ar an oileán. Leis an fhírinne a insint níor chuir siad isteach nó amach ar dhuine ar bith. Ní hionann iad agus na daoine a tháinig ón tír mhór, daoine a mheas go raibh saibhreas le déanamh ar stoc, a cheannaigh cúpla gabháltas ar fhíorbheagán agus a ghlac seilbh ar an oileán gan chead gan iarraidh. Mheas siad nach gcuirfeadh na créatúir a d'fhág isteach nó amach orthu agus go mbeadh sé uilig acu dóibh féin in am ghairid. ('Ac Fhionnlaoich, 1975: 170–1)

[Strangers came and bought houses and farms for little or nothing. They were looking for peace and quiet and they got it. They came from England and Scotland, from Belfast and Dublin. It wasn't difficult for them to acquire a property at a bargain price and before long there was a crowd of them on the island. To tell the truth, they didn't bother any of us. They weren't at all like those people who came from the main-land who thought they could make their fortune on dry stock, who bought up holdings for a pittance and who laid claim to the island without consulting anyone. They thought that the poor creatures who had left wouldn't bother them in the slightest and that the whole of the island would be in their possession before long.]

The West Kerry Gaeltacht has had a long attachment with the Depart-ment of Irish in the National University of Ireland, Cork. Individual students – undergraduate and postgraduate – were and still are often housed with local people, usually at Easter and other offpeak times (and special hostels were purpose-built to accommodate university students). The establishment of Irish colleges for secondary school students from the late 1960s onwards, of course, opened up this kind of educational tourism and instead of individual or small groups being accommodated and integrated to a degree with local households, the pattern changed to the accommodation of much larger groups in grant-aided extensions. Young people growing up in the West Kerry Gaeltacht during this period would be very familiar with the seasonal influx of urban teenagers, and Pádraig Ó Cíobháin in his autobiographical novel *An Gealas i Lár na Léithe* (1992) draws considerably on his experience of this annual phenomenon. Far from being an object of pity or a victim of exploitation, the native young man in this book is firmly in control of the situation. The tourist is feminised and sexualised throughout, becoming either the object of the desiring and aesthetisising native gaze or the means whereby the young male can experiment sexually without the social obligations associated with an emotional attachment to a local woman. Apart from the mother figure, all the female characters in the book are tourists. The central character is seen zooming in on the backsides of the foreign tourists on their rented bikes doing the Slea Head tour or else following in the footsteps of his slightly older mentors by becoming sexually involved with the female students from the city – whose cultural idealism is depicted as fair game for the native male libido. Readers may find this character's attitudes to women less than palatable but what is interesting about them in the context of the subject of this chapter is the manner in which the common stereotype of the exploitative and hedonistic tourist is turned completely on its head. The native who speaks in this book is one who has come to terms with the annual arrival and departure of youthful energy and sexual vitality which, for him, is the drama of the tourist season:

> Cad a bhéarfadh gur bheart gan dealramh é dáileadh mo ghrá ortsa, a Rósailín, a tháinig chugam anuraidh, atá tagtha chugam i mbliana i gcrot eile agus a thiocfaidh arís an bhliain seo chugainn i gcrot bhaineannaigh éigin eile fós? (pp. 289–90)

> [Who could say that it was in vain that I loved you, Rosaleen, you who came to me last year, who has come to me again this year in another guise and who will come again next year in yet another female shape?]

What I have attempted to do in this chapter is present an example of the usefulness of native literary works as sources for the study of tourist–native encounters in a bilingual cultural context.

While much valuable work has been done on the construction and on the consumption of tourist sites, a study which draws attention to native perceptions of such processes may aid our understanding of the complex set of relationships between places, communities and the visitors which they attract. The texts from the West Kerry Gaeltacht region under examination here suggest a highly sophisticated understanding among a native rural population of the social and cultural processes at work in tourist practices and tourist encounters, an understanding which stems in large part from the linguistic awareness of the authors. Though aspects of their accounts suggest that their perceptions are not always shared by other members of their communities, what is evident from the examples cited is that the native gaze is a critical gaze, capable of discriminating between the positive and the negative aspects of tourist activity. It is often cynical, especially when it focuses on the uneven spread of tourist-related benefits or on demeaning native responses to tourist demands or expectations. It can be as intrusive and as objectifying as the tourist gaze itself. Above all, it recognises the exploitative nature of many tourist activities; it is ambivalent about the possibilities for authentic communication between tourists and natives and ultimately looks upon the whole relationship in terms of a drama in which only some get to play the good parts.

Notes

1. All translations from Irish-language sources in this paper are my own. Page references refer to the original text.
2. In 1989 the Blascaod Mór National Parks Act was passed enabling the land on the island to be compulsorily purchased for development as a national park. The compulsory purchase clause in the Act excluded those properties still in the possession of ex-islanders or their descendants. The constitutionality of such a clause was subsequently challenged in the High Court by the present owners of 17/25ths of the island, the consortium An Blascaod Mór Teo. (consisting of Mr Peter Callery, a solicitor from Dingle, his brother James, of Cloonahee House, Elphin, Co. Roscommon, Ms Kay Brooks, widow of a former US diplomat, and Mr Matthias Jauch, of Mercier Park, Turner's Cross, Cork), who claimed that the clause discriminates unfairly against certain landholders in favour of others. A High Court decision of 27 February 1998 ruled in favour of An Blascaod Mór Teo., stating that the Act was invidious, unfair and offensive as it was 'discriminative treatment between two classes of citizens based substantially on pedigree'.

References

(Note: when two dates are provided below (for example 1928/1977), the first one refers to the original year of publication, the second one to the edition used in preparing this article.)

Aalen, F.H. and Brody, H. (1969) *Gola: The Life and Last Days of an Island Community*. Cork: Mercier Press.

Convery, F. J., Flanagan, S., Keane M. and Ó Cinnéide, M. (1994) *Ón Bhonn Aníos: Straitéis Turasóireachta don Ghaeltacht.* An Daingean: An Sagart.

Champetier, Y (1992). LEADER agus Turasóireacht Chultúrtha. *Comhar* 51 (12), 40–1.

Culler, J. (1981) Semiotics of tourism. *American Journal of Semiotics* 1, 127–40.

de Mórdha, M. (eag.) (1998) *Ceiliúradh an Bhlascaoid 1 Bláithín: Flower.* An Daingean: An Sagart.

Dew, J. (1998) The contribution of English scholars. In M. de Mórdha (eag.) *Ceiliúradh an Bhlascaoid 1* (pp. 9–15). An Daingean: An Sagart.

Foster, J. W. (1998) *The Islandman.* In M. de Mórdha (eag.) *Ceiliúradh an Bhlascaoid 1* (pp. 44–58). An Daingean: An Sagart.

Jones, A. (1992) Coimhlint Chultúir agus an Turasóireacht. *Comhar* 51 (12), 42–6.

MacCannell, D. (1973) Staged authenticity: Arrangements of social space in tourist settings. *American Sociological Review* 79, 589–603.

MacCannell, D. (1976) *The Tourist: A New Theory of the Leisure Class.* New York: Schocken Books.

Mac Conghail, M. (1989) Brian Ó Ceallaigh: Páirtí Thomáis Chriomhthain. In A. Ó Muircheartaigh (eag.) *Oidhreacht an Bhlascaoid* (pp. 155–69). Baile Átha Cliath: Coiscéim.

Mac Conghail, M. (1998) Flower, Myles na gCopaleen, Séamus Bán. In M. de Mórdha (eag.) *Ceiliúradh an Bhlascaoid 1* (pp. 16–22). An Daingean: An Sagart.

'Ac Fhionnlaoich, S. (1975) *Ó Rabharta go Mallmhuir.* Baile Átha Cliath: Foilseacháin Náisiúnta Tta.

Nic Eoin, M. (1982) *An Litríocht Réigiúnach.* Baile Átha Cliath: An Clóchomhar.

Ní Chéilleachair, M. (eag.) (1998) *Ceiliúradh an Bhlascaoid 2: Tomás Ó Criomhthain 1855–1937.* An Daingean: An Sagart.

Ní Shúilleabháin, E. (n.d) *Letters from the Great Blasket.* Dublin/Cork: Mercier Press.

Ó Cíobháin, P. (1992) *An Gealas i Lár na Léithe.* Baile Átha Cliath: Coiscéim.

Ó Conaire, Breandán. (1992) Tomás agus Brian. In B. Ó Conaire (eag.) *Tomás an Bhlascaoid* (pp. 229–32). Indreabhán: Cló Iar-Chonnachta.

Ó Coileáin, Seán. (1992) Tomás Ó Criomthain, Brian Ó Ceallaigh agus an Seabhac. In B. Ó Conaire (eag.) *Tomás an Bhlascaoid* (pp.233–65). Indreabhán: Cló Iar-Chonnachta

Ó Coileáin, S. (1998) An tOileánach – Ón Láimh go dtí an Leabhar. In M. Ní Chéilleachair (eag.) *Ceiliúradh an Bhlascaoid 2: Tomás Ó Criomhthain 1855–1937* (pp. 25–43). An Daingean: An Sagart.

O'Connor, B. (1993) Myths and mirrors: Tourist images and national identity. In B. O'Connor and M. Cronin (eds) *Tourism in Ireland: A Critical Analysis* (pp. 68–85). Cork: Cork University Press.

Ó Criomhthain, S. (1969) *Lá dár Saol.* Baile Átha Cliath: Oifig an tSoláthair.

Ó Criomhthain, T. (1928/1977) *Allagar na hInise.* Baile Átha Cliath: Oifig an tSoláthair.

Ó Criomhthain, T. (1929) *An tOileánach.* Baile Átha Cliath: Muinntir C.S. Ó Fallamhain Teo/ Oifig an tSoláthair.

Ó Criomhthain, T. [eag. B. Ó Conaire] (1997) *Bloghanna ón mBlascaod.* Baile Átha Cliath: Coiscéim.

O'Crohan, S. (1992) *A Day in Our Life* (T. Enright trans.). New York/Oxford: Oxford University Press.

O'Crohan, T. (1951) *The Islandman* (R. Flower trans.). Oxford: Clarendon Press.

O'Crohan, T. (1986) *Island Cross-talk* (T. Enright trans.). New York / Oxford: Oxford University Press.

Ó Fiannachta, P. (1998) An Spreagadh chun Pinn. In M. Ní Chéilleachair (eag.) *Ceiliúradh an Bhlascaoid 2: Tomás Ó Criomhthain 1855–1937* (pp. 82–90). An Daingean: An Sagart.

Ó Glaisne, R. (1989) Allúraigh san Oileán. In A. Ó Muircheartaigh (eag.) *Oidhreacht an Bhlascaoid* (pp. 305–20). Baile Átha Cliath: Coiscéim.

Ó Lúing, S. (1989) Lucht Léinn ón Iasacht. In A. Ó Muircheartaigh (eag.) *Oidhreacht an Bhlascaoid* (pp. 143–54). Baile Átha Cliath: Coiscéim.

Ó Sé, A. M. (1992) Turasóireacht Chultúrtha agus Forbairt na Gaeltachta. *Comhar* 51 (12), 20–23.

Ó Súilleabháin, Muiris (1933) *Fiche blian ag fás.* Baile Átha Cliath: Preas Talbóideach.

O'Sullivan, M.(1933) *Twenty Years A-Growing* (M. Llewelyn Davies and G. Thomson trans.). New York: The Viking Press.

Smith, I.C. (1986) Real people in a real place. In *Towards the Human* (pp. 13–70). Edinburgh: MacDonald.

Stagles, J. and R. (1980) *The Blasket Islands.* Dublin: The O'Brien Press.

Ua Maoileoin, P. (1960) *Na hAird ó Thuaidh.* Baile Átha Cliath: Sáirséal agus Dill.

Ua Maoileoin, P. (1983) *Ó Thuaidh!* Baile Átha Cliath: Sáirséal Ó Marcaigh.

Urry, J. (1990). *The Tourist Gaze: Leisure and Travel in Contemporary Societies.* London / Newbury Park / New Delhi: SAGE.

Urry, J. (1995) *Consuming Places.* London / New York: Routledge.

Part 4

Imagining Ireland: The Construction of Tourist Representations

Chapter 9

Next to Being There: Ireland of the Welcomes and Tourism of the Word

MICHAEL CRONIN

Evelyn Waugh once remarked that 'every Englishman abroad, until it is proved to the contrary, likes to consider himself a traveller and not a tourist' (Waugh, 1930: 44). If Waugh was Irish he might have formulated the relationship between travel and self-perception differently. Irish people, at home, until it is proved to the contrary, like to consider themselves writers and not tourists. For the connection between writing and the construction of Ireland as a tourist destination has been one of the most enduring features of Irish tourism since its inception in the late 18th century (Nash, 1993: 86–112). From the Romantic courting of the sublime to the verse extracts stencilled on Aer Lingus plane seats, writing has shadowed the emergence of Ireland as a significant tourist destination. Writing on this writing has largely concentrated on the presentation of anthologies of travel writing on Ireland or on critical studies dealing with published travel accounts on the country (Maxwell, 1954; Ó Muirithe, 1972; Ó Cillín, 1977; Cronin, 1993: 51–67; Harrington, 1991; Fuchs & Harden, 1994; Hadfield & McVeagh 1994; McVeagh 1996; Ryle 1999). However, little attention has been devoted to the area of tourist magazines and journals that no less than books shape responses to people and place. In this chapter, the focus will be on *Ireland of the Welcomes*, the official publication of the Irish Tourist Board which has been in continuous existence since 1952. In particular, we will look at the implication of writers in the Irish tourism project, changing writing practices and what the writing itself can tell us about a society that has changed so dramatically in the five decades of the magazine's publication.

Publicity and the Writer

A central feature of the proactive approach to the development of Irish tourism in the 1950s, stimulated by the promptings of Ireland's Marshall

Plan funders, was publicity (Deegan & Dineen, 1997: 21–5). Tourists could only come to Ireland if they knew about it. And now that austerity was coming to an end in Britain and Americans were increasingly discovering the novelty of air travel, many more might want to know about it. To this end, Fógra Fáilte, was established as the publicity wing of Irish tourism operations under the 1952 Tourist Traffic Act. Although Fógra Fáilte was later subsumed into Bord Fáilte, the initial establishment of a separate body was significant in indicating the perceived need to emphasise the external marketing of the country. Tangible evidence of the new orientation in tourism policy was the decision to produce a regular, bi-monthly publication which would showcase Ireland's attractions as a place to visit. The first issue of *Ireland of the Welcomes* appeared in May 1952 and the reader was duly welcomed by a letter from Seán Lemass, the then Minister for Industry and Commerce. A secular blessing was not sufficient, however, and under the title, 'Seeing What is Good', Pope Pius XII (1952: 23) offered his own imprimatur to the Irish tourism enterprise. He noted:

> Another and more important benefit of tourism is that it refines the senses, enlarges the spirit and enriches experience. One sees, feels and observes. Many things in nature, in art, in regional customs or local traditions which, at first sight, may have seemed strange, not to say irritating or ridiculous, appear merely different and often indeed quite understandable, and at times very wise.

Less the Pontiff be mistaken for a latter-day *philosophe* he is quick to point out the dangers of ethical relativism, 'Not indeed that there should be any sacrifice of principle. The good is ever the good, evil is still evil, truth retains its rights as against error' (Pius XII, 1952: 23). Pius XII might indeed have been anticipating the difficulties of the fledging tourist board in that one of its difficulties was to dispel a number of 'errors' about Ireland (the Irish as feckless, lazy, inefficient) while seeking to promote a marketable version of the 'truth' (the Irish as welcoming, convivial and modernising).

The particular conception of the audience for the publication is eloquently expressed in the advertisements seeking subscribers. In the September–October issue for 1963, the copy begins: 'Ireland today is all you ever hoped, much you never dreamed. *Ireland of the Welcomes* is next to being there. A magazine specifically for those of us who can't be there, but yearn to know how it is.' The advertisement concludes by claiming: 'Here's the full scope of Ireland, as seen through the perceptive, witty or scholarly eyes of such renowned contributors as Padraic Colum, Brendan Behan, Sean Ó Faoláin and Sir Compton MacKenzie' (*Ireland of the Welcomes*, 1963: 35). Nine years later in the March–April issue of 1972, the title of the appeal for subscribers is 'Give your friends a holiday (6 times a year)' and the tone is more direct, less fulsome, 'Share your pleasure in *Ireland of the Welcomes* by giving it as a gift to friends who know or would like to know Ireland' (*Ireland of the Welcomes*, 1972: 4). The magazine thus has a dual function. First, it has a *representative* function in that it represents Ireland to those who cannot be there. Reading the magazine itself becomes a form of tourism, so that holidaying practice for at least part of the readership is seen as primarily substitutive and sedentary. In this way, a touring culture is not constructed *pace* Rojek and Urry through actual visits to sacred sites but through a nomadic encounter with the culture, mediated through print and illustration (Rojek & Urry, 1997: 1–19). The virtual space of reading is in a sense 'next to being there' and of course, 'those of us who can't be there' can refer as much to Ireland's diasporic population as it does to the country's distant if immobile aficionados. The second function of the publication is *rhetorical*. The magazine was initially the responsibility of Fógra Fáilte and the primary aim of that organisation was to persuade people to visit Ireland. Hence, the choice of articles, contributors, illustrations is dictated by an imaginary dimension to tourism discourse, by the way in which the potential Irish tourist is envisaged and what is seen to excite his or her interest.

In the 1963 advertisement, the only names mentioned in the advertisement are those of writers. It is writers alone who legitimise the claims of the magazine to be representative and authoritative in the establishment of a specifically Irish touring culture. Indeed, the history of the magazine might be generically summarised as the passage from literary journal to colour supplement. In the first year of its existence *Ireland of the Welcomes* published articles and poems by Benedict Kiely, Dora Sigerson Shorter, Brendan Behan, Seán Ó Faoláin, Lord Dunsany, Donagh McDonagh and the Reverend Francis Mahony. There were pieces on the 'Gaelic Story-Teller' (J.H. Delargy), Thomas Moore (Brian Gildea), 'Landmarks in the Yeats Country' (Philip Rooney), 'When the Abbey was Young' (Winifred Letts) and Aran's 'Immemorial Cultural Heritage' (Malachy Hynes). It is Benedict Kiely who intuits a relationship between tourism and literature which is closer than many of his colleagues might care to admit. In the first issue of the magazine, Kiely states:

> One of the first pieces of poetry I ever learned, after *Lord Ullin's Daughter* and *The Woman was Old and Feeble and Grey*, appeared as an advertisement in a Tyrone newspaper. It was a resounding verse, and no mockery; and even if it was an advertisement it did not tamper with or inflate the truth:

> Bracing breezes, silvery sands,
> Booming breakers, lovely lands,
> Come to Bundoran! (Kiely, 1952: 6)

The ready availability of cash for prose in hard-pressed times is certainly one explanatory factor for the presence of so many leading signatures in the pages of the publication.[1]

More generally, the role of literary Romanticism in reclaiming large tracts of Irish land for sightseeing and the strength of the travel writing tradition on Ireland throughout the 19th and 20th centuries meant that writers were closely implicated in the presentation of Ireland to the travelling public. Kiely's childhood memory, however, is revealing less of past affections than future dilemmas for the engagement of Irish writers with tourism. In the Tyrone newspaper, poetry, advertising and tourism are conflated in the evocation of Bundoran beauties. The touching naivety of the *aa* rhyming scheme (sands/lands) barely conceals a hard truth about the advertisement itself, it is selling a product and the product is a Donegal seaside resort. This example and the explicit literary content of *Ireland of the Welcomes* from its inception shows that tourism was not simply an industry among others in the Ireland of the period but that it had a strong aesthetic component. In other words, Irish tourism, in addition to being a modernising force while invoking the rhetoric of the pre-modern, also anticipated the post-modern mutation of the Irish economy with its emphasis on the production of aesthetic and informational goods (music, multimedia, software development, craft industries).[2]

The aestheticisation of production and consumption which is a feature of developed economies in late modernity has long been at work in the 'welcome industry' (Lash & Urry, 1994: 111–14). The result is, at times, a generic leakage so that literary prose, advertising copy and real estate hype, for example, become indistinguishable. Mervyn Wall opens a piece in *Ireland of the Welcomes* entitled 'Seascapes' with

> The Waterford and Cork coasts are impregnated with a peculiar sleepy charm. Everything is perfectly in its place – the small clustered towns above the sandy bays, and the rocky peninsulas creeping out to enclose water strewn with islands. (Wall, 1963: 4)

In an article in *The Irish Times* property supplement detailing the charms of Mia Farrow's Irish holiday home, Orna Mulcahy describes the house as

> [a]lmost invisible from the road, it is set in a low hilly landscape, surrounded by ancient stone walls and a patchwork quilt of fields. The Avonmore river runs along the bottom of the property, and a small stream rushes by the house on the east side. (Mulcahy, 2001: 4)

The clustering of platitude ('ancient stone walls', 'patchwork quilt') might mark out the Mulcahy passage as poor literature but the conventional 'sleepy charm' and 'strewn with islands' in Wall's contribution equally show the pressure of stereotype on the sentences of the penman. If the acquisition of property must be aestheticised in terms similar to the descriptive come hither of travel writing then the writer is placed in the position of witting or unwitting provider of aesthetic alibis for far-reaching economic changes of which tourism offers one of the earliest and most telling examples.

The Sports of Kings and Tourism of the Word

Bundoran like Bray and Courtown was the nearest Ireland ever got to a mass seaside resort but the literary tenor of the advertising copy and the contents of *Ireland of the Welcomes* over the years are eloquent in their definition of the market sought by policy makers and the contradictions that arise when development and perception fall foul of one another. An early boast of *Ireland of the Welcomes* was the open-handed egalitarianism of the Irish holiday experience. A 1952 article by Eric G. O'Leary on horse racing in Ireland has as its main title 'They're Off' and the sub-title reads: 'In Ireland the Sport of Kings is Everybody's Business' (O'Leary, 1952: 9–10). Another article in the same issue of the magazine by Tony Gray is entitled 'White Sails in the Bay' and the sub-title again holds out the Republican promise of fraternity of access, 'Yachting in Ireland . . . democratic – inexpensive – thrilling' (Gray, 1952: 17–18). One could argue that what was being advocated was a lower middle-class version of popular democracy. Yachts and horses, the symbol of aristocratic or merchant class leisure pursuits in Britain, might be indulged in across the Irish Sea without the opprobrium of social ridicule. Travel to Ireland, like the ostentatious consumption promised by duty-free shops, allowed the tourist to enter a liminal zone of class where they could relish the sports of Kings on a schoolteacher's salary and be the Queen for a Day. The tone and contents of *Ireland of the Welcomes* were clearly aimed at a highly literate readership who sought the compensation of culture while appropriating the privileges of toffs. Visitors needed to be reassured, however, that this democracy of entitlement tallied with an appropriate perception of the Irish themselves. Regal illusions were not always easy to sustain in a country that had congenitally low income levels and a countryside devastated by emigration. Poverty of appearance had to be subjected to the alchemy of the verb. Ironically, it was a Republican activist, Brendan Behan, who was to make this process most explicit. In an early article for *Ireland of the Welcomes*, 'In the Kingdom of

Kerry', Behan brings the reader on a Sweeney-like skyride through the county. Stopping in Tralee, Behan observes:

> In Tralee, they debated football, politics and the genealogies of great clans. These heirs of old nobility sat and drank pints of stout in the back snug, whose fathers held courts in castles and gave the bard a hearing over wine. (Behan, 1952: 16)

He goes on to note that, '[i]n Caherdaniel, you'll be bedded like a Prince and fed like his father for half nothing and the quarter of that again, if you can sing a song' (p. 16). This is a kingdom with no subjects, only lords and ladies, down on their luck. Behan's breathless prose with its almost parodic pseudo-translation of Gaelic hyperbole does make an important and culturally long-established point. Appearances deceive. In a popular version of the Irish past, the political subjection of Ireland meant that the language and culture went underground with the result that the aristocratic culture of the bards would become the birthright of small farmers and agricultural labourers. The unkempt farmhand might turn out to be a distinguished lyric poet, the lachrymose drinker an expropriated aristocrat. Though this version of the Hidden Ireland is challenged by later scholars like Breandán Ó Buachalla (1993: 48–55), the identification of the Irish countryside with Ireland's noblest cultural traditions allows physical realities (poverty, isolation) to be subsumed into a different and more prestigious framework of reference.

J.H. Delargy writes with reverence of the Kerry storyteller, Seán Ó Conaill, in an article which would be reprinted 21 years later in a special anniversary issue of *Ireland of the Welcomes*:

> He had never been to school, was illiterate so far as census officials were concerned, and could neither speak nor understand English. But he was one of the best-read men in the unwritten language of the people whom I have ever known, his mind a storehouse of traditions of all kinds – pithy anecdotes, intricate hero tales, proverbs and rhymes and riddles, and other features of the orally preserved lore common to all Ireland three hundred years ago. (Delargy, 1952: 3)

Tourists must be convinced that they are, in a sense, among equals, albeit exalted equals. In view of a lingering nationalist hostility to tourism as an abject exercise in flunkeydom, it was important to scotch any suggestion that welcoming visitors to Ireland involved a reversion to the music-hall stereotype with craven natives capering around the Quality. Indeed, as early as 1916 (just over two weeks before the Easter Rising), George Bernard Shaw writing on travel in Ireland for the magazine *The Car* warned potential tourists against comic condescension,

> Irish people are, like most country people, civil and kindly when they are treated with due respect. But anyone who, under the influence of the stage Irishman and the early novels of Lever, treats a tour in Ireland as a lark, and the people as farce actors who may be addressed as Pat and Biddy, will have about as much success as if he were to paint his nose red and interrupt a sermon in Westminster Abbey by addressing music-hall patter to the dean. (Shaw, 1963: 14)

Therefore if Ireland was targeting a particular kind of visitor, the host population in terms of cultural sophistication was presented as equal to if not superior to the task despite what material externals might suggest.

If a large number of the early articles in *Ireland of the Welcomes* stress the Irish talent for talk and their easy familiarity with the literary classics of the Irish canon, it is partly because the Word itself is construed as a tourist attraction. In a country whose built infrastructure had suffered the severe depredations of the Tudor and Cromwellian wars and where there was, at best, indifference to the Anglo-Irish architectural inheritance, one of the difficulties for Irish tourism in the early years was what to show tourists. Once the sublime drama of western landscapes had been exhausted, there was the risk of a visual deficit in a country that was not sufficiently interested in or could not afford 'heritage'. This is where language does not so much come into as create the picture. It is the anecdote of history and the remembered verse and literary fiction which bring a pile of stones to monastic life or transforms a Tralee snug into a Great Hall. For the English writer Kenneth Alsop, text and context merge in the streets of Dublin, 'how can anyone walk down a Dublin street without a dozen times feeling that he is in the middle of a paragraph written by James Joyce, in a poem by W.B. Yeats, in a scene from a play by Sean O'Casey' (Alsop, 1963: 8). It is not so much what Alsop sees as what he imagines he is seeing that counts. This state of aesthetic stimulation is maintained by a complicit population. Alsop declares that, 'the average Irishman's natural instinct for literature and language may have become a cliché from repetition, but it is true'. The pubs which he visits are alive with debates about the respective merits of 'Sam Beckett' and 'Jimmy Joyce' as writers.

This literate utopia makes one important assumption, namely that the tourist is an English speaker. This indeed was overwhelmingly the case until the 1980s when British and American dominance of the Irish tourism market began to recede in favour of tourism from the European continent (Péchenart & Tangy, 1993: 162–80). If the magazine in the 1980s and 1990s begins to rely more and more on photographs and illustrations and place and considerably less emphasis on the Irish as people with a talent for talk and a ready acquaintance with their literary forbears, it is in part because the language world of tourist contact is no longer homogeneous. A shared language and canon allowed the suitably curious British or American tourist to engage in literary banter with the locals. For visitors from other languages and cultures, this camaraderie of reference would be infinitely more problematic.

It has become a sociological commonplace to point to the importance of the visual in late modernity and a great number of heritage attractions place a premium on sight as a way of apprehending experience. However, there is a danger in perceiving tourist experience uniquely from the perspective of visually sophisticated heritage attractions in developed economies. *Ireland of the Welcomes* in the early decades was the product of a poor, peripheral, underdeveloped country. The funds for investment in the heritage panopticon of tourism, the visible, material infrastructure of the centre, sight, attraction were not forthcoming. So, in a sense (and this echoes a familiar tourist complaint about developing countries, particularly about towns and cities), there was not much to 'see'. By emphasising literature and language, however, not only could imagination take up where reality left off but sightseeing could give way to eavesdropping. This was not the wordless communion of musical 'craic' to be celebrated in later versions of Irish tourism rhetoric (which could be passively observed) but an active invitation to engage with language and letters. The benefits of the immaterial to the soul might be immense but in the material world the costs were blessedly low.

Contestation

The Irish Literary Revival and the subsequent fortunes of Irish writers in the post-independence period firmly established the Irish writer as an adversarial figure, whether as advocate of political separateness or as gainsayer of the pieties of land, faith and religion. The rhetorical representation is of the novelist, poet, dramatist as the conscience of the people, a fearless exposer of cant and corruption. Is the decision then to write for a magazine promoting Irish tourism, among other things, a sordid Faustian pact, a cynical sacrifice of principle to the punt, a shameless example of the subordination of the dissenting voice to the promptings of self-interest? This version of the writer as propagandist, as manipulative anti-hero(ine), would be to grossly simplify the actual prose itself and perpetuate reductionist readings of how writing, tourism and identity mesh in tourist publications.

An emblematic figure in the long lineage of contestation in Irish writing in the 20th century is Seán Ó Faoláin. Not only does Ó Faoláin write for *Ireland of the Welcomes* but, as we saw earlier, his is one of the names that figures in advertisements for the magazine. When he writes for the magazine, however, he does not abandon criticism for sanctimony and quietly subverts many of the cultural, political and tourist expectations of the period. Writing in the September–October 1952 issue on 'The Counties of Cork', he casts aspersions on the restrictive definitions of the native:

> Those ubiquitous McCarthys, for example, are mere upstarts as Corkonians. When I think of Cork the names that occur to me are such as the Norman Barrys, Roches, Nagles, Fagans, not to mention such later settlers as the Finsleys and the Coppingers – of Coppinger's Court in the west or Castle Coppinger in the east. (Ó Faoláin, 1952: 7–8)

If Ó Faoláin is proposing a more generous definition of belonging, challenging the conventional categories of natives and newcomers, he also troubles national narratives by claiming that Cork's fabled cosmopolitanism owed less to the intrinsic openness of its inhabitants than to their enthusiasm for Empire. Remembering the city of his boyhood, he states, 'perhaps, it was not really so very international? Perhaps it was just a rather Englished city?' (p. 9). He also tilts at the cherished images of Irish tourism. The Cork writer takes the Romantic movement and the Irish Literary Revival to task claiming that they 'have done as much to narrow as to intensify our enjoyment of Ireland. They have over-concentrated on the picturesque West.' Ó Faoláin continues: '[b]esides, rich land is rich in other things than what the romantics call 'scenery': strong castles, noble houses, planned gardens,' (p. 11).

His redefinition of appropriate objects for the travellers' interests has obvious political implications. If the imagination of cultural nationalism was at home in the western island and the tourism industry commodified the sentiment in presenting the scenery of the western coast as the defining marketing image of Ireland, Ó Faoláin wants to reinstate other traditions, notably the Anglo-Norman and the Anglo-Irish. His tone of opinionated dissent is a recurrent feature of contributions to the magazine. Writing in the same issue on Irish songs of exile, Donagh McDonagh (1952: 15) argues: 'Many of them are good songs by any standard, most of them have qualities of genuine emotion wedded to a good tune, and a great number of them are rubbish'. Stephen Rynne in a later issue is anxious to check tourist petulance with a stern warning:

> Don't be one of those haughty people who say that farmers should cut down their hedges so as to give the tourists better views! Farmers have to live in the country and if they lowered their sheltering hedges, they'd be blown out of the place. After all, this is only an island, 306 miles by 207, not a continent. (Rynne, 1963: 19)

Joseph O'Connor, for his part, in 1996 in the midst of a tourist boom delivers a withering diatribe against the forced travel of emigration, focusing on the Industrial Development Authority poster showing a group of University College Dublin students as Ireland's 'Young Europeans'. He says of the poster: 'It always seemed to me as poignant as any ancient Ulster saga, this pantheon of the departed heroes, so hopeful and innocent, so frozen in their brief moment of optimism' (O'Connor, 1996:)

Critical stances in particular kinds of tourist publications are not only inevitable but necessary. This seeming paradox, that propaganda must engender its own critique to survive, is an important factor in understanding the continued existence of a publication like *Ireland of the Welcomes*. The purpose of criticism is threefold. First, there is the question of credibility. Prose which is uniformly positive excites suspicion. For the article to be taken as a *bona fide* expression of authentic sentiment, it must have the internal tension, the telling disharmony that appears to distinguish the writer's piece from the hygienic banalities of the holiday brochure. Second, there is a fact of the market. Although there has been an exponential growth in the numbers of visitors to Ireland over the last five decades, the type of tourist courted by marketeers has generally been urban, educated and relatively well-off (Cronin & O'Connor, 2000: 170–7). As increasingly self-reflexive consumers of cultural products, these tourists value irony and knowing obliquity. They are more likely to believe what they read and be persuaded to come to Ireland if the writing is not too fulsome and appears, at least, to sabotage the conventional rhetoric of tourism. Third, there is the issue of the writers themselves. Successful writers have no particular need for tourism articles to feature on their curriculum vitae. Propaganda is no great addition to a writing career. For this reason, the risk of disharmony must be allowed if the quality of expression is to be maintained.

That these remarks apply not only to an official national tourist publication such as *Ireland of the Welcomes* but also to a very wide range of influential tourist writing is borne out by the phenomenal success of guide books such as those contained in the *Lonely Planet* and *Rough Guide* series. The guides are bought not because they wish to praise but because they dare to criticise. Telling the reader that a particular restaurant is dirty, over-priced and the serving staff indifferent means that the guide is believed when the reader is told that another restaurant is cheap, cheerful and clean. The writerly tone of the guides with their cooption of the subjective narrative of travel writing, the mixing of formal and informal registers of language and the ironic debunking of tourist–industry speak (if only to generate other myths in their turn) confer legitimacy on their many claims, a legitimacy that is all the stronger (and, therefore, harder to contest) in that external contestation is internalised within the narrative of the guide. So tourism writing cannot be simply dismissed as instrumental hackwork. Its efficacy depends, in part, on its ability to generate and incorporate contradiction. It is this feature of the writing that often puts critics of tourism at a disadvantage as the critique of one year becomes the advertising crib of the next.

Big Houses, Business and Time

Writing against the present is, of course, an invitation to the future. Criticising the way things are suggests how things might be or ought to be. If we return to Ó Faoláin's strictures on scenery, the riches he referred to were eventually to be put on lavish display in the pages of *Ireland of the Welcomes*. A marked difference between the magazine in the 1950s and 1960s and the same magazine in the 1980s and 1990s is the progressive gentrification of Ireland. Brian Inglis in an article on 'Turning Points in Irish History' is sharply critical of the tendency to represent Irish history solely as the unceasing struggle for Irish independence. Writing three years before the 1966 commemoration of the 1916 Rising, he claims that studying Irish history in isolation from what was happening in England was unsatisfactory and misguided. Inglis does acknowledge one traumatic turning point in Irish history as F.S.L. Lyons would a number of years later, the Great Famine. Inglis concludes his article, 'More than a million dead; millions forced to emigrate. It is impossible to assess the exact effect a disaster of this magnitude has on a country; but its scars linger to this day' (Inglis, 1963: 28). How the event is referred to a number of years later in the same magazine is eloquent not only of a general change in historiography but of a shift in perception. The poet and travel writer Richard Tillinghast in his 'Travels through Somerville and Ross's Ireland' introduces us to the new victims of the Famine, 'Following the Famine and the Land Wars, the landowning classes -and the Martins in particular who hung on to their big house with the utmost difficulty – were hard put to earn a living' (Tillinghast 1996: 30). Tillinghast is, of course, correct. Many landlords were seriously affected by the loss of income which resulted from their tenants either starving to death or taking the passage to new and not so new worlds. It is less history that is important here, however, than the presentation of the country to a largely external audience.

If the magazine in the early decades had concentrated on making Downstairs seem remarkably like Upstairs with countless articles emphasising the culture, nobility and self-possession of the common folk, in later years the focus is firmly on Upstairs with Downstairs knowing its place. Two captions to photographs contained in an article on Newbridge House published in the March–April 1987 issue suggest that being down below was not so bad after all: 'The labourers' dining room (upper centre) gives a sense of solid comfort, as Joan Long poses for a picture of homely domesticity in the kitchen (above)' (Burke, 1987: 32–3). The tone is one of benign paternalism as domestics play a game of Happy Families. Peter Harbison offers the readers of another issue pen portraits of four locals who worked on the Glenveagh Estate for its owners in County Donegal and he says of the housekeeper, Nellie Gallagher, 'Her brother was Mr. McIlhenny's liveried butler, a factor which doubtless helped enormously in creating the family atmosphere in the castle, which Nellie describes as always being very friendly' (Harbison, 1987: 40). The Merchant–Ivory nostalgia for the relics of auld dacency is not a uniquely Irish phenomenon as is borne out by the popularity of costume-driven films and television series in Britain and the United States in recent decades and the centrality of stately homes to the heritage industry in England, Scotland and Wales (Lowenthal, 1998). However, there are two factors more specific to Irish conditions.

First, the (Northern) conflict that dare not speak its name in the pages of the magazine led to a discrediting of many of the more exclusivist theses of cultural nationalism with its spoken or unspoken contempt for Anglo-Ireland. It became possible, even desirable, to celebrate and to renovate the 'noble houses' and the 'planned gardens'. Embracing the Anglo-Irish tradition was to establish the pluralist *bona fide* of a new Ireland. Second, a revival of interest in the literature of the Big House, notably in the novels of Molly Keane, Elizabeth Bowen, J.G. Farrell and Jennifer Johnston, led to a recomposition of the literary landscape. The whitewashed cottages of Rosmuc give way to the castles and demesnes. The dogged literalism of tourism means that readers mutate into visitors and a whole new area of tourist accommodation is made available by the writings of the few. Tillinghast intimates this connection in his description of a night spent in the Castle of Mrs M. Salter-Townshend from which the town in county Cork takes its name: 'There are enough creaky floors and trophies of past glory to delight any reader of Molly Keane's novels' (Tillinghast, 1996: 31).

There is another dimension to Big House tourism which is less lyrical and more markedly prosaic, money. If the early representations of the country in *Ireland of the Welcomes* suggested a Republican ethic of inclusiveness where privilege, in a sense, was the property of all, in the more recent versions of Ireland, *Country Life* displacing *Ireland's Own*, there is a sense of exclusivity which can, of course, be purchased but does not have to be shared.[3] In other words, if the spalpeen taking a feed of potatoes in the 'solid comfort' of the kitchen is a poet of genius, it no longer matters. He is hidden not by the culpable ignorance of a colonial administration but by the business savvy of his gentrified compatriots. As we noted earlier, Irish tourism policy-makers repeatedly state that they are looking for income rather than numbers in their marketing drives in order to avoid the adverse effects of mass tourism (O'Donnell, 1992: 33–40). One consequence is that in a world with increasingly wide disparities between the revenues of the rich and the poor, the latter are not worth appealing to unless they are young western backpackers slumming their way to future success. Offering the privilege of old money to the creators of the new means for Irish tourism and its scribes that the big house is big business.

In an editorial hailing the 21st issue of the magazine, the editor Elizabeth Healy declares: 'A milestone such as this is an occasion to look back over those years, at how the face of Ireland has changed for the visiting stranger, and how much it has, in essence, remained the same.' As proof of the eternal essence of Ireland J.H. Delargy's article on the Gaelic storyteller is reprinted and Healy comments: 'It is interesting to reflect that the first article of the first-ever issue[. . .]could as well have been written today as all those years ago' (Healy, 1972: 5). That continuity should be expressed in terms of print is not simply the natural reaction of a magazine editor seeking after some metaphor of the eternal but points to one of the specific functions of a publication like *Ireland of the Welcomes*. In the half-decade of the magazine's existence, Ireland has undergone a process of convulsive modernisation and been the site of a violent conflict which has claimed over 3000 lives. There is little explicit evidence of these events in the pages of the magazine, presumably on the grounds that tourists as temporary refugees from modernity are not enthused by the idea of entering a construction site or a war-zone. So how does *Ireland of the Welcomes* respond to the 'face of Ireland' which 'has changed for the visiting stranger'?

At one level, the response has been instrumental. In other words, Irish modernisation is seen primarily as a function of improved service-delivery. So there are repeated references to better quality food, more comfortable accommodation, more efficient transport services, a greater variety of leisure activities and more diversified shopping experiences. The instrumentalised modernisation is thus treated in isolation from larger changes in the society. It becomes a text without context so that as early as 1952 James Laver (1952: 16) can write: 'Dublin retains, in spite of its efficient bus service and up-to-date hotels, something incredible, primitive and remote'. The other response to social change and political upheaval has been to create a history outside of history. This is articulated in two ways. First, large-scale historical narratives are shunned in favour of a fetishisation of place and the local. This tendency is in keeping with reactions everywhere to the phenomenon of globalisation but in the Irish instance by concentrating on the local, on the parish, historical events are often simply juxtaposed with no larger narrative communicating interpretations that are seen to be hopelessly contaminated by the political tensions of the present. The spatialisation of history leads to the relentless de-historicisation of the here and now, thereby sustaining an illusion of an Ireland which 'has, in essence, remained the same'.

A second rhetorical move is the invocation of literature as a guardian of the immemorial. In the January–February 2001 issue of *Ireland of the Welcomes* Madeleine Humphreys describes a visit to the areas in South Galway made famous by the activities of the writers of the Irish Literary Revival. She introduces her piece with a passage mixing allusion, meteorology and the ethereal:

> In the Spring of 1900 the novelist George Moore went to visit Augusta Gregory in south Galway. Riding a bicycle from the railway station at Gort to the Gregory home at Coole Park he was 'pleasantly ventilated by the late breezes from the Burren mountains. We shall be folklore in time', he mused. Keeping Moore and his compatriots of the Irish Celtic Renaissance in mind I set out to look for ghosts. It was a typical Irish summer's day, soft, warm, grey with intervals of sun and light rain. I felt a common bond with the spirits that filled the air. (Humphreys, 2001: 26)

The article offers brief pen portraits of some of the protagonists of the 'Irish Celtic Renaissance' but there is no politics in their lives, only art as a religion of the otherworld. When the writer comes to the end of her South Galway journey in late evening in the woods of Coole Park, 'it wasn't long before Gods and Fairies folded their wings and perched all around me. I was in the enchanted wood surrounded by historic hills, fairy forts and ancient ruins' (Humphreys, 2001: 31). This sense of timeless arcadia is further strengthened by the following article in the same issue about the workshop in Kilnamartyra which produces miniature reproductions of characters from *The Hobbitt* and *The Lord of the Rings*. The article is entitled 'Middle Earth Country?' and much is made of the relationship between the workshop owner, Lars Edman, and the West Cork countryside so that the reader might answer the rhetorical question of the title by affirming that it is Ireland indeed which is the true Middle Earth Country (Kerrigan, 2001: 32–9).

The selective use of literary texts to remove Ireland from history into a land of fairytale and myth is almost a parody of the Literary Revival. The heroes and heroines no longer stride through the General Post Office creating history out of myth but reappear as diminished figures, literally figurines (the West Cork workshop produces a chess set based on the *Táin*), history subsumed to literary myth to sell the holiday experience of the West. The irony is that literature is repeatedly enlisted by the magazine, although prominent writers themselves no longer feature in any significant way in the publication, the exception being the special issue edited by Derek Mahon for the Frankfurt Book Fair in 1996. This development reflects in part the general professionalisation of writing with magazine publication largely the province of freelance journalists who are rather coyly presented in *Ireland of the Welcomes* as 'freelance writers'. The change also indicates a new intellectual economy where it is media pundits, the heresiarchs of the newspaper columns and the caster folk of the radio and television studios, wheeled on for the grumble over newspapers or the carefully-timed soundbite, who are now occupying what is left of the public sphere in Ireland. Not only are Irish writers less likely to be the subject of the pub discussions prized by English tourists to Ireland decades ago but they are also less likely to feature in any public discussion, marginalised by the professionals of the microphone and the note pad.

On the copper-plate frontispiece of *The Compleat Irish Traveller* produced in 1788, there is a picture of a man in knee-breeches advancing, book in one hand, towards a group of young women, clad in muslin in the classical style and underneath the picture is the caption, 'The Proprietors of the *Irish Traveller* presenting a Copy of that Work into the hand of Futurity to be preserved from the Devastation of Time.' The hand of Futurity has been kind to *Ireland of the Welcomes*. In existence for half a century and with a print run of over 100,000 copies, the magazine looks set to continue as the flagship publication of the Irish Tourist Board. It is a magazine whose history has much to tell us about the particular relationship between literature and tourism in Ireland and, above all, how not even the Irish Traveller can escape from the Devastation of Time.

Notes
1. See Anthony Cronin (1980) for a vivid description of the precarious finances of Irish *litterateurs* in the post-war period.
2. For a discussion of tourism and its role in the development of Irish modernity see Michael Cronin and Barbara O'Connor (2000).
3. That these representations did not, of course, correspond to social reality in the Ireland of the time interests me less here than that there was a felt need to represent the country in this way in the first place.

References
Alsop, K. (1963) Ireland. *Ireland of the Welcomes* 12 (4), 5–8.
Behan, B. (1952) In the Kingdom of Kerry. *Ireland of the Welcomes* 1 (2), 15–17.
Cronin, A. (1980) *Dead as Doornails*. Dublin: Poolbeg.
Cronin, M. (1993) Fellow travellers: Contemporary travel writing and Ireland. In B. O'Connor and M. Cronin (eds) *Tourism in Ireland: A Critical Analysis* (pp. 51–67). Cork: Cork University Press.

Cronin, M. and O'Connor, B. (2000) From Gombeen to Gubeen: Tourism, identity and class in Ireland, 1949–1999. In R. Ryan (ed.) *Writing in the Irish Republic: Literature, Culture, Politics 1949–1999* (pp. 170–7). London: Macmillan.

Deegan, J. and Dineen, D. (1997) *Tourism Policy and Performance: The Irish Experience.* London/Boston: Thompson International Business Press.

Delargy, J.H. (1952) The Gaelic Story-Teller. *Ireland of the Welcomes* 1 (1), 2–4.

Fuchs, A. and Harden, T. (eds) (1994) *Reisen im Diskurs: Modelle der literarischen Fremdefahrung von den Pilgerberichten bis zur Postmoderne.* Heidleberg: Universitätsverlag C. Winter.

Gray, T. (1952) White sails in the bay: Yachting in Ireland . . . democratic – inexpensive – thrilling. *Ireland of the Welcomes* 1 (1), 17–19.

Hadfield, A. and McVeagh, J. (eds) (1994) *Strangers to that Land: British Perceptions of Ireland from the Reformation to the Famine.* Gerrards Cross: Colin Smythe.

Harbison, P. (1987) A memorable quartet. *Ireland of the Welcomes* 36 (1), 40–1.

Harrington, J.P. (ed.) (1991) *The English Traveller in Ireland.* Dublin: Wolfhound Press.

Healy, E. (1972) Editorial. *Ireland of the Welcomes* 21 (1), 5.

Humphreys, M. (2001) The Enchantment of South Galway. *Ireland of the Welcomes* 50 (1), 26–31.

Inglis, B. (1963) Turning points in Irish history. *Ireland of the Welcomes* 12 (2), 25–28.

Ireland of the Welcomes (1963) 12 (3), 35.

Ireland of the Welcomes (1972) 20 (6), 4.

Kerrigan, J. (2001) Middle Earth Country. *Ireland of the Welcomes* 50 (1), 32–9.

Kiely, B. (1952) Approach to Donegal. *Ireland of the Welcomes* 1 (1), 5–7.

Lash, S. and Urry, J. (1994) *Economies of Signs and Space.* London: Sage.

Laver, J. (1952) Strolling down O'Connell Street. *Ireland of the Welcomes* 1 (1), 15–16.

Lowenthal, D. (1998) *The Heritage Crusade and the Spoils of History.* Cambridge: Cambridge University Press.

Lucy Burke, H. (1987) Upstairs and downstairs at Newbridge House. *Ireland of the Welcomes* 36 (2), 32–3.

Maxwell, C. (1954) *The Stranger in Ireland from the Reign of Elizabeth to the Great Famine.* Jonathan Cape: London.

McDonagh, D. (1952) The place in the song. *Ireland of the Welcomes* 1 (3), 15–18.

McVeagh, J. (1996) *Irish Travel Writing: A Bibliography.* Dublin: Wolfhound Press.

Mulcahy, O. (2001) River runs by Mia's Laragh cottage home. *The Irish Times*, 25 January, 4.

Nash, C. (1993) 'Embodying the Nation': The West of Ireland landscape and Irish identity. In B. O'Connor and M. Cronin (eds) *Tourism in Ireland: A Critical Analysis* (pp. 86–112). Cork: Cork University Press.

Ó Buachalla, B. (1993) In a hovel by the sea. *The Irish Review* 12, 48–55.

Ó Cillín, S.P. (1977) *Travellers in Co. Clare 1459–1843.* Galway: Ó Cillín and Brannick.

Ó Faoláin, S. (1952) The counties of Cork. *Ireland of the Welcomes* 1 (3), 7–8.

Ó Muirithe, D. (1972) *A Seat behind the Coachman. Travellers in Ireland 1800–1900.* Dublin: Gill and Macmillan.

O'Connor, J. (1996) Diaspora and exile. *Ireland of the Welcomes* 45 (5) 49–50.

O'Donnell, M. (1992) The role of Bord Fáilte in rural tourism. In J. Feehan (ed.) *Tourism on the Farm* (pp. 33–40). Dublin: UCD Environmental Institute,.

O'Leary, E.G. (1952) They're off: In Ireland the sport of kings is everybody's business. *Ireland of the Welcomes* 1 (1), 9–10.

Péchenart, J. and Tangy, A. (1993) Gifts of tongues: Foreign languages and tourism policy in Ireland. In B. O'Connor and Michael Cronin (eds) *Tourism in Ireland: A Critical Analysis* (pp. 162–80). Cork: Cork University Press.

Pius XII (1952) Seeing what is Good. *Ireland of the Welcomes* 1 (1), 23.

Rojek, C. and Urry, J. (1997) Transformations of travel and theory. In C. Rojek and J. Urry (eds) *Touring Cultures: Transformations of Travel and Theory* (pp. 1–19). London and New York: Routledge.

Ryle, M. (1999) *Journeys in Ireland: Literary Travellers, Rural Landscapes, Cultural Relations*. Aldershot: Ashgate.

Rynne, S. (1963) The little things. *Ireland of the Welcomes* 12 (3), 17–20.

Shaw, G.B. (1963) Bernard Shaw's Irish holidays. *Ireland of the Welcomes* 12 (4), 13–15. Reprinted from *Collier's Magazine*, 10 June 1916 and first published in *The Car*, 5 April 1916.

Tillinghast, R. (1996) Travels through Somerville and Ross's Ireland. *Ireland of the Welcomes* 45 (2) 27–32.

Wall, M. (1963) Seascapes. *Ireland of the Welcomes* 12 (3), 4–7.

Waugh, E. (1930) *Labels: A Mediterranean Journal*. London: Duckworth.

Chapter 10

Home from Home: Diasporic Images of Ireland in Film and Tourism

STEPHANIE RAINS

Introduction: Ireland and the Irish-American Diaspora

The tourism dynamic which this chapter explores is the relationship between the Irish-American diaspora and Ireland itself as a tourist destination for that diaspora. More specifically, I will be concentrating upon the representations of Ireland which were produced by and for the Irish-American market, principally those using the medium of film, both in the form of feature films and promotional films. The chapter will concentrate on the period immediately after the Second World War. From this point on, foreign travel became an increasingly available commodity for consumers from the West, and therefore began its journey to its present position as a marker and definer of modern and, later, post-modern global culture.

Before moving on to discuss these representations in detail, it is worth considering the reasons for exploring the connections between the diasporic tourism industry in Ireland and filmic representations of the country. Due to the importance of Irish-American audiences to the development of the film industry in America, representations of Ireland have not only been a constant feature of Hollywood films from the silent era onwards but these representations have been structured in ways which have reflected the demands and imaginative positioning of that Irish diasporic audience. In particular, this has led to a noticeable filmic positioning of Ireland as 'home', with all the connotations of the familiar, the hospitable and the specific which that implies. Such a dominant metaphor also brings with it, of course, other apparently 'universal' associations such as oppressive expectations, unresolved emotions and the need to leave. However, these other, less optimistic associations of home reinforce, rather than negate, the more welcoming associations, intimately connected as they are with the possibility of return and reconciliation.

The concept of the national 'home', with all the powerful associations it contains, becomes particularly complex for a diaspora which has reached its second, third or even fourth generation since that home was left behind. Such was the case for the Irish-American diaspora by the beginning of the 1950s. While, of course, America was still receiving, and would continue to receive to the present day, many first-generation immigrants, by the end of the Second World War there was established a substantial Irish-American population who had no first-hand experience of Ireland and, in particular, no experience of post-independence Ireland. The negotiation of such Irish-Americans' relationship to Ireland, therefore, becomes one dominated by the concept of a 'home' nation which is not only elsewhere but which is not directly and personally remembered. This negotiation, and all that it entails for the construction of Ireland within the global narrative, must also therefore take place primarily through the production and circulation of narratives and images. It is this moment at which Ireland becomes, for the majority of the world's population who identify themselves as Irish, a home understood through the consumption of narrativised images, rather than first-hand memory or experience, and it is principally through the national representations of film and tourism that these images are illustrated.

The fact that in the second half of the 20th century, tourism and film have been central to the Irish-American relationship to Ireland means that in the absence of other critiques, these have been the principal sources of assessment of that relationship. General criticisms of both points of contact which have been applied within the Irish context include claims of a romanticising determination to engage only with those aspects of Irish culture which confirm the beliefs already cherished in Irish-American communities. Typically, this is believed to be centred around a nostalgic view of Ireland as traditional, politically simplistic and removed from the modern, international culture symbolised by America.

What the criticism of this nostalgic attachment to 'home' ignores, however, is the process by which a diasporic cultural identity, such as that of Irish-America, is constructed within both the spatial dislocation created by emigration and also, very significantly, within the emigrants' experience of temporal dislocation. These dual dislocations occurred when, as a result of their journey to the United States, the emigrants' active participation in Irish culture was transformed into an act of memory and recall alone. And it is within this operation that the links between the touristic and filmic modes of cultural transmission become clear. For example, when discussing the role of narrative in the assimilation of journeys of exile and emigration, Barry Curtis and Claire Pajaczkowska (1994: 212–3) specifically connect the external, physical journeying of travel to the internal, emotional and symbolic journeying of film narrative. Within this connection, they argue for the possibility of the reintegration of split identities and the production of knowledge through a process of subjective and narrativised identification.

> Knowing, travelling and narrative point of view are thus intimately and structurally linked . . . In all journeys, of the body or soul, subjectivity is transformed by an encounter with objectifications, 'different' objects that require different forms of recognition of similarity and difference.

This understanding of the positioning of Ireland within Irish-American diasporic culture must lead to a reassessment of the meanings involved in that diaspora's act of return, whether permanently or, as in the focus of this chapter, through the temporary mode of tourism.

Ireland, therefore, stands in the cultural imagination of its diaspora as a figurative 'home' constructed through memories of disjuncture and dislocation. These memories are then circulated primarily through the narrativised images of film and tourism. Once this is understood, it is clearly not sufficient simply to characterise the Irish-American visitor's experience of Ireland as being one devoid of cultural meaning due to a basis in sentimentality, preconceived ideas and a refusal to engage with contemporary Irish culture. Rather, it would appear that their experience of contemporary Ireland involves an active, if not necessarily conscious, act of negotiation between the temporal and spatial disjunctures inherent in the diasporic relationship to Ireland.

This is not, of course, to suggest that sentiment and nostalgia are not contained within Irish-American approaches to Ireland; rather it is to suggest that within this context at least, such touristic behaviour should be subjected to a more sensitive scrutiny than it has generally been afforded and that, in particular, it should not be equated with a lack of 'authentic' meaning on behalf of the tourists involved. This apparently tense relationship between tourism and its perceived lack of authenticity has been the subject of close scrutiny within cultural analyses of tourism for many years and within many contexts (e.g. Boorstin, 1961; MacCannell, 1989; Urry, 1990). Instead, it will be argued here that in the case of diasporic tourist constructions of Ireland, definitions of 'authenticity' are already unstable, due to the mediated nature of diasporic identity transmission. This is not, therefore, to suggest that diasporic tourism should not be subjected to rigorous critique. Instead, this discussion attempts to demonstrate that a recognition of this instability of meaning and identity is frequently contained within diasporic tourist texts themselves; thus signalling a critical complexity to the use of nostalgia and romanticism within this context.

The Production of Tourism Texts for the Irish-American Diaspora

While, as Figure 10.1 shows, visitors from the United States were a very small proportion of the total visitors to Ireland during 1955–60 (Deegan & Dineen, 1997: 30–1), they did provide a disproportionately large proportion of visitor revenue to the country, undoubtedly making them a desirable target market for both Bord Fáilte and other 'traffic operators' within the tourism industry. At the same time, however, analysis of the average expenditure combined with the average length of stay of US visitors during this period shows that these tourists tended to stay longer and spend less per day in Ireland than in other European countries. As Deegan and Dineen (1997: 27–35) point out, the principal reason for this would have been the considerable number of United States visitors with family ties in Ireland, allowing them to stay with relatives and therefore reduce the costs of their visit.

It is within the context of these industry figures and analyses that the promotional films being produced about Ireland during this time must also be considered. During this period there was a rapid increase in the production of travelogue films about the country. While the majority of such films were commissioned and made by Bord Fáilte, and aimed at the dominant British market, a significant proportion were also produced for the US market. It is noticeable that these films were often produced by American-based, commercial production companies, such as Tribune Films Inc. and Dudley Pictures Corporation. However, these would also have had Bord Fáilte support and assistance during location filming in Ireland.

There is little archival information now available regarding the produc-

Year	1955	1956	1957	1958	1959	1960
US visitor nos	43000	51000	55000	61000	70000	80000
Proportion of total visitors	1.1%	1.3%	1.6%	1.8%	1.8%	1.7%
Revenue from US visitors (IR£)	4m	4.3m	4.3m	5.4m	6.1m	6.8m
Proportion of total visitor revenue	12.9%	12.8%	13.2%	15.6%	16.1%	16%

Figure 10.1 The economy of Irish-American tourism to Ireland

Figures drawn from James Deegan and Donal A Dineen (1997: 30–31).
Visitor numbers and revenue receipts from the United States, 1955–1960

tion and distribution policies behind the travelogues of this era. What is known, however, is that Bord Fáilte had a conception of the US market as being divisible into three distinct niches: the Irish-born, their Irish-American descendants and the non-Irish. The content of the films (which will be discussed in detail later) suggests that they were overwhelmingly aimed at the first two of these groups. The distribution of the films appears to have been controlled by Bord Fáilte and other 'traffic operators' such as airlines and major tour operators. Not only were they shown at conventions and trade fairs run or attended in the USA by these organisations, they were also loaned out to interested groups through Bord Fáilte's lending libraries of travel information. These groups could include diverse social organisations (such as sporting or musical associations) in the USA, who were considering taking a tour group to Ireland. One such type of group known to have been a regular user of these films (along with other promotional material), and a frequent organiser of visits to Ireland, were the Irish-American 'parish associations'. The centrality of the Catholic Church to the Irish-American diaspora, and the large number of Irish clergy working in their parishes, appears to have created a definable audience for the travelogue films.

It is also known that some of the films had limited releases in US cinemas – presumably those based in Irish-American areas, and which would have been practised in actively promoting Irish-themed feature films through the use of other Irish material, as discussed in detail by Casey (1998). Although some of the films may also have been broadcast on US television, it appears that the gradual decline in production of travelogues coincided with the increasing number of network-produced television travel programmes, which would have superseded the use of pre-produced films; as well as the rise of more sophisticated media marketing by tour operators, replacing the *ad hoc* connections between Irish-American organisations and the tourism industry.[1]

Cinematic Representations of the 'Return Home'

In 1952, at the time when international tourism was starting to become a realistic opportunity for significant numbers of Americans, there appeared one of the most popular and enduring representations of the journey home: John Ford's film, *The Quiet Man*. The story of Sean Thornton's return to his ancestral home in the West of Ireland, and his process of adaptation to the local culture; an exercise which is eventually rewarded by a happy marriage to an Irish girl, Mary Kate, *The Quiet Man* was an epic retelling of the diasporic journey of return.

In the film, Sean returns to White O'Morn, the cottage in which he was

born in the village of Inisfree, or 'another name for Heaven' in Sean's own
explanation of his journey. The magnitude of the emotional journey he has
undertaken is expressed in this phrase alone, as he explicitly equates the
return 'home' with a return to Eden. In terms of the wider cultural theme of
the diasporic journey back to the home country, the film's portrayal of
Sean's initial contact with his family cottage is extremely significant. While
it is the place in which he was born, thus making him, in literal terms, a first-
generation emigrant, it is made clear within the film that he has no personal
memories of either Inisfree or White O'Morn. Instead, as he is being driven
into the village upon his arrival, and the cottage is pointed out to him, the
narrative of memory is transferred to his mother, whose voice-over in the
film, as she describes their family life there, takes the place of his own
memory; 'It was a lovely little house, Seaneen, and the roses! Your father
used to tease me about them but he was that proud of them too!'. As Luke
Gibbons (1987: 199–200) comments on this crucial scene in the film,

> These words reverberate in the voice-over through Sean's mind when,
> early in the film, he first apprehends his ancestral cottage, bathed in
> sunlight in the midst of luxuriant verdure. Yet the fact that the cottage
> is revealed to us in a point-of-view shot through Sean's eyes, and that
> little effort is made at maintaining spatial continuity between Sean's
> position and the countryside surrounding the cottage, throws into
> relief the possible fictive status of his vision.

If Sean's vision of 'home' is potentially fictive, his memory of it certainly
is, in that it is an inherited one, passed on to him by his mother, as indicated
by her narrative interruption within the film. But the status of Inisfree, and
by extension of Ireland itself, as the home to which the Irish diaspora is
struggling to return, remains unchallenged within the film by this admission of the collective and inherited nature of the diasporic imagination. *The
Quiet Man* was heavily criticised from its initial release for its apparent
romanticisation of Ireland and its lack of realism. In a contemporary review
in *The New Yorker*, on 23 August 1952, John McCarten complained that
within the film the Irish are: 'just as cute as a button. The people are not only
cute but quaint, and the combination stretched out for something more
than two hours, approaches the formidable . . . '. And in its preview of the
film on 19 May 1952, *The Irish Independent* commented: 'Clearly Republic
Pictures had their eye on the American market when they went to work in
Co. Galway and perhaps that is the excuse for the exaggerations . . .
American audiences should like all of it; we will like some of it very much.'

However, contained within *The Quiet Man*'s representation of that
attachment to memories and images of the individually unexperienced
'home' was a serious assessment of the diasporic experience. The film is a

portrait of Sean's attempts to reconcile his Irish and American senses of identity. The strength of his identification with a home he has never known is demonstrated in his very decision to 'return' and to reject his American experience. The difficulties inherent in this action, however, are played out within the film's treatment of his developing relationship with Mary Kate. In that romantic relationship, which serves as a marker of Sean's emotional homecoming, lies the film's representation of his slow adaptation to Irish culture within Ireland, as distinct from the diasporic Irish cultural identification which he has maintained in America.

What is also made clear within the film, however, is that an understanding of this cultural difference between the diaspora and the homeland is always already an inherent part of diasporic Irishness. The Irish-American 'sentimentality' for Ireland, of which *The Quiet Man* itself was so vigorously accused, is shown within the film to already contain an understanding of the inherent division between the diasporic image and the reality of experience. So Sean's instinctive response to his first, Edenic vision of Mary Kate caught in the sunlight between the trees is: 'Hey, is that real? She couldn't be'. This is an example of what Gibbons (1987: 200) sees as

> the ability of certain strains in Irish romanticism to conduct a process of self-interrogation, to raise doubts at key moments about their own veracity, which cuts across any tendency to take romantic images as realistic accounts of Irish life. This suggests that it is not so much realism which offers a way out of the impasse of myth and romanticism, but rather a *questioning* of realism or any mode of representation which seeks to deny the gap between image and reality. (Emphasis in the original)

Within the diasporic context of Sean's questioning of realism and representation in *The Quiet Man*, the film demonstrates the subtleties actually contained within the Irish-American negotiation of cultural contact with Ireland. As Sean reveals in his reaction to Mary Kate's appearance, he already recognises that his understanding of Ireland, informed as it is by his mother's memories and other received images, is an unreliable source in terms of realism. What he is also recognising, however, in his very decision to return to Inisfree, is that however 'unrealistic' is his connection to Ireland, it remains nevertheless a powerful force in his personal identity, and therefore remains culturally valid in its meaning for him as a member of the Irish diaspora.

The Quiet Man's emphasis on the extent to which Sean is consciously seeking a return to the past is demonstrated within the opening shots of the film, in which he is shown arriving by train and then transferring to

Michaeleen's horse-drawn cart. As J.A. Place (1979: 196–7) describes it as follows:

> Sean is seen through the window [of the train], looking through its frame at the quiet village . . . A pony cart (in contrast to the moderness of the train) is framed through another window. It is like looking at a picture of the past and then walking into it as Sean passes through the window.

This explicit use of modes of transport as both an establishing device in the narrative of return, and also as an indicator of the complex negotiation of history and time for the visitor, was a recurring feature of promotional tourist films about Ireland during this period. Mia Gallagher (1989: 26), in her discussion of the use of landscape in Bord Fáilte's films, describes this as a framing device which attempts to resolve the tension between 'a cinematic drive for narrative and the timelessness insisted on by spectacle'. This resolution, she argues, is achieved through the depiction of arrival (and departure) in order to make the experience of the films, in themselves, into 'imaginary visits to Ireland' for the viewer.

Touristic Representations of the 'Return Home'

The theme of the Irish-American's 'return', most likely for the first time, was a central feature of many of the tourist promotional films produced by and for the Irish-American market during the 1950s and 1960s. What is most striking about these particular films is the extent to which, unlike travelogue films produced for other markets, they borrow their format so directly from the Hollywood feature film tradition. This format includes the use of fictional characters, surprisingly detailed narratives and photography which makes direct reference to mainstream feature films. This is in notable contrast to travelogue films about Ireland produced for the British market, which, although there are occasional narrative themes, generally tend to be 'informative' in a very specific way about the facilities and opportunities for holidays in Ireland. The distinctive nature of the films produced to promote Ireland as a destination for American tourists is, therefore, worth examining in detail in order to explore the specific appeal which the country is seen to have for its diaspora.

The Irish in Me, made in 1959, deals explicitly with the subject of the Irish-American diaspora who have no direct knowledge of Ireland. It is heavily narrativised, centring on the fictional story of Sheila, a 12-year-old American girl travelling not only to meet the grandfather she has never seen before but also the nation to which she 'belongs'. The film, which is narrated by her grandfather, follows her from her arrival at Shannon

Airport, through an exploration of Dublin alongside him and then on a journey into the country to meet her extended family.

Sheila's understanding of Ireland through the stories she has heard from her father in America is made clear within the film's narrative. During her tour of Dublin, she is shown refusing to enter the Hugh Lane Gallery of Modern Art, while her grandfather's voice-over describes her reasoning as being that the Ireland of her father did not include museums. Immediately after this, however, she is taken to The Abbey Theatre and shown enjoying the experience. This selective consumption of Irish culture would seem to fit the classic representation of the tourist who arrives in a new destination guaranteed to find exactly and only a justification of their preconceived notions and therefore to leave with no 'genuine' understanding of or feeling for the place they have visited. It is precisely these patterns of tourist experience which have been characterised as inauthentic and 'unseeing', as opposed to the Romantic traveller, whose yearning for truth made his or her experiences authentic (e.g. Boorstin, 1961; Hewison, 1987; Lowenthal, 1985). And within the context of this example, Sheila's specific rejection of the Hugh Lane Gallery in favour of the Abbey Theatre appears to confirm the nostalgic gaze's separation from the modern.

However, the continued narrative of *The Irish in Me* suggests that for the Irish diaspora the consumption process cannot be emptied of meaning. Sheila, on her visit to her extended family in the country, is shown making friends and exploring the countryside with Sean, a boy of similar age from her family's village. After a day of climbing trees and playing in rivers, her now absent grandfather's voice-over declares:

> Deep in the heart of Ireland, Sheila becomes in spirit what she is in heritage – an Irish girl come home to the land of her forefathers. She cannot give a name to the thing she feels in her heart – it might be called pride, or a love of country. To Sheila it is a nameless joy – a feeling of belonging with the Irish boy Sean. There is deep contentment . . . and then the summer is gone. It is time to return home . . . she takes Ireland with her.

So for Sheila the experience of Ireland is one of spiritual home-coming, rather than 'mere' touristic pleasure. And indeed the narrative of the film itself almost obstructs the process of tourism which it is designed to promote, through its concentration upon the fictional characters and their relationships. It is certainly far removed from other tourism films of the period, such as *Carefree Ireland*, produced for English visitors, which detail fishing opportunities, good roads and designated tourist attractions. *The Irish in Me*, in fact, through its engagement with Sheila's selective inheritance of Irish culture, is recognising and screening the act of negotiation between diasporic memory and contemporary reality which is an essential part of the Irish-American visitor's experience of Ireland.

Another travelogue film of the period, *Honeymoon in Ireland*, made in 1963, follows a format of more obvious use to Irish tourism as an industry, in that it adopts a narrative tour around Ireland, thus highlighting the country's attractions to foreign tourists. However, here too the highly developed narrative and fictional characters around which the film is constructed appear to obscure its explicit marketing techniques, pointing again to an understanding of visits by Irish-Americans as being more complexly motivated than those by non-Irish tourists. The film follows Mary, a fairly recent emigrant from Cork, and Bill, her American husband, on their honeymoon in Ireland. The voice-over consists of their conversation as they travel around the country. Delivered in the past tense, the impression given is of their joint re-telling of their trip to friends back in the USA, with the images serving in place of holiday photographs. This format, combined with the content of their narrative, means that within the film, Mary explains Ireland to Bill and Bill 're-interprets' this for a non-Irish audience. The relationship which the film establishes between the Irish girl and her new American husband points to a complex understanding of the positioning of Irish-Americans within wider American society and the implications of this for the international 'meaning' of Ireland itself.

The film opens with a scene of the newly-weds on board an Irish International Airlines plane, bound for Dublin airport. Bill is openly distracted by the attentions of a glamorous Irish air hostess, musing on the voice-over about the attractions of Irish girls, until Mary is forced to remind him that she too is Irish, in order to regain his attention. The underlying point of this exchange within the narrative is soon made clear to be, not so much Bill's susceptibility to the erotic charms of Irish women, even on his honeymoon, but in the question of the pair's ethnic and emotional origins, both as a couple and as individuals. Immediately after this incident, while still on the plane, Mary begins a sentence with the words 'We Irish . . . ', only to be cut off by Bill's insistence, 'You're American now', to which she responds forcefully, 'Oh, don't be ridiculous'. It is not clear, at this stage of the film, whether her identity is seen as questionable because of her emigration or because of her marriage to a non-Irishman. Mary's sense of loss at leaving Ireland is made clear later on when the film's jocular tone is disrupted upon their arrival in Cork, her home town. She says: 'I felt terribly sentimental in Cork, and we didn't talk very much. I little guessed when I was here last, that when I came back I would be on my honeymoon. I so hoped Bill wouldn't laugh at me for being so solemn.'

Mary's anxiety that her American husband will not understand her feelings for 'home' is, therefore, a continuation of the debate begun on the plane about her identity and the challenge posed to it by a non-Irish husband. The resolution within the film of this painful barrier between the couple, however, suggests significant implications for Ireland itself, as well as for individual Irish emigrants. This resolution occurs at the very end of the film, as the couple are preparing to board another plane to leave Ireland. Mary again expresses sadness at leaving 'home' and this time Bill too shares this feeling of loss, to the extent of delivering double-edged praise for the advent of modern travel in Ireland, when he declares that at least air-travel makes leaving easier, because it removes the painful experience of having to watch the shoreline disappearing. With this statement, Bill, as a departing tourist, is positioning himself firmly within the historical experience of colonial emigrants, for whom the act of departure from Ireland to the USA was one of leaving home, rather than returning to it. He is, therefore, eliding the apparently profound division between the migrant exile and the tourist, as his ostensible act of return becomes his point of departure.

What this narrative resolution of the film appears to suggest, therefore, is that rather than Mary's marriage to Bill having made her an American, Bill has instead become Irish, not due to the legalistic fact of marriage, but through the emotional and cultural experience of his visit. It also suggests, by implication, that if his apparent return is actually his departure, then his arrival was itself an act of return; again reinforcing the concept of Ireland as an archetypal 'home', to which even the first visit is a return. What is most significant about the representation of this theme within *Honeymoon in Ireland* is that it is seen to apply even to non-Irish visitors. Unlike Sheila in *The Irish in Me*, Bill is not coming 'home to the land of . . . forefathers' and the film's narrative makes it clear that it is not through his new wife's Irishness that his visit is a return. Rather it is through an inherent quality of Ireland itself that Bill experiences the country as 'home'.

Modernity and Diasporic Memory

This cross-generational possibility of closing the circle of emigration by completing the journey 'home' through tourism again raises interesting questions about the nature of the concept of time and memory under the colonial experience of emigration, exile and diaspora. The understanding that, for the Irish diaspora, even a first visit to Ireland is a return, contains within it the clear implication that under these conditions, time is not to be understood in purely linear terms and that memory is of more than personal, first-hand experiences. This implication complicates the classic touristic trope of depicting the journey through space to the tourist destination as also being a journey back through time. As O'Connor (1997: 75–6) among others has commented, such a representation of the destination is typical of tourist imagery and certainly has been particularly striking in Irish tourism, no matter which category of tourists have been the target market. The depiction of Ireland in terms of a pre-modern idyll for visitors (and, by implication, for the Irish too) is one of the most consistently recurring themes of the nation's tourist imagery. This process has its roots within colonial imaginings of Ireland, in which the land and its people were co-opted into the Romantic vision of unspoilt landscapes and equally unspoilt inhabitants, whose culture had not been fractured by the 'civilisation' of modernity. Thus Ireland, for the imperial visitor, represented the possibility of cultural renewal, even while this positioning of the Irish and their land also provided justification for a continuation of the imperial project. The leisurely pace of Irish life, and its promise to the visitor of the opportunity to escape from the pressures of modern, work-dominated life, is a central feature of Irish tourism's representation of the country. So the 1966 film, *Ireland Invites You*, produced by Bord Fáilte, begins with the statement,

> This is Ireland, a green island set in the seas like a gem of a rare beauty, a haven of undisturbed peace in a restless world, a land of infinite variety of scenes, an ageless, timeless place where old beliefs and customs live on beside the spreading tide of human progress.

Such images, of a country apparently cut off from the instability and loss of cultural authenticity which is associated with the modern world, are typical of the tourist advertising of many countries. As MacCannell (1989: 3) points out, it is precisely this possibility of recapturing the lost 'authenticity', which the West has believed to have existed in its own 'golden age' of Edenic innocence before the onset of modernity, which inspires many tourists in their choice of destination. MacCannell asserts:

> The progress of modernity ('modernization') depends on its very sense of instability and inauthenticity. For moderns, reality and authenticity are thought to be elsewhere: in other historical periods and other cultures, in purer, simpler lifestyles. In other words, the concern of moderns for 'naturalness', their nostalgia and their search for authenticity are not merely casual and somewhat decadent, though harmless, attachments to the souvenirs of destroyed cultures and dead epochs. They are also components of the conquering spirit of modernity – the grounds of its unifying consciousness.

If one of the principal motivations of tourists is to attempt to step back across the historical divide between themselves and the time which they perceive as having been more 'authentic' and, in particular, as having possessed a cultural coherence, then it is obvious that potential destinations will seek to market themselves as still existing in this mythical past. Therefore, the descriptions of Ireland as 'a haven of undisturbed peace in a restless world', and the accompanying images of undeveloped landscapes and such indicators of pre-modern lifestyles as thatched cottages and horse-drawn transport, are consistent with attempts to commodify a nation's history which are common within the tourist industry across the world.

However, when the audience for these images of Ireland is the Irish diaspora, it would seem that there is more to this process than the 'inauthentic' commodification of the past. If that diaspora's memory is understood to be collective and cross-generational, then the images of Ireland as 'traditional' and un-modern are not necessarily anachronistic within the terms of their process of memory and recovery. While the Ireland described by *Ireland Invites You*'s voice-over may not be 'timeless', it was perhaps not unreasonable to recognise that for diasporic tourists, their contact with Ireland, constructed as it was as an 'original' return, was primarily governed by the events of a previous era and, therefore, a recovery of memory which was simultaneously personal and historically collective. Again, this process is a result of the diasporic narrative of images and memories created by the cultural dislocation of emigration discussed earlier.

Such a touristic act, therefore, cannot be so easily dismissed as to characterise it in terms of an uninformed and romanticised consumption of 'heritage' without context or meaning, as critics of tourism often attempt to do. An indication of the greater complexity of the experience of diasporic tourists can be seen in the representations of modernity within the very tourist texts which also contain such 'traditional' images of Ireland. Despite the emphasis upon the country's apparently 'timeless' qualities, the process of modernisation is not only screened within the promotional tourist films, it is actively eulogised, and often in contexts which have no obvious relevance to the practice of tourism.

Honeymoon in Ireland, for example, actively plays with the image of Ireland as a pre-modern idyll of peasant life. When Bill and Mary, the honeymoon couple, first arrive at Dublin Airport, it is explained that Mary has already arranged for a hire car to be waiting for them. This information is immediately followed by a shot of a 'vintage' 1930s car waiting outside the terminal building as the couple emerge. After lingering on this car for a moment, the camera then follows Bill and Mary past it, to the brand-new red open-top sports car which is to be their hire car. In this visual joke, the film simultaneously acknowledges and challenges the currency of the 'thatched cottage' image of Ireland presumed to be familiar to the American visitor.

This example of the inclusion of modernity within tourist narratives does at least have obvious connections to the practice of tourism in which the industry was required, in its construction of national representation, to balance the advantages of promoting pastoral and pre-modern images of Ireland against the need to reassure visitors (particularly, perhaps, those from America) that their holiday will not be marred by a lack of 'modern conveniences'. The same motivation would appear to be in evidence in another promotional film, *O'Hara's Holiday* (although the exact date of the film is unknown, the Irish Film Archive classify it as dating from the 1950s and the film's visual clues strongly support this classification). The eponymous hero, a New York policeman visiting Ireland for the first time, begins an extended eulogy to Shannon Airport. His explanation of the principles of duty free shopping as being a modern Irish invention – and one of great benefit to the world – appears at first to be located purely within the internal logic of tourist promotion. However, after explaining that 'Shannon isn't just an airport – it's an idea', O'Hara goes on to describe some of the finer points of the tax incentives for foreign companies setting up and investing in the airport complex, a narrative which is accompanied by a number of distinctly unpastoral shots of modern industrial development at Shannon. Following this, *O'Hara's Holiday* then easily returns to images of nearby Bunratty Castle, with its romantic and historical associations.

This blending of the modern and the traditional in the representation of Ireland to its diaspora points towards the need for a more careful interpretation of the description in *Ireland Invites You* of the country as 'an ageless, timeless place where old beliefs and customs live on beside the spreading tide of human progress'. The crucial wording in this description, therefore, appears to be the use of the term 'beside', suggesting parallel and simultaneous time within the visitor's experience of the nation. This, in turn, appears to reflect the complex experience of time and memory of the 're-turning' Irish-American, in which the Ireland they encounter is both their own present and the past of their collective diasporic memory.

The nature of that collective memory, for a second or third generation Irish diaspora, is significant within the context in which it is generated and reflected in their contact with Ireland itself. By the nature of cross-generational cultural transmission, much of the understanding and experience of Irish-Americans' Irish identity is necessarily through the medium of the image, be it film, photography or narrative. This process is even more pronounced in the diasporic 'recollection' of Ireland (as distinct from their diasporic Irish identity within America) for those generations who have never previously been there. In the 20th century and for Irish-Americans in particular, while a considerable amount of their cultural identification would have come from narratives within their community such as family and other first-generation immigrants, they would also have acquired an extensive exposure to images of Ireland, primarily through the medium of film.

Narrative and Diasporic Identity

As described earlier, the use of fictional characters, strong narrative and even flash-back sequences in the tourist films of the 1950s which were designed to appeal to the growing market of Irish-American visitors to Ireland indicates a recognition by the industry of the importance of filmic images as a source of community identity formation. The use of these devices appears to be predicated on an explicit understanding that, for second- and third-generation Irish-Americans, the principal source of their images of the 'home' country had been that of Hollywood films and, as such, their concept of that home was already structured by narratives and fictional characterisation. A particularly striking example of the 'cross-fertilisation' between the feature film industry and the tourist industry in Ireland is an American-produced tourist film of the 1950s, *The Spell of Ireland*.[2] Narrated principally by Jack McCarthy, the film, which at 58 minutes was uncharacteristically long for a travelogue, is structured in the form of a tour around Ireland, highlighting not only the major tourist attractions of different regions but also facets of Irish life which are clearly considered to be of interest to the audience even though they do not have obvious connections to tourist activity.

The narrator, who does not appear within the film, acts as a guide for the audience through the travelogue. It is noticeable that the film's journey around Ireland is geographically disjointed; rather than constructing its movement in the form of a tour which visiting tourists might follow, it jumps from location to location and doubles back on itself. This is unusual for films constructed as a tour of the country and suggests that rather than providing practical information for visitors to Ireland, it has instead constructed the nation as a location in a filmic sense, in which geographical positionings are secondary to the events being shown in them.

The Spell of Ireland is not constructed around a narrative in the same way as *Honeymoon in Ireland* or even *O'Hara's Holiday* is. The narrator not only does not appear within the film but neither is he narrating for the viewer the 'story' of a particular journey to Ireland as those other films did. Instead, *The Spell of Ireland* appears to be inspired, to a large extent, by the documentary tradition of American television and also by the spirit of entertaining education which informed the *National Geographic*'s project, as described by Lutz and Collins (1993). There is a scene of traditional Irish dancing at a crossroads, for example, which has anthropological overtones in its lengthy and unnarrated camera shots. There is also a lengthy episode of the film shot at a Croagh Patrick pilgrimage. This section of the film is dramatically untouristic in its focus on the dedication, devotion and physical suffering of the pilgrims in appalling weather conditions, showing them collapsing, encountering accidents on the mountain due to exhaustion and being rescued by medical teams. The musical score and the tone of Jack McCarthy's voice changes significantly during this section of the film to one of sombre respect and awe for the devotion of the pilgrims. The pilgrimage is not portrayed as being accessible to tourists as a potential source of entertainment or pleasure and is instead treated as a serious religious experience. This reinforces the documentary nature of *The Spell of Ireland* and its apparent aim of informing its audience about the culture of Ireland.

However, in the later section of the film, the 'tour' reaches Donegal, which the narrator describes as his home county, therefore having special memories and associations for him. At this point, not only the tone but the entire structure of the film changes abruptly. Unintroduced, Helena Carroll (a well-known member of The Irish Players theatre group in the United States) takes over the narrative in the guise of Jack McCarthy's mother, reminding him of his childhood and family home. In a direct reference to the scene in *The Quiet Man* in which Sean Thornton returns to Inisfree and first sees his family cottage, the narration of *The Spell of Ireland* continues: 'Ah yes, Seaneen, you've been gone a long time, but your roots are still in Ireland. You were born in that little cottage and it was your sister who kept the cottage going for all you wains . . . '. The film then continues for the next ten minutes to portray the narrator's childhood, in the form of a flashback using staged footage of scenes from village life in Ireland, still narrated by his 'mother', who like McCarthy himself, remains unseen on screen. This flashback sequence takes the form of childhood 'memories' of gathering hay in the fields, village festivals and specific individuals, such as a young man whom the narration informs us is now a policeman in New York. The flashback sequence (and his mother's narration) ends with the words, 'Ah, Seaneen, those were your happy, carefree days in Ireland', and the film then continues its documentary tone, moving immediately on to scenes of the horse-show at the Royal Dublin Showground, including shots of President O'Kelly's attendance, before showing an interview with Eamon de Valera about his continuing aspirations for a united Ireland.

This departure from the documentary travelogue style of the preceding sections of the film indicates a number of manoeuvres within the text. First, there is the sudden introduction of a fictional narrative at the point at which the narrator announces that within the film he has returned to his home, as opposed to the documentary tone of the earlier sections. Second, there is the expectation that the audience will be so familiar with *The Quiet Man* that the film's reference to it remains unexplained. Significantly, this reference occurs at the very moment at which the narrator drops the role of an objective and informative guide to the facts of Irish life in order to adopt a more personal and evocative narration of his own history. Not only is his voice displaced by that of this mother in order to effect such a transformation but without explanation, she refers to him as Seaneen, rather than Jack. This introduction of a clearly fictional and narrativised section into the film at the very point at which the subject of individual history and memory is raised points to the centrality within that diasporic memory of the fictional narratives of Hollywood films such as *The Quiet Man*. And within both *The Quiet Man* and travel films such as *The Spell of Ireland*, there is a significant manoeuvre in which diasporic memory is delineated as non-individual and always already fictionalised through the inherited, second-hand processes by which it is acquired.

Conclusion

In conclusion, I would suggest that the Irish-American diaspora's engagement with Ireland is not indicative of an anti-modern romanticism that is to be compared with a realistic and modern Irishness. Rather, in this context, the nostalgia evident within the diasporic gaze should be seen as the self-interrogating framework through which the diaspora negotiates a reconciliation between its narrativised collective history and its engagement with contemporary Ireland.

I would also suggest that the act of tourism, as well as its associated texts, particularly the visual ones, forms an essential and inherently meaningful aspect of this reconciliation. As this chapter has described, the convergence between widely available international tourism for many US citizens in the aftermath of the Second World War, and the rapid expansion of the American-born Irish population, created an important new dynamic in the relationship between Ireland and its largest diaspora. Where, prior to this era, that diaspora's understanding of their cultural relationship to the 'old country' had been predominantly constructed through the use of narratives (fictional or historical), the advent of mass tourism provided the opportunity for those narratives to be experienced within the context of contemporary Ireland. This experience appears to have had a significant impact upon both the structures of the Irish tourism industry itself and upon the diasporic relationship to the country. On the one hand, the centrality of narrative themes and forms to the currently dominant cultural and heritage attractions of the present-day tourism industry could be argued to have many of its roots in the highly specific needs of diaspora tourists. These tourists' contact with Ireland was preceded by and predicated on a circulation of collective narratives. This has perhaps influenced the contemporary reliance upon narrativised cultural attractions. On the other hand, the modern relationships and identity constructions negotiated between Ireland and its diaspora may be attributed, at least in part, to processes of tourism. That process of diasporic tourism to the 'home' country has allowed for an exploration of the complex temporal and spatial connections between Irish and Irish-American culture.

Notes
1. For information on the production and distribution policies regarding the tourism films of this period, the author is grateful for the assistance of both Bill Morrison and Derek Cullen of Bord Fáilte.
2. The exact date of the film is unknown. Its US distributors advertise it as 'a visit to the Ireland of the 1940s' and indeed some of its sequences may well be from that period. However, the visual clues of other sections, along with the film's few historical references, suggest that the film was completed and released in the 1950s, most probably during the administration of de Valera's 1951–54 government.

Filmography
Carefree Ireland (1959) Colm O'Laoghaire (dir.). Bord Fáilte, Ireland.
Honeymoon in Ireland (1963) Bord Fáilte, Ireland.
Ireland Invites You (1966) James Mulkerns (dir.). Bord Fáilte, Ireland.
The Irish in Me (1959) Herman Boxer (dir.). Universal International Colour/Dudley Pictures, United States.
The Quiet Man (1952) John Ford (dir.). Republic Studios, United States.
O'Hara's Holiday (1950s) Peter Bryan (dir.). Tribune Films Inc., Ireland/United States.
The Spell of Ireland (1950s) Danny Devlin (dir.). Celtic Films, United States.

References
Boorstin, Daniel (1961) *The Image: A Guide to Pseudo-events in America*. New York: Harper & Row.
Casey, Marian (1998) *Ireland, New York and the Irish image in American popular culture, 1890–1960*. DPhil. thesis, New York University.
Curtis, Barry and Pajaczkowska Claire (1994) 'Getting there': Travel, time and narrative. In George Robertson (ed.) *Traveler's Tales: Narratives of Home and Displacement*. London: Routledge.
Deegan, James and Dineen, Donal A. (1997) *Tourism Policy and Performance: The Irish Experience*. London: International Thomson Business Press.
Gallagher, Mia (1989) Landscape & Bord Fáilte Films. *Circa* (Dec./Jan.) 43.
Gibbons, Luke (1987) Romanticism, realism and Irish cinema. In Kevin Rockett, Luke Gibbons and John Hill (eds) *Cinema and Ireland*. London: Croom Helm.
Hewison, R (1987) *The Heritage Industry*. London: Methuen.
Lowenthal, D (1985) *The Past is a Foreign Country*. Cambridge: Cambridge University Press.

Lutz, Catherine A. and Collins, Jane L. (1993) *Reading National Geographic*. Chicago: University of Chicago Press.

MacCannell, Dean (1989) *The Tourist: A New Theory of the Leisure Class*. New York: Schoken Books.

McCarten, John (1952) *The New Yorker*, 23 August.

O'Connor, Barbara (1997) Myths and mirrors: Tourist images and national identity. In Barbara O'Connor, and Michael Cronin (eds) *Tourism in Ireland: A Critical Analysis*. Rpt. Cork: Cork University Press.

Place, J.A. (1979) *The Non-Western Films of John Ford*. New Jersey: Citadel Press.

The Irish Independent, (1952) 19 May.

Urry, John (1990) *The Tourist Gaze: Leisure and Travel in Contemporary Societies*. London: Sage.

Chapter 11

Photography, Tourism and Natural History: Cultural Identity and the Visualisation of the Natural World

JUSTIN CARVILLE

Introduction

What does the discipline of natural history have to do with tourism? On the surface very little except that naturalists were required to travel in order to carry out fieldwork on surveys. These travels may have been a simple trip along the coast or into a neighbouring county or a major expedition to the European colonies (Wilson Foster, 1997a: 321–5). Either way throughout the 19th century naturalists became part of the growing number of tourists, trippers and travellers who criss-crossed Europe, North America and the Colonies on the expanding rail and sea networks. It is not just these physical aspects of travel that linked natural history to tourism however. Throughout the Victorian-era, physical mobility came to be equated with social mobility as the middle classes turned to tourism as another popular leisure activity. However, as the 19th century came to a close legislative changes in the length of the working week combined with cheaper rail fares, brought the middle classes increasingly into contact with the working classes who flocked to seaside resorts on the weekends and bank holidays (Urry, 1990: 16–42). This middle class embrace of tourism thus brought with it anxieties concerning class distinctions and fear of encounters with the lower classes outside of the domestic and industrial workplaces of the home and the factory floor. In order to distance themselves from this other class of tourist, the middle classes pursued activities that made their class position clear to both themselves and others while travelling in the natural world. Natural history was just one of a number of activities that could be used to signal class and social standing.

This chapter sets out to explore the role of natural history in middle-class tourism in Ireland. In particular, it takes as its focus the intersection of representations of tourism in photographs and natural history travelogues produced for the amateur natural historian. The examination of photography here will not just be on its use as a popular leisure activity of the middle and ascending classes but on its use to represent the activities of the tourist while travelling in the natural world. Tourism, photography and natural history would appear to sit comfortably with one another as inter-related activities in which the natural world has increasingly been brought into contact with the cultural. As tourism and natural history have brought culture to bear on the physical aspects of nature, photography has taken the natural world into the life spaces of society. In this seemingly reciprocal act nature has been transformed into its opposite and the natural world has come to be understood through the cultural.[1] The social construction of nature has been embedded in Ireland's social and political past. From literary texts to cartography, nature in Ireland as it has been represented through images from the scientific and cultural world has never been distant from the concerns of political and cultural identity (Andrews, 1997). This chapter looks at the social construction of nature in Ireland through its representation in tourism and natural history and sets out to explore the connections between cultural identity and the natural world. In particular it examines the use of photography in scientific and tourist accounts of the natural world and questions the popular belief that there is a clear distinction between the scientific and tourist discourses that framed the photographic image in the late Victorian and early Edwardian era.

The rise of natural history as a popular leisure pursuit amongst the urban ascending and middle classes coincides with a cultural revival that incorporated the study and collection of Irish folklore, antiquities and literature throughout the closing decades of the 19th and opening decades of the 20th century. The relationship between scientific field study and this cultural revival has been examined by a number of cultural historians, in particular John Wilson Foster and Sean Lysaght within the context of Ireland's literary culture (Wilson Foster, 1987; 1990: 61–9; 1991: 92–103; 1997a; Lysaght, 1989: 68–74; 1997a; 1998). However, little attention has been given to the relationship between natural history and the nation's visual culture. The articulation of cultural and national identity cannot simply be reduced to the relationship between intellectuals and their thought. Identity is mediated and formed through the material world in which it is expressed and experienced. Amongst the numerous volumes of journals, books and reports produced to promote tourism and the study of nature, numerous illustrations and photographs are to be found. This chapter therefore sets to examine the use of photography in Irish natural history and tourist publications. In particular, it focuses on the relationship between William Lloyd Praeger and Robert John Welch, who individually and collectively produced a number of travelogues, brochures and illustrated articles for Ireland's railway companies and natural history organisations, designed to promote tourism and rail travel for the Irish naturalist.

Central to the concerns of this study is the role of photography in natural history at a time when both the discipline's amateur traditions were being questioned amid growing concerns over leisure and class distinctions. The examination of photography in natural history, therefore, will not solely revolve around the recording of specimens from the natural world, it will also examine the use of photography to present a self-image of the naturalist in that world. An essential feature of the establishment of cultural identity is recognising one's outward appearance in the material forms of cultural expression. It is only through the acknowledgement of one's embodied outward appearance in what Mikhail Bakhtin calls the 'plastic pictorial world' that a sense of cultural identity can be fully realised (Bakhtin, 1990: 28). As Luke Gibbons (1996: 10) notes, this emphasis upon the material forms of cultural practices have:

> important consequences in reconsidering the relations between culture and history in Ireland, particularly as they impinge on the deeply contested issues of cultural and national identity. It is clear from this approach that identity does not just involve consciousness, or even self-consciousness, but also the realm of representation, i.e. the capacity to be realised in material form.

Interest in Irish cultural and national identity by the Protestant middle classes was, by and large, self-serving. Their interests were not directed at the nation as a whole but in a particular group and community of people whose overriding concern was for administrative and economic independence rather than complete political autonomy. As a consequence, their forms of literary and visual representation were produced for and consumed by this particular group of people, largely the Protestant industrial and commercial classes. Recent theoretical writings on the photographic image have tended to focus on the discourses of representation or the contexts in which the flow of meaning has been conventionalised through the photographic image. Such critical approaches have been at the expense of a consideration of the photograph as a tangible object. That is to say, as a physical object that is exchanged freely or commercially between individuals or groups, who have an interest in these discourses of representation (Sekula, 1982). From this perspective, it is important to note that the codes that are identifiable in these images are part of a system of exchange between a particular group of people, and it is within this exchange that the photographs become meaningful. Photographs exist, are consumed and ultimately reside in life spaces such as the family album, the wallet or the drawing room wall. For those who are either represented in or are consumers of these photographic images, it is in these types of domestic spaces which exist between the margins of the public and private sphere that photographs, despite critiques of their conventional uses, have a very real and significant role to play in the understanding of cultural identity.

In the discussion that follows, I wish to examine the function of photography in establishing a sense of cultural identity amongst the emerging middle and ascending classes particularly within the contested fields of amateurism, leisure and tourism. It is through these links of amateurism, leisure and representation that this study will explore the relationship between tourism and natural history during the closing decades of the 19th and opening decades of the 20th century.

Tracing Natures: Photography, Tourism and Natural History

The discourses that have come to define tourism's and natural history's representations of the natural world have themselves, in turn, been naturalised through the photographic image. Photography's status as a trace of the real, its indexical relationship to its referent, the 'thing' photographed, is not merely a result of the discourses in which the photograph operates and is put to use. Throughout the 19th century the ontology of the photographic image was conceived as the instantaneous or spontaneous production of nature. From its very conception photography's inventors struggled to articulate photographic reproduction through images from the natural world. From William Henry Fox Talbot's (1839) description of objects 'delineating themselves' to Sir John Herschel's coining of the term photography, the descriptive history of the medium has been bound up with metaphors of nature (Batchen, 1993). The articulation of photography as a discursive practice, as it emerged during the early 19th century, was rooted in the Enlightenment's concern with the natural world (Batchen, 1991: 15–17). Unlike other forms of representation, literary and visual, photography was not considered as a conventionalised means of representing nature, it was nature itself.

This mapping of nature onto photography has, of course, had a significant impact on the cultural interpretation of photographic representations of the natural world in both natural history and tourism. If photography's use in tourism and natural history are considered separately however, their representations of the natural world would appear to have very little in common. Tourism's representations of the natural world have predominately been articulated through the gaze upon the landscape. From personal snapshots to consumerist picture postcards, tourist representations of nature have traditionally been associated with visual mastery of the natural world. Here nature is framed by the ocular metaphors of representation. Each tourist may bring their individual stories to the photograph's representation of the landscape but such stories are embedded with the descriptive tropes of 'picturesque' and 'picture perfect' that assist the tourist to make sense of their experience of natural world.[2]

Such photographs are also entirely mutable and open to interpretation, existing uneasily between the private domain of the tourist's memory and the public sphere of cultural determination. Natural history's representation of the natural world, however, would appear to be immune to the kinds of shifting cultural determinants associated with tourist photography of the landscape. If tourist representations are concerned with the whole of nature, natural history could be said to be interested in its parts. Unlike the picturesque tourist, the natural historian's representations of the natural world is premised on observation of the immediately visible objects of nature. In natural history the objects of nature in order to become known are collected, accumulated and then separated out into their discursive categories (Foucault, 1989: 157). Through these positivist discursive practices, natural history photography has been brought through the natural world into the seemingly impartial framework of scientific knowledge.[3] Within this epistemological framework, natural history photography is merely a vehicle through which the objects of nature delineate themselves upon the blank space of the photographic image. The mimetic function of photography, that is to say its ability not only to represent but to replicate, also came to be used as a means to naturalise the evolving discourses of the physical and social sciences. As Roland Barthes (1977: 21) reminds us, it is photography's ability to take on 'the objective mask of denotation' that has given it that special status as a trace of the real.

Within Victorian culture then, it could possibly be argued that there can be identified a clear distinction between conceptions of photography in the world of science and those in the realm of picturesque tourism. In natural history, photography is regarded as an objective trace of the natural world, the instantaneous production of nature itself. In tourism, photography is seen as an 'interpretive' representation of nature, extending and altering the trace of natural world to fit it into the cultural. Such a rigid demarcation however, fails to acknowledge the mutability of the photographic image. The photographic trace of nature may leave distinct lines across the page but the boundaries between the systems of exchange in which they operate are far from clear.

Natural history and tourist photographs are themselves represented through their own set of distinct discourses, the latter through the language of culture, the former the language of science. An examination of natural history in Ireland during the two decades on either side of the turn of the 19th century, however, reveals that the representation of nature is in no way insulated from the types of cultural influence we expect to find in tourist representations of the natural world. As Sean Lysaght (1997a: 440) has argued, the field of natural history cannot be isolated from the concerns of cultural and political identity. Even scientific nomenclature is not impervious to the cultural relationships people have with the natural world. For a particular group of amateur natural historians who travelled across the country to study and classify the nation's geology, flora and fauna, the boundaries between tourism, natural history and cultural identity increasingly collapsed and merged in their written accounts and visual representations of the natural world. In the preface to his *Tourist's Flora of The West of Ireland* for example, Praeger (1909: vi) writes of the districts covered:

> The Burren, the Cliffs of Moher, Lough Derg, the Aran Islands, Conemara, Achill, Lough Gill, Ben Bulben, Lough Erne, are names widely known to the scientific and non-scientific. To the botanist these names suggest visions of alpine plants growing in sheets down to the edge of the Atlantic, of meadows filled with the Canadian 'Blue-eyed Grass', of wild bogs clothed with beautiful heaths unknown elsewhere in the British Isles, of limestone ledges bright with the blossoms of Arenaria Cilitata, pods full of the curious flowers of the American Pipewart, and lakeshores starred with the golden heads of Inula Salicina.

Praeger's descriptive account of these western regions slides in and out of the scientific observation and identification of flora and the gaze of the picturesque tourist. For Praeger, the natural historian's identification of botanical features would appear to be concomitant with the tourist's gaze and his/her visual mastery of the natural world.

Like Praeger's text, Welch's photographs, which appeared as illustrations in many travelogues produced for the amateur natural historian, were not devoid of the duality of botanical and tourist discourse. Welch's photographs of *Dryas Octopela* near Black Head Co. Clare (Figure 11.1), which appeared in *A Tourist's Flora*, is not typical of the type of botanical illustration that isolated the specimen for the scrutinising gaze of the natural historian. Such images, like Welch's photographs of *Spiranthes Romanzoviana* (Irish lady's-tresses) (Figure 11.2), identified by Praeger during a sustained period of botanical field-work in Armagh during the summer of 1892, is more indicative of this type of natural history illustration (Lysaght, 1998: 33–4).

Such imagery was produced with very different uses and contexts in mind, the latter within the institutionalised framework of the scientific

Figure 11.1 Robert John Welch's *Dryas Octopela* near Black Head, Co. Clare from *A Tourist's Flora of the West of Ireland*, 1909. (Reproduced by courtesy of the National Library of Ireland.)

archive, the former in the increasingly commercialised field of tourism. Scientific illustration, however, was not such a static and rigid practice. As observation of botanical specimens moved out of the institutionalised spaces of the museum and the academy into the natural world itself, scientific illustration had to evolve to incorporate the changing discourses of natural history. There was a discernible shift in natural history illustration during the 19th century, which impacted upon the constituted spaces in which the objects of nature were scrutinised (Knight, 1998: 113). A shift that saw the act of representing natural history specimens displaced from the scientific institution, only to emerge in the more expansive spaces of the natural world itself. Such theoretical problems in the discourse of scientific representation also become visual ones that had to be resolved in scientific illustration. The divergent discourses of tourism and botanical classification were thus not so polarised as to be incorporated in Welch's photographs of *Dryas Octopela*. The photograph establishes and attaches a sense of location to the scientifically classified botanical specimen. It situates the identified object of the natural historian's scrutinising gaze within the broader spatial field of the landscape.

Figure 11.2 Robert John Welch '*Spiranthes Romanzoviana*' 1892. (Photograph reproduced with the kind permission of the Trustees of the Museums and Galleries of Northern Ireland.)

The establishment of location in Welch's photograph has a dual function here. First it provides a visually represented space that accommodates the antithetical gazes of the natural historian and the picturesque tourist. It is interesting to note that the positivist and Romantic conceptions of the gaze have been formulated within similar historical junctures. Foucault's (1975: 107) conception of the 'clinical' or 'observing' gaze, as he articulates it in *The Birth of the Clinic*, becomes embedded within the deep structures of the medical sciences throughout the late 18th century, around the same period when the eye began to displace the ear as the dominant sensory experience of tourism. As Judith Adler (1989: 22) has noted, it was not until the 18th century that the Romantic gaze began to dictate the ritual of the tourist's appropriation of the landscape. The landscape in Welch's photograph is thus represented as a space in which the scientifically trained eye of the natural historian and the aesthetically cultivated gaze of the tourist intersect.

Second, Welch's photograph of *Dryas Octopela* puts Praeger's discourse into pictures, bringing the scientific appropriation of the landscape into a material visual form that the ascending and middle-class amateurs could recognise as culturally significant. Drawing attention to the contrasting position of Praeger's scientifically mediated landscape to that which sits more comfortably with nationalist sentiments, Sean Lysaght (1989: 71–2) has demonstrated that the Protestant socialised landscape with its emphasis on discipline and order has, at its roots, the mapping of Ireland's botanical and geological territory as something which has its own identity within the broader spectrum of natural history. Welch's pictorial representation places the botanical specimen within the Western Irish landscape, providing the generically named object with an indigenous location. For the amateur naturalists who accompanied Praeger in his tourist travelogues into the rural landscape, the collection and identification of Ireland's geology and botany was one of a number of outlets in which to express their interests in all things Irish. Welch's photograph provided a pictorial emphasis to Praeger's scientific/picturesque rhetoric that the amateur natural historian could recognise as an expression of their shared understanding of the Irish landscape.

Amateurism, Photography and Natural History

Today, the notion of amateurism carries a certain derogatory inflection in its common usage and is generally understood to have two distinct meanings. On one hand, it has retained that connotation of something which is done outside of one's profession. In this sense it is associated with individual or group activities carried out beyond the workplace. On the other hand, it is also understood to categorise ineptness, associating it with the activities of dabblers or dilettantes and not serious devotees. Throughout most of the 19th century, however, amateurism had a very different set of meanings that brought it well beyond the sense of an avid enthusiast. For those who were geologists, botanists or astronomers, being an amateur was considered as something very special indeed. Unlike its contemporary pejorative meaning, amateurism retained the notion of having the education, leisure and means to apply oneself without the need of financial gain to a chosen activity. Significantly, it was considered as something which necessitated the investment of labour outside of the regulated measures of production with many modern professions in the sciences and arts originating as just one of the cultivated interests of the aristocratic gentleman (Sebbins, 1979: 21).

The rise of natural history in Ireland, particularly in Belfast and later in Dublin during the mid- to late-19th century, occurred during a period when the traditional amateur disciplines associated with the arts and sciences were steadily being professionalised and incorporated into the bureaucratic structures of the universities and academies throughout Britain and Ireland (Bennett, 1997: 39). The 1877 Dublin Science and Art Museum Act, for example, saw the Science and Art Department at Westminster take control of the Royal Dublin Society's library and major scientific collections ushering in a more bureaucratic and centralised administration (Jarrell, 1983: 339). However, these administrative changes rarely brought about a cultural transformation in the organisation of these activities. In his study of the organisation of science in Britain throughout the 18th and 19th centuries, Morris Berman (1975: 34) has argued that although the professional middle classes eventually prevailed in their struggle for control of the cultural and scientific world over the aristocracy, they conformed to the old order rather than rebelled against it. The amateur ethos of many scientific and cultural fields thus remained in place throughout the 19th century.

Whether or not Irish natural history was as subsumed into the administrative structures of the professional institutes as their British counterparts is open to debate (see Bennett, 1997: 39; Lysaght, 1997a: 157; MacLeod, 1997: 9–13); but certainly within the country's field clubs, the amateur ethos appears to have prevailed. Membership of the Belfast Naturalist Field Club, which was founded in 1863, was almost exclusively made up of the mostly Protestant middle classes[4] and as with its counterpart, the Dublin Naturalists Field Club founded 23 years later, retained its links to the amateur traditions normally identified with the 18th-century aristocracy.[5]

Photography, too, had become subject to fluctuating changes in its social organisation during the last two decades of the 19th century. Soon after the announcement of the Daguerreotype in Paris and Fox Talbot's 'photogenic drawing' in London, the aristocratic amateurs established themselves as arbiters of photographic style and technique. As a result, developments in photographic equipment and processes throughout photography's initial years were largely the result of experimentation by the aristocratic gentlemen who combined photography with their other scientific and artistic activities.

Although the historical canon is dominated by the names of aristocratic gentlemen during the early period a significant number of women also made valuable contributions to photography's early development. In an Irish context there are a number of prominent examples of amateurs who combined photography with their other scientific interests. Louisa Tenison along with her husband Edward King Tenison became one of the first people in the Britain and Ireland to acquire a licence from Fox Talbot in 1851 (see Davidson, 1989; McKenna-Lawlor, 1998). One of Ireland's most celebrated amateur scientists and photographers of the Victorian era, Mary Countess of Rosse, took up photography as early as 1842. Countess Rosse, who along with her husband had a long association with photography, attempted to combine an interest in astronomy with photography from an early stage. After some initial setbacks, the Rosses managed to take photographs of the moon through the great telescope at Birr castle in 1854, after Lord Rosse forwarded calotypes to Fox Talbot seeking technical advice on how to best achieve their aim (McKenna-Lawlor, 1998: 22).

By the mid-1880s, however, the aristocracy had lost its monopoly on the social organisation of photography. The increased industrialisation and manufacturing of photographic plates and equipment, combined with the foundation of photographic clubs and societies throughout most European cities, brought photography into the cultural sphere of the nascent middle classes who quickly incorporated it into their repertoire of leisure activities. Apart from the major photographic societies such as the one founded in Dublin in 1854, which later became the Photographic Society of Ireland,[6] many other amateur organisations established photographic societies and committees to document their members' activities. The natural history organisations were no exception and from the late 1880s the Belfast Naturalists Field Club, in particular, became interested in systematically organising the photographic activities of its members. These committees and photographic sub-sections of the Field Clubs became outlets for continued experimentation in photography by amateurs who wished to explore its capabilities and restrictions in recording the natural world. A paper read at the Belfast Natural History and Philosophical Society in 1889, for example, gave details of the results obtained by John Brown (1989: 86) in producing figures by the discharge of electricity through an induction coil onto photographic dry plates. The *Irish Naturalist* also published a paper by Greenwood Pim in 1892, outlining details on how to record botanical specimens without the aid of a camera (Pim, 1892: 25–8). Both Brown and Pim's cameraless images are, in Pim's own terminology, concerned with 'obtaining photographic transcripts of natural history'[7] those traces of nature that had pre-occupied conceptions of photography during its initial years.

The first committee appointed to record the antiquities of the North of Ireland systematically and organise the photographic activities of its members was established after a motion forwarded by Robert Lloyd Praeger at the Belfast Naturalists Field Club's 27th annual meeting in 1890 (Anon 1890/91a: 231–3). The Committee, which when established consisted of William Swanston, George and John Donaldson and the Belfast Naturalists Field Club President William Gray, reported its progress at the club's following annual meeting, outlining details of instructions which had been issued to members regarding procedures to be followed in their photographic activities. The recommendations made in the committee's report had already been pre-empted by Swanston who, at a meeting during the winter session of the club in January 1889, made a number of detailed suggestions for the use of photography in the club's geological, archaeological and botanical excursions. Swanston's paper (1888–89: 131–2), which began by complimenting the pedagogical role of the Club's reports and proceedings reproduced in the popular press for the wider public, put forward an argument for photography's use in recording the archaeological remains of the country's monuments.

> Photography is a comparatively new art-science, and the more recent introduction of dry plates has so simplified it, and made it easily available for field use, that it has suddenly sprung into prominence and taken a firm hold on the public taste. As one of the popular and fascinating pursuits, archaeology, where truthfulness in delineating every detail is such an essential, is especially a field in which photography can render aid. Our district –which, be it remembered, is all Ireland – is particularly rich in monuments of its early inhabitants – monuments too, with a character and richness almost impossible to delineate with pencil and brush, but for which the camera seems specially designed.

Swanston's main concern was the lack of a clear categorisation for those Field Club members who combined photography with their diverse field work in archaeology, botany and geology. Almost in exacerbation he later states of these growing band of naturalists:

> At present there is no place for them; they do not fit into any departments properly. True the club has a series of photo albums, and offers annually prizes for these; but there is a lack of system even in this. (Swanston, 1888/89: 133)

It would appear that it was the task of the natural historian not only to collect, categorise and put into some semblance of order the natural world, but also his own place within it. Yet regardless of this need for a systematic and clearly defined role for photography in natural history, Swanston's conception of it belied such taxonomic desires. Despite focusing attention on its optical veracity, Swanston's conception of photography is still that of a bastardisation of art and science. It is a concept that dominated opinion on photography throughout the Victorian era. Photography thus appealed to Victorian public taste, attracted as it was to its cultural significance as a Romantic form of representing the familiar and everyday. A value judgement could thus be placed on photography that revolved around the pleasure of looking and popular notions of leisure. This Romantic idealism that can be identified in Victorian conceptions of photography was also accompanied by the philosophical discourse of positive realism (Kolakowski, 1972: 60–89). Popular consciousness of the medium was thus simultaneously rooted in conceptions of photography as fact, an object of the Victorian culture of realism.

It would be wrong, however, to consider these conceptions of the photographic image, Romantic and positivist as being polarised within the Victorian attempts to articulate the photographic image. The language of art and science frequently merged and became indistinct in descriptive accounts of the medium throughout the Victorian era, an anomaly that is clearly evident from Swanston's account of the photographic image earlier. This not only had an effect on how Victorian society came to classify photography within the wider visual culture, it also had a bearing on the way photography was put to use in various social and scientific disciplines. Within the social sciences in particular, conventions from portrait painting were adapted for anthropological and criminological studies. In natural history too, photography borrowed the conventions of landscape painting and illustration. More significantly, however, the type of photography practised by amateur naturalists that would normally be classified as 'scientific' also falls into the category of tourist imagery, not only through the conventionalised representation of the natural world but also by the representation of themselves in that world.

The Naturalist, Tourism and the Visualisation of Leisure

In his study of leisure in the mid-Victorian era, Peter Bailey (1978: 76) has remarked that in a work-orientated value system, leisure in the eyes of the Victorian middle classes represented the irrepressible preoccupations of a parasitic ruling class or the reckless carousing of the working class. As one writer quoted by Bailey (1977: 14) in an earlier study curtly remarked in the Dublin University Magazine (Keningale Cook, 1877: 174–92):

> From being Machines, fit only for machine work or inert quiescence, the masses are given the liberty of being man –gentlemen indeed, if that term be applied the possession of leisure, the power of being 'at large' – a coveted attribute of gentility.

As with the issue of amateurism, leisure for the middle classes was a contested terrain that simultaneously embraced and rejected certain elements of the culture of the aristocracy, and the collective mass of culture of the working classes. A nascent bourgeois ever vigilant to maintain 'social frontiers of class', thus approached leisure with a certain amount of suspicion (Bailey, 1977: 15).

The ethos of application and dedication which had underpinned Victorian amateurism also contributed to middle-class efforts to solve the dilemmas they foresaw in the realm of leisure. The life-space of leisure in the

Victorian era became a site in which the moral legitimism of the middle class could be affirmed. Leisure became subject to the imperatives of work discipline and activities which best reflected the physical and moral exercising of body and mind were pursued. The idleness and over consumption associated with the nobility and working classes was seen in stark contrast to the self-discipline and refined behaviour of the leisured bourgeois. Leisure afforded the middle classes the opportunity to display their social standing and natural history became one of those disciplines in which social mobility and moral propriety could be expressed while touring and travelling. Naturalists could thus differentiate themselves from other groups of tourists that they encountered on their travels in the natural world. For naturalists in particular, the natural world only became meaningful through the social interaction that took place between fellow tourists, and it was through this social experience of the natural world that naturalists could segregate themselves from other groups of travellers.

Although it has been noted that membership of the Dublin Naturalists Field Club was predominantly made up of those of ascendancy background, the Naturalists Field Clubs, in both Belfast and Dublin reflect the middle-class's desire to legitimise leisure socially (Lysaght, 1998: 40). With a few notable exceptions such as Robert Bell, a steel riveter at the Belfast shipyard of Harland & Wolff (Wilson Foster, 1990: 62), the Field Clubs mirrorred the cultural hegemony of middle-class tourism and leisure witnessed throughout the closing decades of the 19th century.[8]

Largely under the guidance of Praeger, the Field Clubs carried out numerous excursions into the rural North and West of Ireland culminating in the hugely ambitious Clare Island Survey between 1909 and 1911 (Guiry, 1997: 177–7; Lysaght, 1998; Scharf, 1915). With the establishment of the Irish Field Club Union in 1894, joint excursions between the four main Field Clubs in Belfast, Cork, Dublin and Limerick were organised, requiring greater emphasis upon careful planning and organisation. As a result, the activities of the natural historian became subject to the timetables of the railway companies and the rigid schedules of Field Club itineraries. The work of the naturalist thus became bound to the measured time of the tourist and traveller, while maintaining its links to a rigorous work ethic.

This work-orientated leisure was also something that necessitated visibility. Even if it was carried out in the domestic spaces of the home, leisure was required to be open to public scrutiny. The activities of the naturalist and tourist thus had to revolve not just around visual consumption of the natural world but also the production of it. The act of representing the natural world, either through the collection and accumulation of lists of natural history specimens, or representations of the landscape through sketching and photography, became part of the spectacle of leisure for

Figure 11.3 Robert John Welch 'Slieve Commedagh'. (Reproduced by permission of the Royal Irish Academy © RIA.)

fellow travellers to witness. Praeger's tourist guides provided the amateur naturalist with systematic and regulated tours and itineraries in which their work-orientated leisure could be displayed. Writing in a guide for the Belfast and Co. Down Railway Company in 1898, Praeger (1898: 18) gives the following summary for those hunters of the picturesque view:

> County Down is a capital district for artists and photographers, being usually well provided with railways and other modes of conveyance traversing all the finest scenery in the district . . . [*sic*] . . . The low, receding shores of Strangford Lough, with its multiple tiny islands and occasional ruins of fine old castles, will suit those who wish for peaceful seascapes.

Praeger's guide not only identified and listed the natural world to be scrutinised by the botanical tourist but also the landscape to be gazed upon by students of the picturesque. Like many other travelogues produced throughout the 19th century, his guide was a lesson in the rules of touring and looking. The picturesque was not immediately recognisable to the individual tourist, it was only through the aesthetic cultivation of the eye, and education in the rules of harmony and proportion that the picturesque gaze could be achieved (Adler, 1989: 22). It was a guide not only in what to look at but also how to look at it and to underline the lesson in a visual frame. His view of Slieve Commedagh for example (Figure 11.3), provided the frame, like the Claude glass before it, through which the natural world should be observed.

Imaging the Naturalist

Photography, which had become a leisure activity in its own right, was also an essential feature of other leisure activities, recording for public approval the popular pastimes of the urban bourgeois. The use of photography by the Naturalists Field Clubs during the last two decades of the 19th and first two decades of the 20th century, thus centred not only on the recording of geological and botanical specimens or picturesque views identified during organised field trips but also used to document the Field Club members themselves, either carrying out fieldwork or at leisure in the natural world. Robert John Welch, a photographer by profession, had become the unofficial photographer of the Field Club movement recording the activities of participants at most of the Irish Field Club Unions Triennial conferences. Welch, whose photographic work ranged across topographical landscapes to ethnography, produced a vast body of work recording Field Club members themselves.[9]

Two photographs of the Irish Field Club Unions (IFCU) outing in Rosapenna, Donegal, during the final IFCU Triennial Conference in 1910 are typical examples of this type of imagery. The two photographs, the Irish Field Club Union 'At Lough Salt' (Figure 11.4) and 'Afternoon Tea in Barnes Beg' (Figure 11.5) appear, on the surface, inconsequent to the serious business of fieldwork that brought these people to the natural world in the first place. The Field Club members after all, are merely taking a respite amidst the systematic surveying of the landscape, momentarily stopping to acknowledge their mastery of the natural world. The significance of these images, however, lies not simply in the fact that they represent a particular group of tourists in the landscape, although the form of representation is central to the argument that follows. The photograph itself should also be considered as an object and attention should not focus solely on the objects represented in it. Welch's photographs, such as those of the naturalist as tourist in Rosapena, came to be exhibited at Field Club Triennial Conferences, mounted in field club albums and displayed in the houses of Field Club members. These were spheres of social life, where the material forms of cultural expression were used as affirmations of cultural and national identity.

The recognition of cultural identity through the material forms of culture is also locked into the acknowledgement of one's self-image in such forms of representation. This recognition of self-image is not just a case of

Figure 11.4 Robert John Welch 'IFCU at Lough Salt' 1910. (Reproduced by permission of the Royal Irish Academy © RIA.)

identifying one's physical appearance in its represented forms. It is also dependent upon the sense of being embodied in such forms of representation. This embodied self can only be envisaged or perceived as the other sees it. It is useful at this stage to introduce Mikhail Bakhtin's elaborate theorisation of the relationship between self and other. In a series of disjointed texts published collectively as *Art and Answerability*, Bakhtin (1990: 27) explores the experience of one's own exterior. The outward appearance of the self that can only be experienced in the field of visual perception through the other.

Bakhtin (1990: 23) suggests that our physical presence in the material world enables us to experience this world from a unique subject position that is unavailable to other human beings. That is to say, our field of vision as 'bipedal hominids with a binocular, forward-projecting mode of sight' (Gardiner, 1999: 60) gives us an 'excess of seeing' which allows us to experience the world as others cannot. When we experience another human being in the physical world, we see and know things that are inaccessible to that other human being's gaze (Evans & Turner, 1977).[10] But this position is also

Figure 11.5 Robert John Welch 'Afternoon tea in Barnes Beg', 1910. (Reproduced by permission of the Royal Irish Academy © RIA.)

restrictive. The flip side of this unique subject position is also true as Bakhtin (1990) puts it: 'As we gaze at each other, two different worlds are reflected in the pupils of our eyes'. The other can thus experience our place in the world, a place that we are incapable of seeing. To affirm our outward appearance in the material world as an object amongst other objects, we must vivify our own exterior 'out of the other and for the other human being' (Bakhtin, 1990: 30). To attempt to vivify one's outward appearance through the self, that is to say through emotional and internalised perceptions of outward appearance, is to experience one's exterior through the sense of vision as scattered and fragmentary (Bakhtin, 1990: 28). As Gardiner states it is not simply a matter of returning or reciprocal gazes that allows the self to be envisaged through the other (Gardiner, 1999: 61). To envisage an outward appearance and have it affirmed in the 'plastic pictorial world', there must be dialogical relationship between the self and other through the everyday social interaction that takes place in the material world.

What I am suggesting here is that Welch's photographs functioned as objects through which the middle-class naturalist's exterior presence in the

natural world could be affirmed. They present the exterior image of the naturalist in the physical world, as they perceive the other to see it. These
images are an attempt to present a self-image of the middle-class naturalist
as tourist. Moreover, they also set out to identify these middle-class tourists
with the rural landscape. Throughout the 18th and much of the 19th centuries, the rural landscape within visual culture had largely been the domain
of the peasant and the landowner.[10] Landscape painting had traditionally
been preoccupied with the representation of ownership and agrarian
labour, aspects of the landscape that the urban middle classes had not traditionally been identified with. Even when the illustrated press came to
record the changing urban landscape in the 19th century, the factory
worker and street pauper were its primary subjects. Throughout 19th-
century visual culture in Ireland, the ascending and middle classes had literally remained out of sight in representations of the landscape,.

While Welch's photographs may attempt to reaffirm to the middle class
its desire to legitimise work-orientated leisure by imaging them as the
other sees them, the dialogical exchange between self and other is collapsed
upon itself. The photographs do not present the amateur naturalist as they
are perceived by the other but how they perceive the other sees them. The
photographs in this mutual system of exchange are co-authored between
Welch and his subjects. As Bakhtin (1990: 35) himself claims, photographs,
as with other representations of the self that are created for selfish reasons,
such as a reflection in a mirror, are from a position of only a 'possible other',
who lacks any standing of his own. Indeed Bakhtin (1990: 34) states of photographs in general;

> A photograph of oneself also provides no more than material for colla-
> tion, and once again we do not see ourselves here – we see only our own
> reflection without an author. True it no longer reflects the expression of
> a fictitious other, i.e., it is purer than the reflection in a mirror; neverthe-
> less it is fortuitous, artificially received, and does not express our
> *essential* emotional volitional stance in the ongoing event of being.
> (Emphasis in original)

This lack of author to which Bakhtin is referring to is the absence of the
other's reaction to the outward appearance and exterior presence of our
being in the world that is required for a coherent image of the self as a corporeal subject amongst other corporeal subjects in that world. In their
attempts to construct a coherent image of themselves, the middle class
tourists abstracted their physical appearance in the natural world to reaffirm their own perceptions of their place in it. As in an earlier image of
Praeger by Welch, 'The Kerry Cowboys' (Figure 11.6), the construction of a
self-image was an attempt by the middle classes to image their position

Figure 11.6 Robert john Welch 'The Kerry Cowboys'. (Photograph repro-duced with the kind permission of the Trustees of the Museums and Galleries of Northern Ireland.)

within the natural world, as one of taming wilderness through the scientific and cultural activities which displayed their civilising influence upon nature. Such grand visions necessitated a vehicle through which they could be affirmed and photographs provided that immediacy in which the process of inner affirmation could be shared and exchanged between a social group with shared interests in such representations of self-image.

Conclusion

Mass produced tourist imagery, particularly photographic views and picture postcards, brought the middle and ascending classes for the first time into the sphere of visual representation of the natural world. While painting had been established as the dominant form of representation of landed gentry and rural peasantry (although it must be said that the latter had little control over how they were represented),[11] photography became the means by which the emerging classes forged an identity with the rural

landscape. Photography's ubiquity also ensured that this newfound identification with the landscape was established relatively quickly amongst
their own class.

This middle-class identification with the natural world was set against
that of the aristocracy and rural peasantry. The landowner colonised and
designed the natural world, extending and altering its space to fit it into the
framework of the picturesque (Andrews, 1989: 3). The natural world was
emptied of all traces of labour except for the compositional decisions of the
landscape designer. Eamonn Slater (1993: 30–32) has noted that this picturesque landscaping became an important feature of Irish tourism during the
19th century. Ownership of the cultivated picturesque landscape by the
colonising landlord was used in 19th century travelogues as a means to differentiate between the land that was laboured in by the native peasant
tenantry and that which was the reworked land of the landlord's demesne.
As Raymond Williams (1993: 120) has stated: 'A Working country is hardly
ever a landscape', and certainly for the landowning aristocracy and the
colonial tourist, the picturesque gaze necessitated the displacement of
labour from their field of vision over the natural world.

This conception of the picturesque landscape from the perspective of the
aristocracy and colonial tourist is based on a gaze upon the natural world
that is at a distance, outside of the framed landscape itself. But for the middle-class domestic tourist there was a desire to embody themselves in
representations of the landscape in order to confirm their shared cultural
identity within the natural world. The middle-class tourist's experience of
the natural world was fragmentary and disjointed. Engagement with the
natural world was encountered through fleeting images from travelogues
and photographs, articulated through leisure and amateur activities and
constructed through the discourse of natural history. It was through these
fragmentary discourses that the middle classes attempted to construct a
homogeneous and unified sense of identity within the rural landscape.
Tourism for the middle-class domestic traveller did not just revolve around
individual visual consumption of the natural world, visual mastery had to
be witnessed by fellow travellers. The middle-class tourist became an
essential figure in representations of tourism throughout the late 19th and
early 20th century. Picture postcards and tourist photographs did not just
represent the picturesque view but also the tourist presence in the landscape during the act of visual consumption of the natural world around
them.

As I have argued in this chapter, tourism was not just about visual consumption of the natural world but also the representation of it. Tourism for
the amateur natural historian involved a set of cultural representative practices. From the production of systematic lists of flora and fauna to visual

representations of the natural world through sketching and photography, tourism provided the middle classes with the opportunity to appropriate the natural world in order to establish a place within it.

Notes

1. For a critical analysis of the relationship between nature and culture within philosophical and social discourse see Eder (1996).
2. For a contemporary perspective on the reading of photographs by tourists see Crawshaw and Urry (1997).
3. For an account of scientific positivism in the 19th century see Kolakowski (1972).
4. For a history of the BNFC see Campbell (1938).
5. For an account of the rise in popularity of natural history throughout the 19th century see Allen (1976).
6. For a history of the Dublin Photographic Society which later became the Photographic Society of Ireland see Merne (1954).
7. See forthcoming article by the author.
8. The term is borrowed from Antonio Gramsci (1971).
9. For a brief survey of Welch's career see Evans and Turner (1977).
10. For a survey of landscape painting throughout this period see Klingender (1968).
11. On the political and ideological issues associated with landscape painting and class relations see Barrell (1980) and Bermingham (1980).

References

Adler, J. (1989) Origins of sightseeing. *Annals of Tourism Research* 16, 7–29.22

Andrews, J. H. (1997) Paper landscapes: Mapping Ireland's physical geography. In J.W. Foster (ed.) *Nature in Ireland: A Scientific and Cultural Study*. Dublin: Lilliput

Andrews, M. (1989) *The Search for the Picturesque: Landscape Aesthetics and Tourism in Britain, 1760–1800*. Aldershot: Scolar.

Bailey, P. (1977) A mingled mass of perfectly legitimate pleasures: The Victorian middle class and the problem of leisure. *Victorian Studies* 21.

Bailey, P. (1978) *Leisure and Class in Victorian England: Rational Recreation and the Contest for Control 180–1885*. London: Methuen.

Barthes, R. The photographic message. In *Image- Music Text*, trans. Stephen Heath, London: Fontana.

Batchen, G. (1993) The naming of photography: 'A mass of metaphor'. *History of Photography* 17.1.

Bennett, J. (1997) Science and social policy in Ireland in the mid-19th century. In Bowler & White (eds) *Science and Society in Ireland: The Social Context of Science and Technology in Ireland, 1800–1950*. Belfast: Institute of Irish Studies.

Berman, M. (1975) Hegemony, and the amateur tradition in British science. *Journal of Social History*.

Brown, J. (1889) Figures produced by electric action on photographic dry plates. *Proceedings of the Belfast Natural History and Philosophical Society*.

Davidson, D. (1989) *Impressions of an Irish Countess: The Photography of Mary, Countess Rosse*. Dublin: The Birr Castle Scientific Heritage Foundation

Diprose, R. and Farrell, R. (ed.) *Cartographies: Poststructuralism and the Mapping of Bodies and Spaces*. London: Allen & Unwin.

Foucault, M. (1975) *The Birth of the Clinic: An Archaeology of Medical Perception*, trans. A.M. Sheridan Smith. New York: Vintage.

Foucault, M. (1989) *The Order of Things: An Archaeology of the Human Sci*ences. London: Routledge.

Gardiner, M. (1999) Bakhtin and the metaphorics of perception. In I. Heywood and B. Sandwell (eds) *Interpreting Visual Culture: Explorations in the Hermeneutics of the Visual*. London: Routledge

Gibbons, L. (1996) *Transformations in Irish Culture*. Cork: Cork University Press.

Guiry, M. D. (1997) Robert Lloyd Praeger and the Major Surveys. In J. Wilson Foster (ed.) *Nature in Ireland: A Scientific and Cultural Study*. Dublin: Lilliput.

Holquist, M. and Liapunov, V. (eds & trans.) (1990) *Art and Answerability: Early Philosophical Essays by M.M. Bakhtin*. Austin: University of Texas Press.

Jarrell, R.A. (1983) The Department of Science and Art and Control of Irish Science, 1853–1905. *Irish Historical Studies* 23.92.

Keningale Cook, J. (1877) The labourers leisure. *Dublin University Magazine* 22

Knight, D. (1988) *The Age of Science*. London: Blackwell.

Lysaght, S. (1989) Heaney vs. Praeger: Contrasting natures. *Irish Review* 7.

Lysaght, S. (1997) Contrasting natures: The issue of names. In J. W. Foster (ed.) *Nature in Ireland: A Scientific and Cultural Study*. Dublin: Lilliput.

Lysaght, S. (1997) Science and the cultural revival, 1863–1916. In Peter J. Bowler and Nicholas White (eds) *Science and Society in Ireland: The Social Context of Science and Technology in Ireland, 1800–1950*. Belfast: Institute of Irish Studies

Lysaght, S. (1998) *Robert Lloyd Praeger: The Life of a Naturalist*. Dublin: Four Courts.

MacLeod, R. (1997) On science and colonialism. In Bowler & White (eds) *Science and Society in Ireland: The Social Context of Science and Technology in Ireland, 1800–1950*. Belfast: Institute of Irish Studies.

McKenna-Lawlor, S. (1998) *Whatever Shines Should Be Observed: quicquial nited notandem*. Dublin: Santon.

Pim, G. (1892) Photographing objects of natural history without a camera. *The Irish Naturalist* 1.2.

Praeger, R. L. (1909) *A Tourists Flora of the West of Ireland*. Dublin: Hodges Figgis.

Praeger, R.L. (1898) *Belfast & Co. Down Railway Company. Official Guide to County Down and the Mourne Mountains, with plates by R.J. Welch*. Belfast: Marcus Ward for the Belfast and Co. Down Railway Company.

Proceedings of the Belfast Naturalists Field Club, (1890/91) *Annual Meeting*. Series II, Vol. III, Part III.

Scharff, R. F. (1915) The Clare Island Survey. *Irish Naturalist* 24

Sebbins, R. A. (1979) *Amateurs: On the Margin Between Work and Leisure*. London: Sage.

Sekula, A. (1982) On the invention of photographic meaning. In V. Burgin (ed.) *Thinking Photography*. London: MacMillan.

Slater, E. (1993) Contested terrain: Differing interpretations of Co. Wicklow's landscape. *Irish Journal of Sociology* 3.

Swanston, W. (1888/89) Photography as an aid to the club word. *Proceedings of the Belfast Naturalists Field Club* Series II, Vol. III, Part II.

Talbot, W.H.F. (1839) Some account of the art of photographic drawing, or, the process by which natural objects may be made to delineate themselves, without the aid of the artist's pencil. In Beaumont Newhall (ed.) (1981) *Photography: Essays and Images*. London: Secker & Warburg.

Urry, J. (1990) *The Tourist's Gaze: Leisure and Travel in Contemporary Societies*. London: Sage.

Williams, R. (1993) *The Country and the City*. London: Hogarth

Wilson Foster, J. (1987) *Fictions of the Irish Literary Revival: A Changeling Art*. New York: Syracuse University Press.

Wilson Foster, J. (1990) Natural history, science and Irish culture. *Irish Review* 9.

Wilson Foster, J. (1991) Natural science and Irish culture. *Eire-Ireland* 26.2.

Wilson Foster, J. (1997) Natural history and modern Irish culture. In Peter J. Bowler and Nicholas White (eds) *Science and Society in Ireland: The Social Context of Science and Technology in Ireland, 1800–1950*. Belfast: Institute of Irish Studies.

Wilson Foster, J. (1997) Out of Ireland: Naturalists abroad. In J. W. Foster (ed.) *Nature in Ireland: A Scientific and Cultural Study*. Dublin: Lilliput.

Part 5

Tourism Policy: Historical and Contemporary Issues

Chapter Twelve

Tongue-tied: Language, Culture and the Changing Trends in Irish Tourism Employment

JULIETTE PÉCHENART

Introduction

'Whether we like it or not, by the year 2002 there will be more overseas people working in tourism here than Irish people' (Humphreys, 1999). Even if Denis Moylan, chief executive of Catering Recruitment Consultancy, was proved wrong, the marked shift in the workforce in the hotel and catering industry in Ireland in recent years will undoubtedly pose new challenges for the tourism industry in Ireland as a whole.

In the late 1980s, one of the issues facing the tourism industry in Ireland was the lack of foreign linguistic competence among Irish employees in the industry. Studies were undertaken and syllabi were drawn up (Péchenart & Tangy, 1993:162–80). Foreign-language learning materials were published in order to equip the Irish workforce with enough French, German, Italian and Spanish to cope with the increase in continental European tourists coming to Ireland (Péchenart *et al.*, 1995; Fischer & Crosbie, 1995; Clark & Manselli, 1995; Ponte Miramontes, 1995). Ten years on, the tourism industry in Ireland faces a very different language problem: as the industry experiences an 'acute skills shortage' and has to recruit staff overseas, there is a lack of English language competence among some non-Irish employees in the tourism industry (CERT, 1998: 7).

This chapter will analyse the implications of such a dramatic change in a relatively short period of time. The chapter will begin by examining the reasons for a shortage of Irish staff. It will then go on to explore what happens when staff are recruited overseas. The final section of the chapter will attempt to demonstrate why the recruitment of overseas employees presents new challenges for the tourism sector and will conclude with an examination of measures that might be taken to integrate non-Irish staff into the tourism workforce.

Acute Skills Shortage in the Tourism Industry in Ireland

For the tourism industry in Ireland, 1998 was a record year. Ireland attracted 5.7 million visitors, an increase of 10.7% on 1997 (CSO Principal Statistics – Travel and Tourism) and tourism generated IR£2.3 billion in foreign exchange earnings, a 9% increase on 1997 (CSO Principal Statistics – Travel and Tourism). According to a report in *The Sunday Business Post*, the hotel sector was extremely active in 1998, with 50 new hotels being added to the existing 730 establishments throughout Ireland (Hughes, 1998). A report in *The Irish Times* was even more specific and estimated that at the end of 1998 there were about 32,500 hotel rooms in the country and this figure represented an increase of around 7% over the 1997 figure. In Dublin alone 20 new hotels opened or increased in size during 1998 and this added 1500 new rooms and brought the total of rooms available to 9,200. This represented an increase of almost 20% over the 1997 figure, and 44% over the 1996 figure (Keena, 1999).

The same growth is found in the restaurant sector. The *Employment Survey of the Tourism Industry in Ireland*, carried out for CERT, the State Tourism Training Agency and published in 1998 estimated that in 1997 there were 1890 restaurants in the Republic, an increase of 16% on 1996 (CERT, 1998: 14). The trend was set to continue in 1999 with further new restaurants and hotels opening. Seventy-seven new hotels were planned for 1999, for example the 200-bed Four Seasons Hotel and the 250-bed Bewleys Hotel in Ballsbridge, the Sheraton Hotel in Dublin's College Green to name but a few (Hughes, 1998).

CERT's survey also showed that in the two years since 1996, employment in the hotel sector had increased by 20%. The report states that in 1997, 50,133 employees worked in the hotel sector, 46,402 working in hotels and the remainder in guesthouses. The projected employment growth rate for 1999 was of 9% in the hotel sector alone (CERT, 1998, 9:3). The same survey found that in 1997 33,587 people were employed in the restaurant sector and it anticipated a 17% employment growth in 1999 (CERT, 1998b: 6). However, these figures should not mask the acute skills shortage experienced in the tourism sector. The greatest skill shortage identified in hotels related to waiting and bar staff (1337) and to qualified and commis chefs (923 and 587 vacancies respectively). There was also a shortage of 384 managers and supervisors in hotels (CERT, 1998a: 7). The survey also identified a severe skills shortage in the restaurant sector, particularly for qualified and commis chefs (1225 and 1208 vacancies respectively). A shortage of an estimated 996 waiting staff and 793 general kitchen staff was also reported as well as a shortage of 189 managers (CERT, 1998b: 7). A more recent survey published by CERT in January 2000 _Employment Survey of Tourism and Catering Sectors in Ireland 1999_ predicted there would be 9000 job vacancies in the state's hotel and restaurant sector by summer 2000 (Ingle, 2000). The long-term projections as published in July 1999 in CERT's study _Hospitality 2005_ predict that an additional 105,000 workers would be needed in the hotel and restaurant sector by 2005 if the current high growth rate continues (Mc Iver Consulting & Tansey Webster Stewart, 1999).

This skills shortage is not confined to the tourism sector only. It is now an issue for the economy as a whole in Ireland, especially 'the highest growth sectors in Ireland in terms of job creation – teleservices, financial services, electronics, software, hotels and catering, tourism and construction' (Hughes, 1999). There are at present 1.5 million people at work in the Republic and the unemployment rate currently stands at around 5%. However, the CSO (Central Statistics Office) predicts that only 50% of all new jobs being created can be filled from the natural increase in the population. If this prediction is correct, then, as the unemployment rate continues to fall, skills shortage will become an even bigger problem (Hughes, 1999). The fall in the unemployment rate because of a buoyant economy and the competition from other growth sectors is not the only reason for the staff shortfall in the tourism industry. As an article in _The Irish Times_ puts it (Holland, 1998) 'this 'acute skills shortage' is put down variously to anti-social hours, low wages and burn-out – all of which, in turn, contribute to the increasingly prevalent perception of the industry as a short term, transitory career option'.

In order to counterbalance this shortage of staff, CERT initiated a number of initiatives in 1998 in order to fill the vacancies. The Chairman of CERT, Mr Eamonn McKeon outlined the initiatives as follows: IR£20 million capital investment programme in the Institutes of Technology to expand the number of training places for new entrants; Tourism Days nationwide and in the UK; an intensive promotion during the National Tourism Careers Roadshow in November 1998 to target school leavers (CERT, 1999). These initiatives were repeated and expanded in 1999: a second National Tourism Careers Roadshow was organised and was supplemented by a promotional campaign on breakfast TV and the national press; a special campaign to promote careers in the industry to adults was launched in November 1999 (CERT, 2000). The unemployed and full-time mothers wishing to return to work were also targeted. For example, Eileen O'Meara Walsh, chairwoman of the Irish Tourist Industry Confederation (ITIC), estimated that about IR£100 million should be spent on training and reskilling and should focus primarily on the over–35s and married women

(Mulqueen, 1999). But this was not enough and in its 1998 survey, CERT stated that intense competition for recruiting and retaining staff, at a time when the sector was undergoing unprecedented expansion, was leading many operators to consider recruiting non-Irish staff. According to the survey, 46% of hoteliers and 10% of guesthouse operators had recruited staff from outside Ireland in 1997. Some operators had actively targeted specific countries such as Spain, France and Germany. Others were relying on the annual influx of students to Ireland, particularly during the months of June to September (CERT, 1998a: 40). The survey also stated that 31% of restaurateurs had recruited staff from outside Ireland (CERT, 1998b: 25).

Recruiting from Abroad

The recruitment of staff, whether from Ireland or from abroad, seems to be the main problem facing restaurateurs and hoteliers in a period of unprecedented growth (Holland, 1998):

> While the consumer may face queues, the proprietor faces the heart-ache of whether he or she has the staff to cater for the demand. Both owners and managers describe the business as enormously stressful, with staffing the greatest source of this pressure. Many are obsessed with the question of having to go abroad to recruit staff.

In some instances, even recruiting from abroad does not solve the problem as was the experience of an upmarket and successful Dublin restaurant *Mange tout* which had to close down in March 2000 because of difficulty in getting and retaining staff (Keena, 2000). Fast food outlets also experience problems recruiting and retaining staff and some evenings they just have to close early not for lack of business but because they cannot find enough staff to stay open (O'Kane, 2000).

As there are no official data giving a breakdown of countries of origin for staff employed in the tourism industry, one has to rely on other sources of information to build up a picture of the geographical origins of the new tourism workers in Ireland. One source of information is private recruitment agencies. Indicative of changing trends is that a number of these private recruitment agencies have opened foreign offices to recruit staff abroad. In an interview with *The Irish Times* (Humphreys, 1999), Mr Denis Moylan, chief executive of the Killarney-based Catering Recruitment Consultancy, said: 'Last year [1998], we brought in 600 people from Europe, which was twice what we brought in 1997, but I could have easily found places for 2000'. His agency now recruits staff from Germany, Spain, France and Norway and has opened offices in Sweden and Finland recently. His plans are to recruit workers in Poland, Hungary and the

Czech Republic in the future. Connie Rothschild, director of MTR recruitment in Dublin, says that her company is increasingly going to the UK to recruit. She has advertised in France and Germany as well (Holland, 1998). Frank Fitzpatrick who manages the family business (four Fitzer's restaurants in Dublin, a restaurant in Powerscourt, Co. Wicklow and a film catering company) says that his staff comes from France, Spain, America, England, Australia and Italy (Holland, 1998). One well-known hotelier Conrad Gallagher has even bought a five-bedroom house near Dublin's city centre as a base for the workers he recruits from abroad (Holland, 1998).

An advertisement posted on 12 April 2000 in _The Irish Times_ (2000) for 'JS Hotel Personnel, a specialist division of JacksonStone Recruitment' states: 'We are currently sourcing experienced, English speaking candidates, through partnerships with local consultants in Estonia, Czech Republic and Malaysia'. A more recent development is for foreign-based recruitment agencies to target Ireland and find jobs for their clients in Ireland. For example, the Brittany-based agency, Recruitment Connections was established at the beginning of 2000 and so far 'has sent 20 French people to the Republic to work as lorry drivers, barmen, waiters, porters, cooks and managers' (Marlowe, 2000).

Not only private recruitment agencies, hoteliers and restaurants but also large state organisations such as FÁS, the Irish Training and Employment Authority, recruit from abroad. From the 2–6 June 1999 FÁS took a stand at the training and apprenticeship trade fair in Cologne in Germany to inform workers about job opportunities in Ireland. This was followed by a series of roadshows in Britain, France, Benelux, the USA and Canada. The aim was also to target Irish people currently working in Germany. According to Seán Connolly of FÁS, 'on behalf of employers, we're raising awareness among Irish ex-pats and other EU nationals who have the appropriate skills and languages' (Hughes, 1999). FÁS will continue to train people in Ireland but believes the initiative of anticipating further skills shortage is a prudent one. For some critics, FÁS is encouraging immigration when it should concentrate its energies on training the existing Irish workforce. For others, Irish policy in the area should be positive and pro-active they argue for an immediate relaxation of stringent Irish immigration laws to help meet current labour shortages (_The Irish Times_, 1999). According to the _Labour Force 2000_ survey from the Chambers of Commerce of Ireland published in June 2000 (Yeates, 2000):

> Fellow EU member-states were by far the most favoured for finding foreign recruits. Fifty-five per cent of companies with shortages had recruited staff in England, Scotland and Wales, and the same percent-

age had recruited staff in continental EU states. Seventeen per cent of companies had recruited staff in North America.

As it is, when prospective employees come from European Union countries, the problems are relatively minor but they become more significant when workers come from non-EU countries. This has been the recent experience of the Galway Chamber of Commerce and Industry which had plans to bring 400 Canadians from Newfoundland to alleviate the staffing shortage in the city's tourism industry. Only 50 made the journey in May 2000 as the others experienced delays in securing work permits (*The Irish Times*, 2000b).

FÁS' latest initiative has been to get jobs for asylum-seekers already in Ireland. In May 2000, FAS opened its first training unit for asylum-seekers in Tallaght and opened a second one in Blanchardstown at the end of June 2000. According to Mr Frank Donnelly, director of the Tallaght unit, '35 of the first group of 100 people to attend the unit had found a job within weeks. They include accountants, computer programmers, welders, bookkeepers, warehouse workers and *hospitality industry staff*' (my emphasis) (Haughey, 2000). In order to be eligible to work, asylum-seekers must have applied for refugee status before July 1999 and must have been waiting for a year for a decision. By July 2000, 4100 asylum-seekers were permitted to work. The Irish Small and Medium Enterprises Association (ISME) is of the opinion that with more than 15,000 asylum-seekers in the state and a backlog of about 11,000 applications, all asylum-seekers should be allowed to work after three months (Haughey, 2000). However, it is unlikely under the existing political dispensation that the work scheme for asylum-seekers will be radically changed in the near future.

When the Irish Tourist Industry Confederation published its five-year plan for the industry in May 1998, the plan emphasised the fact 'that in economic terms the industry is almost entirely native-grown: there is no need to import expensive materials – apart from the odd bottle of French wine' (Dunne, 1998). This is no longer the case for the Irish tourist industry in that it is not only the odd bottle of French wine that must be imported but large numbers of French, German, Italian, Spanish and workers from further afield.

What Happens When Hotels and Restaurants Recruit Abroad?

We ordered those spritzers and they arrived quickly, along with a big chrome basket of brown and white bread. The waiter was back in a flash to recite 'ze speshills of ze day'.

Couldn't understand a word except zat zere wur shallots involved somewhere along the lines. He repeated them all over again but we were none the wiser.

Much later, a friend joined us for a drink. When asked for a glass of house white the same waiter nodded, jotted it down on his pad and then asked him how would he like it cooked – medium or rare. This sort of thing is a bit wearing after a while. Even if you can speak a bit of Spanish or Italian, it cuts no ice with the waiter or waitress from deepest Portugal or Latvia. God be with the days when the waiter would start off in Franglais and then lapse into a broad Dublin accent so that everyone could relax.

Despite the language barrier, the service was extremely prompt. (Mulcahy, 1999a).

I found them in the bar sipping dry sherry, although this happy state hadn't been reached without difficulty. The young French barman didn't know his pale from his cream and had made a couple of false starts. In the end, they got what they wanted and declared him to be a decent fellow all the same. (Mulcahy, 1999b).

As these two quotations from *The Irish Times* food critic suggest, recruiting non-Irish staff and especially non-Anglophone staff is often seen as posing its own problems. In 1993, we had written:

Tourism is very much a labour intensive industry and it involves a high level of cross-cultural and linguistic contact in all its sectors be they transport and travel, accommodation and catering and the more recent sectors of leisure / recreation facilities.

If Ireland wants to compete successfully in international markets, it must ensure a high quality of service. That service can only be enhanced if the Irish can communicate with their customers.

It is now widely accepted in the export field that hosts must be prepared to speak their customers' language if they do not want to lose business. The Irish tourist industry must recognize that, as more and more visitors from other European countries come to this country, it cannot rely on the foreigner's ability to speak English. (Péchenart & Tangy, 1993: 164)

However, ten years later, the fate of the Irish tourist industry depends not so much on the ability of its guests but of its employees to speak English. The recruitment of non-Irish staff is not, of course, a completely new phenomenon but in the past, staff were largely back-of-house, the most notable example being French chefs. The radical change in recent

Table 12.1

Front-of-house staff	Tourist/client
I Irish (anglophone) May or may not have foreign language competence	(a) Irish (anglophone)
	(b) Non-Irish and Anglophone(e.g. American, English, Australian, Canadian)
	(c) Non-Irish and non-anglophone(e.g. French, German, Italian, Spanish, etc.)May or may not have linguistic competence in English
II Non-Irish and Anglophone (e.g. American, English, Australian, Canadian, New-Zealander) May or may not have foreign language competence	(a) Irish (anglophone)
	(b) Non-Irish and Anglophone(e.g. American, English, Australian, Canadian)
	(c) Non-Irish and non-anglophone(e.g. French, German, Italian, Spanish, etc)May or may not have linguistic competence in English
III Non-Irish and non-anglophone (e.g. French, German, Spanish, Italian, etc) May or may not have linguistic competence/fluency in English	(a) Irish (anglophone)
	(b) Non-Irish and Anglophone(e.g. American, English, Australian, Canadian)
	(c) Non-Irish and non-anglophone(e.g. French, German, Italian, Spanish, etc.)May or may not have linguistic competence in English

years is that non-Irish staff now occupy front-of-house positions such as waiters, waitresses and receptionists.

As Table 12.1 shows, the linguistic permutations in contact between front-of-house staff in the tourism industry in Ireland and tourists/clients have increased with the recruitment of non-Irish staff.

Only ten years ago, most of the tourist/client encounters were in the I(a)–(c) categories and the potentially problematic ones were in Ic, depending on whether the Irish staff had any or no competence in a foreign language and/or whether the foreign tourist had any or no English. As more and more Irish staff get some training in foreign languages, the hope is that problems arising in the Ic category will become less common. In the new millennium, potentially problematic encounters from a *linguistic* point of view between staff and clients could still occur in Ic as well as IIc, III(a)–III(c). Staff recruited from English-speaking countries as in II should have no problem performing the tasks associated with their job, at least from a linguistic point of view. However, they might experience the same problems as Irish staff when dealing with tourists not speaking English. Whether they themselves speak any or no foreign languages could affect their performance in doing their job.

The most problematic category, from a linguistic point of view, we would argue, is the third one. As no extensive research has been carried so far on the breakdown of numbers between these three categories of staff and on the linguistic competence, in English, of staff in category III, it is difficult to make generalisations. Much of the evidence is anecdotal but the repeated observations of food critics and certain journalists' reports in the print media point out to the challenges facing tourism policy-makers in Ireland for whom the employment of non-Anglophone staff is a very new development:

> Many of the staff working in these establishments [80 restaurants in the Temple Bar area of Dublin] are part-time or temporary: students with holiday jobs, _or foreigners trying to learn English_. (Greene, 1999; my emphasis)

> Many of the positions are also being filled by foreign students _wishing to improve their English_. (Hughes, 1998; my emphasis).

> And as the same weary tourists sit in a restaurant struggling to explain to the _barely English-speaking_ [my italics] waiter that they don't want a full dinner, just a main course from the (as yet, unpresented) à la carte menu, and the waiter gazes back, uncomprehending like Manuel from _Fawlty Towers_, pleading 'A la carte? A la carte? What dish it . . . ', they're bound to wonder if this is one of those unplanned 'magic moments with people' they read about somewhere. (Sheridan, 1999)

Training

The first question to be asked in relation to trends in tourism employment relates to training: Are the staff trained to do their job, whether in their home countries or in Ireland? Views seem to differ on this issue. According to Mr Moylan from Catering Recruitment Consultancy, 'they [the staff he recruits from abroad] are all very well trained, sometimes more so than Irish staff. Ninety per cent of them would have completed courses and might be looking for overseas experience' (Mulcahy, 2000). However, CERT in its 1998 survey identified substantial requirement needs for training. According to the findings of the survey, only 34% of hotels and 3%

of guesthouses had an action plan for training and only 20% of hotels and 2% of guesthouses had a budget allocation for training (Humphreys, 1999). For restaurants, only 18% of them had an action plan for training and only 6% had a budget allocation for training (CERT, 1998a: 42). Frank O'Malley, secretary of the hotel and catering branch of the trade union SIPTU, is quite critical of the situation:

> The new breed of employer has no commitment to training and gives no indication that he or she wants to invest in employees. The problem is that this is grand in the short term. Employers get away with paying low rates, often relying on the tips to pay the wages; they get away without investing in training and, even though the service might be sloppy or the waitress *unable to speak English,* everyone is happy while the economy is booming. (CERT, 1998: 28; my emphasis)

The second issue that arises relates to how the linguistic competence (in English) of the potential employees is assessed and who does the assessing. Is it done by the employers themselves or by language professionals? What sorts of test(s), if any, are given to the candidates? Is it enough to ask somebody to read a menu in English and explain a few words/dishes? How are these candidates going to perform under stress or in an unforeseen situation? How will they cope with accents, linguistic differences? Can they answer the telephone?

One company in Ireland, Dublin City University • Language Services (DCU • LS) was established in 1993 to respond to the growing need for languages in the Irish business world. It has developed a Linguistic Competence Evaluation Test for recruitment agencies and employers who wish to assess the linguistic abilities of prospective employees. So far, it has mostly tested candidates for Teleservices positions in sectors including Information Technology, Finance, Banking, Tourism and Leisure. Its evaluation techniques consist of an oral test by telephone or in a face-to-face situation and a written test if needed. Candidates are then judged to be at Elementary, Pre-intermediate, Intermediate, Upper Intermediate or Advanced level or having near-native competence. It has been their experience that candidates below level Upper Intermediate are not in a position to use the language in which they are being tested in a professional context (see Appendix 1). As some employees in the tourism industry find it difficult to carry out their jobs or some tasks associated with their job because of linguistic deficiency, employers could avail themselves of services such as the one offered by DCULS or similar companies.

One organisation, FÁS, has begun to address this issue. In its new unit set up to help asylum-seekers find work, the unit tests them for competence in the English language. It then puts together a portfolio for employers with an indication of English-language competencies. According to its director Mr Donnelly, 'between 80 and 85% of job seekers attending the unit have 'functional-to-good' English, while the remaining 15 to 20% would have difficulties because of their poor English' (Holland, 1998). Those whose English is not good enough are referred to classes where they get basic language skills.

Linguistic misunderstandings between staff and clients appear to be increasingly common in the context of tourism service in Ireland. Linguistic misunderstandings also occur between staff themselves as the workforce becomes more multicultural and as non-native speakers use English to communicate with each other. As the proprietor of the Dublin restaurant _101 Talbot_ writes in a letter to the Editor in _The Irish Times_, 'The problem is with their [non-nationals] language skills. Poor understanding of English leads to all sorts of confusion for both restaurant customers – and _kitchens_' (Haughey, 2000; my emphasis). So the problems are not confined to the front-of-house activities. They happen behind the scenes as well. According to Dr Patrick Wall, the FSAI (Food Safety Authority of Ireland) chief executive: 'Staff could be a food business's greatest liability if their incorrect actions, as a result of poor knowledge of food safety practices, caused a food-poisoning outbreak' (Letters to the Editor, _The Irish Times_, 2000c). As large numbers of foreign nationals are employed to work in the food industry, Dr Wall stressed that employers had a responsibility to train the staff appropriately and at the request of McDonald's fast-food restaurants, the FSAI has produced educational material in Spanish. 'English-language literature may not be the appropriate way to train staff', said Dr Wall (O'Sullivan, 1999). CERT has adopted a similar approach and in order to alleviate some of the problems encountered by non-Irish staff in the industry, it has developed an induction pack for these workers. Initially produced in French, Italian and Spanish, it covers customer care and operational hygiene as well as advice on living and working in Ireland (O'Sullivan, 1999).

Cross-cultural Capability/Cultural Awareness

The service, for example, could find no decent sense of rhythm on the busy night we were there. Initially too slow in taking our order and bringing the wine list, it then became too quick, with waiters removing plates before all the dishes were finished. This is a forgivable mistake, of course, especially on a busy night, but it was the off-handedness of the young French waiters looking after us, which was disappointing. They simply made no effort to engage us in any way during the meal, and while I appreciate that this may be _a cultural difference regarding the_ *nature of the service,* the fact is that such a cool style of service doesn't suit the rest of Jo Olive's. (McKenna, 1999; my emphasis)

In this encounter, what seems to have struck the food critic and journalist John McKenna is not the lack of linguistic competence of the French waiters but the manner, the 'off-handedness' in which they were doing their job which he attributes to a 'cultural difference'. By drawing the attention to the cultural difference of these particular waiters, McKenna has drawn attention to an area of great interest and scholarship in recent years, intercultural communication or cross-cultural capability. These French waiters did not behave in a way appropriate for an Irish client. In this case, this did not develop into a 'critical incident' that is to say 'a situation where there is a communication problem between people of different cultures. In other words, something goes wrong because the people involved don't understand each other's culture' (McKenna, 1999). But their manner did display a lack of cross-cultural awareness and sensitivity to cultural differences. As front-of-house staff in a restaurant setting, it is not enough to be linguistically competent. The staff also have to be interculturally competent.

As more and more people travel to foreign countries either for cultural visits, as students, on work placements or for work/jobs, many researchers in the area of language learning and teaching have turned their attention to intercultural communication, that is the integration of the cultural component into the process of language teaching and learning (Tomalin & Stempleski, 1993: 84). For example, there has been a growing interest in monitoring the Year Abroad. This is the year spent by students studying in a foreign culture. This experience can have positive as well as negative (culture shock, social isolation) sides as well as language and cultural outcomes (Chambers & O'Baoill, 1999; Killick & Parry, 1999; Parker & Rouxeville, 1995). Researchers like Elizabeth Murphy-Lejeune (1997: 212–22; 1998) have advocated the 'ethnographic bridge' as a means to cross languages and cultures. She states:

> Participation in the daily life of a social group different from one's own prompts strategies such as observing unfamiliar cultural practices, reflecting on these and comparing them with the familiar practices one is used to, analysing the differences between culture 1 and culture 2, finding an explanation for the observations made, placing these observations in a specific context, trying to make sense of the whole picture, etc. All these represent the various steps both anthropologists and strangers follow in order to understand societies different from their own. (Murphy-Lejeune, 1997: 212–22)

Veronica Crosbie, building on the work done by Murphy-Lejeune, has developed, implemented and evaluated a pilot module in Intercultural Communication designed specifically for the BA in European Business non-Irish students at Dublin City University. In a recent article, Crosbie (1999: 130) describes the students as having a fairly good command of English but also

> as 'competent fools', in that they can misread situations or bring their own cultural values and modes of expressions to bear in their dealings with the new cultural environment. Examples of this include making a request, which can be perceived by the host culture as issuing a command.

Activities and tools have been developed so that students become more able ' 'capable travellers', in that they can read and interpret cultural signs and symbols and interact with relative ease in a 'third space'(Crosbie, 1999: 144).

The research done by Barbara Lazenby Simpson in the context of 'The Refugee Language and Training Project' in the Centre for Language and Communication Studies in Trinity College Dublin would be of great benefit to the training of non-Irish staff in the tourism industry. This project aims at 'learners, who come from a wide range of language and education backgrounds, [and who] are engaged in developing the specific language knowledge and communication skills which will enable them to pursue further training and/or compete for and gain employment' (Lazenby Simpson, 1999: 272).

It is now time to introduce these approaches to the training of non-Irish recruits in the tourism industry, not only the French, German and Spanish recruits but also for the USA, English, Canadian and Australian recruits. The implicit assumption is that because the latter are English-speakers, there should not be a problem. However, as Michael Cronin (2000: 25) points out:

> Common language on the other hand can produce a fiction of cultural immediacy . . . The illusion of understanding is all the greater because translation is not believed to be a problem. The traveller to another country with a different language anticipates translation difficulties and, because the language is different, it is assumed that naturally the culture is different. However, there can result a genuine sense of bewilderment if a seeming transparency of language gives way to cultural opacity.

However, even if the staff are professionally, linguistically and inter-culturally trained, will this be enough for the employees to want to stay in

Ireland and work long term in the tourism industry? If the experience of foreign teleworkers in Ireland is anything to go by, one cannot be sure that they will. Having interviewed many workers in call-centres in Dublin, a journalist asserts that many of the foreign workers are not so happy with what they find when they come to the Republic (Mulcahy, 1999c). A Dutch employee at American Airlines call-centre thinks: 'They [the foreign workers] come over here not knowing what to expect and are disappointed with the salary, the culture and the cost of living. The ones that stay usually have a relationship tie here' (Mulcahy, 1999d). When interviewed, the general manager of Xerox Ireland identified that transport and housing were among the most serious issues facing new recruits when they come to the Republic and he added: 'They just can't understand the Irish system' (O'Dea, 1999).

How Will Irish Tourism Meet the Challenge of the Recruitment of Non-Irish Staff?

The then Minister for Tourism, Sport and Recreation, Dr James Mc Daid, at an Irish Tourist Industry Confederation (ITIC) dinner in Dublin in November 1998 referred in his speech to the poor holiday-maker performance in recent years from major Continental European markets and said:

> Market research had confirmed that the uniqueness of the Irish holiday experience lay *in the personal and warm interaction that a visitor has with the Irish people*. As the industry matures and becomes more commercially driven, there may be a natural tendency for less attention to be given to the personal touch. (McDaid, 1998, my emphasis)

In the first study to address the future strategic direction of the industry *Hospitality 2005* published by CERT in July 1999, the consultants had warned:

> For any service industry, competitive advantage is achieved through people – the knowledge and skill they invest in delivering service to customers. In the hotel and restaurant sector, this is particularly the case. The 'moment of truth' in this industry is the interface of front-line staff with the customer.

When tourists come to Ireland, they have expectations of what they will see, of the people they will meet. As Barbara O'Connor (1993: 70) states:

> Tourist imagery has been constructed by selecting and promoting certain aspects of culture as tourist 'markers'. These historically have included the scenery, the beauty and the Irish people and they are

regarded as an essential ingredient in the publicity package. (O'Connor, 1993: 72)

O'Connor (p. 73) adds:

One of the consequences of this emphasis on people as part of the tourist package is that Irish people become more inscribed within tourist expectations. Tourists expect a certain type of behaviour and are disappointed if these expectations are not met.

This view was reiterated in an opinion article published in _The Irish Times_ where the journalist stated that the most important element in Irish tourism is the quality of the Irish welcome (Anon., 1998b). In the same newspaper, a German tour operator was complaining that the service was unacceptable in many three-star Irish hotels and he added that his clients would not mind paying more if they could have a higher degree of service, including the all-important contact with Irish owners and staff (_The Irish Times_, 1998a). O'Connor in 1993 regretted the lack of empirical evidence for Ireland to assess the quality of the local/tourist relationship whether in casual or more formal encounters. The same is largely true today. No ethnographic study has yet been carried out to assess the quality of the non-Irish/tourist relationship in a formal setting be it in a restaurant or in a hotel. However, according to an interview in April 2000 with Mr. John Dully, chief executive of Bord Fáilte, he said:

We are getting complacent because of our success. We need to alert people to the need to work hard at this. The friendliness of the Irish people and a clean, unspoilt environment are fundamental to our success. It's what people expect and are told by us to expect. It's a fast track to failure if we lose that. (Burke, 2000)

And in the same article, Ms Darina Allen, owner of the famous Ballymaloe Cookery School and Restaurant and a vocal proponent of sustainable tourism, echoes Mr Tully when she says: 'The Irish welcome is what brought people here in the first place. We need to be hugely careful not to ruin what people come here for' (Burke, 2000). The _Hospitality 2005_ report notes:

As the labour market tightens, the role of foreign labour is likely to become more important. This issue was highlighted in industry interviews. There is a greater concentration of foreign workers in the Dublin region than in rural Ireland; however, the number of non-Irish working in the major tourism centres is rising as the labour shortages bite. In general, the industry welcomes employment of non-national labour, but identified issues as follows:

The industry must ensure that *the friendliness and relaxed approach that are central to the Irish tourism product are maintained as the number of non-nationals increases* [my emphasis].

The success in integrating non-nationals depends on language ability, experience, the position they will occupy and the location of the business (Mc Iver Consulting & Tansey Webster Stewart, 1999: 26)

However, as the tourism industry's dependence on non-national staff increases and as staff shortages are more acute, all the experts in the sector do not share the same concerns about the impact of a high level of non-national staff on the Irish experience of holiday-makers. For example, Ms. Eileen O'Mara Walsh, chairwoman of the Irish Tourist Industry Confederation, said at a conference organised by it in March 2000 that generally consumers wanted good service, smiling service and professional service. She added:

> They'd prefer to get that from someone with broken English than get it slapped down by some Irish person in a hurry . . .. While using more local staff in front-of-house activities could boost the Irishness of the experience, it doesn't matter where employees are from so long as they are efficient and friendly. (O'Kane, 2000)

In 1993, O'Connor had posed the question about changing markets and changing images in the tourism sector and how these were translated in the representation of Ireland abroad. She had already identified that the 'emphasis on people as part of the tourist package . . . has been lessening somewhat in recent years' (O'Connor, 1993: 82). In 1999 and 2000, for example, Ireland was marketed in France as 'Irlande – un art de vivre' and this promotion focused on aspects of gracious living such as game angling, golf and visits to great gardens. The emphasis on Irish people is played down and the emphasis on the scenery and landscape is reinforced.

Conclusion

As this chapter has attempted to demonstrate, there is an acute skills shortage in many sectors of the Irish economy and especially in the tourism industry. Many employees have been recruited from abroad and this trend is set to continue in the future. We have identified three challenges with respect to the recruitment of non-Irish staff. First of all, some of the staff, like their Irish counterparts, are not properly trained for their jobs in restaurants and hotels. Second, they are not always equipped with the adequate linguistic expertise, namely English, to carry out the tasks associated with their job effectively. Third, they might not be aware or sensitised to intercultural differences, e.g. appropriateness of certain discourse/behaviour in a given situation. It has been argued by researchers that it is possible to have achieved a very high level of linguistic proficiency whilst having a relatively low level of sociopragmatic proficiency. This can result in such speakers using language which some people may interpret as inappropriate, incomprehensible or even offensive. As the recruitment of non-Irish staff seems ineluctable, the Irish Tourism Industry and the State Training Tourism Agency (CERT) could draw on the experience and expertise of researchers in the new interdisciplinary area of Languages for Cross-Cultural Capability or Intercultural Communication and direct their resources to appropriate linguistic and intercultural training for new employees. The work of researchers in the UK, France and in Ireland would be a major source of inspiration for people dealing with the changing trends in the Irish tourism employment and attempting to deal with these changes in a positive and inclusive manner.

If tourists coming to Ireland have various expectations about their holiday experience, including an interest in meeting 'Irish people', then it will be necessary to radically rethink approaches to host/tourist encounters in Irish tourism where the distinction between 'natives' and 'newcomers' breaks down in the new multicultural and multilingual Ireland.

References

The Irish Times (2000a) Advertisement for JacksonStone, 12 April.

The Irish Times (1999) Immigration proposed to rescue economy, 19 April.

The Irish Times (2000b) Visa delays for catering staff, 17 May.

Burke, S. (2000) Welcoming mat begins to show signs of wear, 17 April.

CERT (1998a) *Employment Survey of the Tourism Industry in Ireland, Volume 1 – Hotels and Guesthouses*. Dublin: CERT.

CERT (1998b), *Employment Survey of the Tourism Industry in Ireland, Volume 2 – Restaurants*. Dublin: CERT.

CERT (1999) *Review of Year 1998*. Dublin: CERT.

CERT (2000) *Review of Year 1999*. Dublin: CERT.

Chambers, A. and O'Baoill, D. (eds) (1999) *Intercultural Communication and Language Learning*. Dublin: The Irish Association for Applied Linguistics/The Royal Irish Academy.

Clark, A. and Manselli, C. (1995) *Benvenuti – Italian for the Tourism Industry*. Dublin: CERT.

Cronin, M. (2000) *Across the Lines: Travel, Language, Translation*. Cork: Cork University Press.

Crosbie, V. (1999) Mapping the intercultural space: A BA in European Business Case Study. In Konstantin Theile and Ciarán Ó hÓgartaigh (eds) *International Business Education – Partnership, Patterns and Prospects for the 21st Century*. Dublin: Oak Tree Press.

Dunne, J. (1998) Confederation wants state to reward tourism. *The Irish Times*, 22 May.

Fischer, D. and Crosbie, V. (1995) *Tourismus auf Deutsch – German for the Tourism Industry*. Dublin: CERT.

Greene, S. (1999) Waiting in vain. *The Irish Times*, 10 April.

Haughey, N. (2000) FÁS gets jobs for asylum-seekers. *The Irish Times*, 5 June.

Holland, K. (1998) The waiting game. *The Irish Times*, 29 December.

Hughes, E. (1998) 5,000 jobs in the hotel sector, but who will fill them? *The Sunday Business Post*, 20 December.

Hughes, E. (1999) Working in IT-Overseas recruitment. *The Sunday Business Post*, 22 June.

Humphreys, J. (1999) Agency to open foreign offices in bid to fill vacancies in tourism industry. *The Irish Times*, 11 January.

Ingle, R. (2000) Hotels and restaurants expect 9,000 job vacancies in summer, find survey. *The Irish Times*, 27 January.

Keena, C. (1999) Supply of new hotel rooms is now ahead of demand. *The Irish Times*, 10 June.

Keena, C. (2000) Shortage of staff closes successful Dublin restaurant. *The Irish Times*, 23 January.

Killick, D. and Parry, M. (eds) (1999) *Languages for Cross-Cultural Capability – Promoting the Discipline: Marking Boundaries & Crossing Borders*. Proceedings of the Conference at Leeds Metropolitan University: 12–14 December 1998. Leeds: Centure for Language Study, Leeds Metropolitan.

Lazenby Simpson, B. (1999) Developing cross-cultural capability at the interface between language learning and employment: A study of refugee language learners in pre-vocational language courses. In D. Killick and M. Parry (eds) *Languages for Cross-Cultural Capability – Promoting the Discipline: Marking Boundaries and Crossing Borders*. Proceedings of the Conference, Leeds Metropolitan University, 12–14 December 1998. Leeds: Centre for Language Study, Leeds Metropolitan.

The Irish Times (2002c) Letters to the Editor, Restaurant staff. 30 March.

Marlowe, L. (2000) Recruitment agency in France focuses on employment in Ireland. *The Irish Times*, 12 May.

McDaid, J. (1998) Irish Tourist Industry Confederation (ITIC) dinner. Reported in *LINK*. Dublin: Bord Fáilte.

McIver Consulting and Tansey Webster Stewart (1999) *Hospitality 2005 – A Human Resource Strategy -Building A Sustainable Future Through People*. Dublin: CERT.

McKenna, J. (1999) All things to all people – almost. *The Irish Times*, 6 March.

Mulcahy, O. (1999a) Lolling over a long, lazy lunch. *The Irish Times*, 22 May.

Mulcahy, O. (1999b) So much space – and not a complaint. *The Irish Times*, 19 June.

Mulcahy, O. (1999c) Lord of the lunch. *The Irish Times*, 7 August.

Mulcahy, O. (1999d) Great food, but where is the sea? *The Irish Times*, 14 August.

Mulcahy, O. (2000) From atmosphere to zest. *The Irish Times*, 8 January.

Mulqueen, E. (1999) Tourism chief wants to build business off the beaten track. *The Irish Times*, 2 July.

Murphy-Lejeune, E. (1997) Language and culture crossing: The ethnographic bridge. In A. Coulson (ed.) *Exiles and Migrants: Crossing Thresholds in European Culture and Society* (pp. 212–22). Brighton: Sussex Academic Press.

Murphy-Lejeune (1998) *L'étudiant européen voyageur, un nouvel 'étranger' – Aspects de l'adaptation interculturelle des étudiants européens*. Unpublished PhD thesis, Université de Nancy II.

O'Connor, B. (1993) Myths and mirrors: Tourist images and national identity. In B. O'Connor and M.Cronin (eds) *Tourism in Ireland – A Critical Analysis*. Cork: Cork University Press

O'Dea, C. (1999) Republic is home to one-third of Europe's army of teleworkers. *The Irish Times,* 8 October.

O'Kane, P. (2000) Short order staffing becomes a tall order. *The Sunday Tribune,* 2 April.

O'Sullivan, K. (1999) Language problems mean safety risks in food trade. *The Irish Times,* 20 November.

Parker, G. and Rouxeville, A. (eds) (1995) *The Year Abroad. Preparation, Monitoring and Evaluation.* London: AFLS/CILT.

Péchenart, J., Pyle, D., Rantz, F. and Tangy, A. (1995) *Parlez Tourisme! French for the Tourism Industry.* Dublin: Gill and Macmillan.

Péchenart, J. and Tangy, A. (1993) Gifts of tongues: Foreign languages and tourism policy in Ireland. In B. O'Connor and M. Cronin (eds) *Tourism in Ireland – A Critical Analysis.* Cork: Cork University Press.

Ponte Miramontes, D. (1995) *Hablando de Turismo – Spanish for the Tourism Industry.* Dublin: CERT.

Sheridan, K. (1999) Frosty Fáilte. *The Irish Times,* 23 January.

Tomalin, B. and Stempleski, S. (1993) *Cultural Awareness.* Oxford: Oxford University Press.

The Irish Times (1998a) Encounters with the country and people. *The Irish Times,* 21 August.

The Irish Times (1998b) Opinion: 'Tourism booms'. *The Irish Times,* 31 December.

Yeates, P. (2000) Survey finds unfilled jobs exist in 40% of businesses. *The Irish Times,* 9 June.

Appendix 1

DCU • LS Linguistic Competence Evaluation Outline of test structure

Oral Test

Ten–fifteen minute interview involving a series of questions designed to ascertain the candidate's ability to communicate in the target language. Questions are of both a general and job specific nature. A short dictation of names, addresses and numbers is included. Candidates are evaluated on the following points:

- vocabulary (general and professional)
- grammatical accuracy
- pronunciation
- accent & intonation
- appropriacy i.e. use of formal/informal language
- listening comprehension
- telephone manner
- technical knowledge (where relevant)

Written Test

The following areas are assessed:

Word endings
Prepositions
Verb forms / tenses
Conjunctions / word order
Reading comprehension
Composition
Spelling & punctuation
Vocabulary – use of formal / informal structures, idioms etc.

DCU • LS LANGUAGE ASSESSMENT SCORE SHEET

Name: Recruited by:
Date: Time of Assessment:
Language: Assessed by:

FINAL SCORE (1 ELEMENTARY – 5 NEAR NATIVE):

General conversation (score between 1–5)
Vocabulary range:
Level of fluency:
Level of comprehension:
Level of accuracy (applies to syntax and grammar):
Quality of accent:
Adequacy of register (familiar, formal, idiomatic expressions etc.):
Overall impression (1–5):

Questions on job the candidate is <u>applying for</u>/currently doing (score between 1–5)
Vocabulary range (relating to the position):
Level of fluency:
Level of accuracy (applies to syntax and grammar):
Overall impression (1–5):

Role-play, comprehension of numbers, dates, spelling (score between 1–5)
Level of comprehension:
Level of confidence:
Level of accuracy:
Numbers:
Spelling:
Overall impression (1–5):

Telephone manner (confidence in dealing with the caller etc.) (score between 1–5)
Overall impression (1–5):

Report:

DCU • LS LEVEL TABLE	
Level 5: Near -Native Competence Fully Professional Standard	Accent, fluency & accuracy are very close to those of an educated native speaker of the language. Customers will barely be aware they are not dealing with a native speaker and do not have to modify their speech in order to conduct business with this person. There are practically no errors (in terms of grammar, syntax, vocabulary or pronunciation) in this person's speech and if they do occur, they do not interfere with communication. The candidate has a high level of listening comprehension and will rarely need to ask for clarification. He/she is deemed to be able to work with great efficiency and ease in a professional capacity
Level 4: Advanced Professional standard	A candidate at this level is slightly less competent than a candidate at level 5, perhaps because of a less impressive command of grammar and specialised vocabulary or perhaps because he/she uses less complex structures . He/she cannot be mistaken for a native speaker but can conduct business effectively. There are some occasional errors but they do not interfere with communication and the candidate is always able to repair any break in communication that might occur. The candidate's listening comprehension for details (numbers, names etc.) is 100% accurate.

DCU • LS LEVEL TABLE	
Level 3+: Upper Intermediate Can conduct routine business in the language	Candidates at this level are judged to have the necessary linguistic skills in terms of accent, fluency & accuracy to deal with customers for routine, predictable calls. The customer may have to make some allowances at the level of speaking (speed, complexity of language) & listening but communication is unhampered. Comprehension of details is high (spelling, numbers etc.) but candidates might need to request clarification or repetitions for more complex situations.
Level 3: Intermediate Not suitable to conduct business professionally in the language	Candidate has a sound knowledge of the basic grammatical structures and can communicate using a limited vocabulary. He/she requires consolidation of structures and vocabulary building. This candidate would not be at the required level to deal with customers in a professional context but is deemed to be able to progress quickly to a higher level of competence with further training.
Level 2: Pre-intermediate Not suitable to conduct business professionally in the language	Candidate has retained a grasp of the basic grammatical structures and a limited vocabulary. He/she can understand simple sentences at a slow pace and can formulate very basic responses.
Level 1: Elementary Not suitable to conduct business professionally in the language	Candidate has studied the language in the past and retains some of the basic structures and a minimal vocabulary. Comprehension and expression are very limited. This student generally understands simple questions but responds in native language.

© DCU • LS, Dublin City University, Dublin 9.

Chapter 13

'Not Only Beef, But Beauty. . .': Tourism, Dependency, and the Post-colonial Irish State, 1925–30

SPURGEON THOMPSON

> The national bourgeoisie will be greatly helped on its way towards decadence by the Western bourgeoisies, who come to it as tourists avid for the exotic. . . The national bourgeoisie organizes centers of rest and relaxation and pleasure resorts to meet the wishes of the Western bourgeoisie. Such activity is given the name of tourism, and for the occasion will be built up as a national industry.
> (Frantz Fanon, 1963)

At the moment of independence, as Frantz Fanon (1963: 152) puts it: 'The national middle class discovers its historic mission: that of intermediary'. The ideological expression of the condition of being the post-colonial 'intermediary' is precisely tourist discourse. In Ireland, the magazines, the brochures, the guides, the penny-journals, the newspaper articles and promotional films, the postcards and trinkets are all part of the 'historic mission' of being intermediate, of being the go-between, the coordinator, the second-level bureaucrat for the British bourgeoisie. Cajoling English tourists into visiting the country that their army had recently ransacked expresses exactly, indeed epitomises, the general attitude of the Irish post-colony's[1] new bourgeoisie toward the British bourgeoisie. This is the internally conflicted reasoning of the post-colonial bourgeois: the British Army had burned much of downtown Dublin to the ground in 1916; they had set Cork's city centre on fire; they had terrorised the countryside for three years; yet the British bourgeoisie possesses finance capital. Therefore, invite them to gaze at the scenery, to play golf, to hunt, to fish and to be entertained by native wit. That way they may be encouraged to invest more money in the Free State economy. Everything, according to this depoliticising, history-occluding logic, depends on the British bourgeoisie's initiatives and centres around 'attracting' their attention and interest. Such vacuous reasoning is not unusual, however. It is, rather, a predictable result of the conditions that prevail in the course of decolonisation, as Fanon so clearly elucidates. Locked into economic dependency upon the bourgeoisie of Great Britain, it is natural that the post-colonial élite should choose to develop tourism.

While tourism was, by no means, a priority for the new state, a small but rich section of the state´s élite moved ahead with its promotion. This section consisted of hotel, transport and railway owners. In January of 1925, the Irish Tourist Association (ITA) was founded at a meeting chaired by the Minister for Industry and Finance (Duggan & Dineen, 1997: 10). It consolidated three separate tourist organisations that had existed since the late 19th century in order, primarily, to pool their dwindling resources (*The Irish Times*, 3 March 1925).[2] Its first president was an American lawyer, Howard S. Harrington, living in Dunloe Castle, Killarney (*Irish Travel*, Sept. 1925: 9[3]; *Irish Travel*, July 1926: 243[4]). At its foundation, several sources expressed an unbounding optimism about the goals of the association. *The Irish Times* (3 March 1925) praised the new tourism industry, that is, 'what a great practical railway authority recently declared to be "almost as capable of endowing Ireland with wealth as her agriculture"'. Claims like these would be repeated by tourism promoters and by no means should be granted any credence. Until 1997 tourism would not become a larger industry than agriculture in Ireland (even then, only slightly). It in no way constituted the same kind of economic potential in this period and the talk of 'practical railway authorities' was far from practical or authoritative. It was the empty talk of advertising, the expression of a grand fantasy.

But it was largely supported by the state-sympathetic press. *The Irish Times* editorial 'Free State "Publicity"' (23 March 1925) put it almost poetically: 'We are reminded to-day of another national asset. Ireland can offer the world not only beef, but beauty . . .'. Of course, 'the world' here means Britain: 90% of Irish exports were to Britain in 1925. And 90% of tourists to Ireland were British. *The Irish Times* cannot say it openly but it means to say that it can offer *Britain* 'not only beef but beauty'. Furthermore, the rhetoric of *The Irish Times* helps to elevate tourism to the status an industry, as worthwhile and valid as cattle-ranching. Tourism was not by any means an industry in this sense, being entirely dependent on the British economy's fluctuations, as well as the travelling trends of the middle classes there. In 1925 tourism was not an industry but a desire that expressed the stunted sentiments of the new élite. It should be understood more as a mass-cultural expression of this desire rather than as an important component of the economy.

One of the first steps the ITA took was to begin the publication of a monthly magazine, *Irish Travel*. Unlike the northern tourist agency (The Ulster Tourist Development Association, founded in 1923), the ITA's strategy included not only press visits, brochures and local guides but the production of a fairly substantial magazine. The monthly publication series of *Irish Travel* would remain unbroken until 1953 when it was replaced by *Ireland of the Welcomes*, the magazine of the Irish Tourist Board. The magazine was as much a piece of promotional literature aimed at English tourists as it was a 'shop journal' aimed at hotel owners and the Irish public in general. We have evidence that it was read in America as well and that some of its articles were farmed out to literary magazines there.[5] It is within the pages of *Irish Travel* that the ideological project and history of the ITA can be ascertained most reliably.

But before turning to the pages of the ITA magazine, there is one source for the early days of tourism promotion that is crucial, for through it we can see that there was a pronounced divide between the wealthy board members of the ITA and the bureaucrats that they hired to produce their brochures and magazine. It is through this source that one should view the material produced by the ITA. C.S. Andrews's *Man of No Property* (1982) describes and explains the early years of tourism with a high degree of accuracy. Andrews worked for the ITA first as an accountant and then managing the production of *Irish Travel* from its earliest days, and stayed with it through 1930. Aside from providing a detailed narrative of the formation of the ITA, Andrews describes its staff, important events related to it and the perception of tourism in Ireland at the time. What is absolutely central about Andrews' account, however, is the fact that he reveals that every member of the ITA staff had been a member of the IRA in the Civil War; they had, each of them, taken up arms against the post-colonial state because they did not recognise it as legitimate.[6] The secretary of the ITA, J.P. O'Brien, had fought with the IRA during the Civil War and decided to set aside every post in the organisation for ex-IRA volunteers. In effect, the office was staffed with devoted subversives, ex-members of an illegal guerilla army, while the board of the organisation was anything but this. As Andrews describes: 'It consisted of what was commonly referred to as men of substance who were connected in some way with the tourism business. They were all strong supporters of the Free State regime and some were active politically' (Andrews, 1982: 70). The political convictions of the staff were kept completely hidden from the board. This was difficult to maintain, as Andrews recounts, since he was harassed continually by the Criminal Investigation Department (CID, a special, armed branch of the police force), being regularly picked up in an unmarked car and brought to prison, where he would sit all day with no explanation for his detainment.

Others among the staff were subject to the same treatment. Hiding this from the influential board members would have been difficult. In any case, however, the divide between the board and the staff was, if unspoken, all the more enduring for being so.

Andrews (1982: 70) explains that there may have been good reasons for the board not to pry into the politics of their bureaucrats:

> Having regard to the political climate of the time I thought O'Brien showed great loyalty and courage in surrounding himself with a coven of ex-IRA men who had opposed the government in arms even though, with the exception of myself and that only in the political sense, they were no longer involved in the resistance movement. Certainly the political associations of the staff were never questioned by the board. This may have been due to the fact that the ITA as an organization was insignificant nationally or, more probably, to the government's anxiety to diffuse the causes of opposition and encourage Republicans to return to normality.

Normality, in other words, could be bought by hiring subversives into semi-state agencies, giving them jobs instead of prison cells. Andrews' speculation is, no doubt, correct about this. It is a form of 'peace and reconciliation' to invest in subversives rather than to police them; it is also less expensive. At the same time it gives former rebels an interest, a stake in normality and the consolidation of state power.

There is one more fact that Andrews reveals, however, that complicates the picture. As Andrews (1982: 73) explains: '[In 1927] I appointed Frank Ryan who later became a folk hero of left-wing Republicanism in Ireland and famous for his involvement in the Spanish Civil War. . . He was working for me for some time before I became aware that Frank Ryan was an active IRA member.' Ryan was an active member of the Dublin Brigade of the IRA while he was working at the ITA; he used the office of the ITA to store IRA documents, as a cover for his activities, and as source of much needed income. In fact, as his biographer Sean Cronin reports, Ryan was editing and contributing articles to *Irish Travel* at the very same time that he was publishing an illegal, Irish language Republican newspaper *An t-Óglach* (Cronin, 1980). This led to some problems with the special branch of the police, the CID: 'One day', Andrews (1982: 74) recounts, 'a senior CID officer and his aides entered the office, went straight to Frank Ryan's desk and unearthed a file of IRA documents'. They later came and arrested Ryan, only to release him shortly afterwards. It is clear from Andrews' description, although he does not mention it, that the CID had kept the office under surveillance, otherwise they would not have known exactly where the IRA documents would have been stored, i.e. which desk was Ryan's (Cronin, 1980).[7]

To give some sense of what it meant to be an active IRA member in 1927, it should be recounted that it was in the summer of this year that Kevin O'Higgins, a leading member of the new parliament (also responsible for the executions of some 70 Republican prisoners in 1922), was assassinated by the IRA. In 1926, the IRA had been raiding police stations throughout the new state, guards at prisons keeping IRA prisoners were shot and the prisons raided, and some CID detectives were fired upon.[8] In years previous, the IRA had kept up a campaign of shooting policemen (those who harassed the IRA) and in 1924 they shot a British private, on leave from his duties on Spike Island (a British Army base that remained after decolonisation) – as presumably 'a tourist' – in Cork. The importance of IRA documents, as well, cannot be underestimated. The kind of documents Ryan would have been hiding in the ITA office included such items as reports of republican courts of inquiry and letters to and from members and leaders of the IRA. Tim Pat Coogan (1994: 35), in researching the history of the IRA, found that what was _prima facie_ a secret organisation at this time, 'churned out mimeographed documents in vast and incriminating quantities, inevitably to be found or seized by the authorities'. While produced in massive amounts, these documents were the backbone of the guerilla army's organisational structure. Frank Ryan was only a junior member at this point but would rise to prominence within the organisation in the following years– after he had left the ITA. Ryan's later fame would be built on the fact that he led a section of the Irish International Brigade to Spain to fight Franco's fascists in December of 1936. He was captured, imprisoned and sentenced to death. He lost his hearing and fell badly ill in Franco's prisons while awaiting execution but due to international pressure was eventually released only to die later while a passenger in a German submarine. Ryan was, in short, a committed revolutionary.

Yet, as Andrews (1982: 75) recounts: 'The text for the [1927] series of local tourist brochures and guide books was written jointly by Frank Ryan and myself, although Frank's main preoccupation was with the production of an omnibus _Guide to Ireland_.' That an active IRA volunteer, committed to overthrowing by force the post-colonial state, replacing it with a socialist republic, and driving the British from Northern Ireland, wrote the first 'Ireland Guide' is more than a little unusual. It raises key questions about the complexity of the conditions of production of this kind of mass culture in a post-colonial context. Obviously, Ryan had not been 'bought out' by the post-colonial bourgeoisie; in fact, he was using his new job writing tourist brochures and compiling the _Guide to Ireland_ as a way to make himself appear 'normal'. The 'cover' that a respectable job as a bureaucrat could provide for him was undoubtedly invaluable; yet the fact that his job was to *write* tourist brochures and a guide for English tourists raises other questions about how he negotiated or viewed his unusual position.

In one view, Ryan becomes a sort of player; the discourse he produces for tourists becomes an elaborate ludic performance, a show put up both to distract English visitors and to enable subversive activities to continue unwatched. He is thus like the figure of Michaeleen Flynn, the epitome of the stereotypical stage Irishman in John Ford's film, *The Quiet Man* (1952). Flynn acts the part of the over-loquacious, leprachaun-like 'guide', who takes John Wayne back to his family homestead in a jaunting car; yet we find out later in the film, in a throwaway line, that he had recently been active in the IRA. On the outside, Flynn is an over-acted stereotype but behind the kitschy exterior is a revolutionary. Ryan's case is, of course, much more complicated than this. But this is one way to read his activities. Another way to read them is as those of an oppressed, even hunted subject with few choices. They were the actions of a revolutionary desperate for work and looking for any position that would get him access to production and layout facilities for the publication of subversive materials, as well as the paper and mimeographing materials for the duplication of IRA documents.[9] He certainly could not find work in the bourgeois newspapers' offices, so he turned to a minor tourist agency's office. Understanding his choices in this way makes it possible to read the texts that Ryan produced not as those of an elaborate mask but as those of somebody who had no choice but to write in a manner and for a purpose that would be at least unsatisfying to him, if not degrading. His writing becomes a sort of record of repression, the stereotypes and clichés produced by him the imprint of the imperatives of the new bourgeoisie. Indeed, Andrews uses strong words to describe how he himself, being a committed subversive as a member of an outlawed political party, saw his work. Andrews (1982: 69) says: '[T]hough I had no enthusiasm for what I really felt to be a demeaning occupation there was nothing better on offer'. And again, 'I felt no pride or satisfaction in working in tourist development. I thought it a shoddy business and more associated with national mendicity [beggary] than with legitimate industry'. And again (p. 72), 'I believed neither in the possibility nor desirability of an Ireland swarming with tourists. I could not rid my mind of the notion that Ireland's role in tourism lay in the supply of still more jarveys, gillies,[10] waiters and chambermaids.' With such evident disaffection in evidence, it is difficult not to conclude that the ex-IRA men working there felt as he did, that even Ryan felt demeaned by his work but continued to do it.

While it may be attractive to view the situation as one in which a group of committed radicals used the ITA as a cover for their political convictions,

I do not, finally, subscribe to this interpretation. This view becomes untenable, starts to unhinge rapidly when one looks closely at the material the ITA published. Alternatively, I take the critical view that the bourgeoisie was able to successfully impose its will, its mandate to assert 'normality' in the ITA's propaganda and to produce an image of Ireland for English consumption that accords neatly with the travel writing and tourist discourse that attended at least a century and a half of British colonialism. Finally, it was the role of the 'intermediary', the imperative to give the smiling welcome to the British middle and ruling classes, the production of what Fanon calls 'centers of rest and relaxation and pleasure resorts', that would impose themselves upon even those bureaucrats with the most oppositional of politics. The board of hotel and railway owners would finally be able to assert their cramped, unambitious vision over the entire staff of the ITA. The political is not only pushed into the past but the very people who would lead political struggles would be compelled by economic necessity to advance the larger project of depoliticisation on behalf of the new bourgeoisie. This can be seen clearly in the ideological project represented in its brochures and guides, in the pages of *Irish Travel* and in the activities of the organisation generally.

To begin, take the following introduction to the *Ireland Guide* almost certainly written by Frank Ryan:

> Ireland! What varied emotions are stirred, what memories are evoked by the very name! Scarcely a country of its size in the world holds such a combination of attractions for the holiday-maker, in its wonderful diversity of scenic beauty; its soft balmy health-giving air; the richness and romance of its historical associations; its wealth of monuments to the glorious and remote past – and, over all these, the glamour of that indescribable atmosphere which imparts to an Irish holiday something which is never quite found elsewhere. (Irish Tourist Association, 1930: 2)[11]

With the knowledge of Ryan's political commitments at the time of writing this in mind, it is possible to read this passage as deliberately evasive, speaking through what it leaves out rather than through what it includes. Important omissions include, of course, any characterisation of the people of Ireland as friendly, hospitable, comic, etc., that freight most of the travelogues and guidebooks produced in these years. Omitted, as well, from Ryan's introduction is any comment on the recent past. The only significant concession, ultimately, to colonialist discourse here is the sentence about the 'indescribable atmosphere', which makes holidays in Ireland unique. Even this is not much of a concession. It is possible to see in these omissions and in the deliberate vagueness of phrases such as 'varied emotions are stirred' or 'indescribable atmosphere' a sort of struggle against the imperative Ryan would have felt to conform more to accepted stereotypes for his English readers. Yet while this way of reading Ryan's text is compelling, it is nonetheless impossible to miss the cliché after cliché embedded in it: 'richness and romance,' 'wonderful diversity of scenic beauty', 'wealth of monuments' – this is certainly not the language of revolution. It is the bureaucratically produced, ideological wet blanket thrown over revolution. It is the stock of clichés pulled out to give legitimacy to the status quo and to emphasise the prevalence of normality. Take another example from the 1927 brochure for County Wexford, *Wexford and Its Historic Sights,* written by Ryan and Andrews: 'Gorey, in the north, has its memories of rival occupations during the '98 Insurrection. A good golfing centre, it is also the station for the sea-side resort of Courtown, three miles away' (ITA, 1927a: 4). A crucial site of a 1798 Rebellion battle is transfigured into 'a good golfing centre' useful because it is nearby a local resort. Or Cork, the heart of dissident republicanism in Ireland, becomes, in a brochure written by Ryan and Andrews: 'Picturesquely situated in a hollow encircled by the hills and sea, Cork has strong claims to be the most charming city in Ireland' (ITA, 1927b: 4). It is precisely the fact that such writing appears 'harmless' and normal that is the register of its political function – i.e. to naturalise the legitimacy of the status quo and indeed the new state. In this kind of writing, Ryan and Andrews demonstrate the limits of resistance, the point at which compromises are made to those in power. But the ITA is far more open about naturalising the legitimacy of the status quo in its other publications, especially in *Irish Travel.*

I will begin the survey with a quote from Sir Felix Pole, General Manager of the Great Western Railway of England, in an article entitled 'To the People of Killarney', included in the first issue of *Irish Travel,* in September 1925 (p. 8):

> Nature has given to Killarney the most exquisite scenery, but the people of the district must now heartily co-operate, or we cannot maintain our side of the work. Traders, hotel-keepers, and restaurant owners must make a fast and lasting friend of the tourist . . . Killarney as a tourist resort has to be re-introduced to the public. Never before has it had to face such clever opposition as that which prevails elsewhere. It has powerful business rivals, who are ready to make the most of adverse reports.

The opening issue of *Irish Travel* was directed almost entirely at 'the people' of Ireland, just as this quotation is directed at the 'people' of Killarney. The articles are dominated by a similar tone to Sir Felix Pole's here, who, in his mild warning, is encouraging the people of Killarney to conform to his company's interests; i.e. to make a 'fast and lasting friend of the tourist', to 'heartily co-operate', otherwise 'powerful business rivals' will take Killarney's tourism traffic away from it. Implicit in his warning is that 'adverse reports' must be countered by positive ones, i.e. the image of Ireland must be doctored, corrected in the press, just as was being done in the north. The editor of *Irish Travel*, J.P. O'Brien in 1925, has set the tone for the magazine's and the ITA's ideological project here. This project is centred around modernising Ireland's tourism industry to meet the needs of the British bourgeoisie, represented here by the railway manager Sir Felix Pole. In order to do this, the agency must actively combat the 'adverse reports'. It must make the post-colony appear modern, respectable and above or beyond politics.

Before moving on to look at this active campaign, we should attend briefly to Sir Felix Pole. In fact, while in general encouraging conformity with his company's interests, he is also responding directly to a specific labour dispute. The boatmen-guides of Killarney, upon hearing that the ITA's American President, Howard Harrington, was going to introduce motorboats onto the lakes in the district, protested strongly, to the point of preparing to go on strike. Of course, the boatmen are staunchly determined to resist the innovation because the introduction of machinery, as always, puts people out of work. With Pole's warning to 'heartily cooperate', Harrington, in the typical fashion of the bourgeoisie, counters the protesting boatmen with the charge that the 'welfare of Killarney' should not be 'jeopardised by the ill-advised attitude of a small section of her people'(*The Irish Independent*, 25 October 1925). Normality, defending the interests of the post-colonial bourgeoisie, the status quo, these all guard the 'welfare of Killarney', not labour disputes.

As with the Ulster Tourist Development Association, the ITA must press politics into the past. The lead article in *Irish Travel's* third number exemplifies the tendency. 'Is Ireland Safe?' asks its headline. Then:

> Irish readers will rub their eyes in wonder when they read the heading of this article . . . Many readers abroad still think Ireland a land with a turbulent, unsettled population who do not know how to enjoy the gifts that have been bestowed upon them in such profusion. We who live in Ireland know that the country has passed through its ordeal of fire and sword and has settled down to the ways and habits of peace. Even when it was rent by war, the visitor who came on business or pleasure found its people courteous and hospitable . . . Ireland is perhaps the most peaceful country in the world to-day. It has its own social, political, financial and economic problems to solve, like every other country, but it can be truthfully said that it is not inhabited by a

turbulent, unsettled people. There is no turbulence; there is no rioting, and there is practically no crime in Ireland beyond the very ordinary offences that arise out of the conditions of modern civilization. In the face of this fact it is ridiculous to suggest that Ireland is not a safe place for any visitor. The scare stories that have been published recently are laughed at in Ireland. We would ask our readers to join in our laughter. .. 'Ireland is probably the safest country in the world for visitors,' wrote George Bernard Shaw some time ago when conditions were less settled than they are at present. Of course the great dramatist was only saying what everybody in Ireland knew to be a fact. . . etc. (*Irish Travel*, November, 1925: 1)

The sheer repetition in this article of reassurances should make any attentive reader nervous, suspicious that what is denied so vehemently is precisely what the writer has to hide. And the assurance not once, but twice that Ireland *even at war* is safe for visitors, should draw suspicion as well – what need is there to include such information if the country has 'settled down to the ways ... of peace'? Is it to suggest that the visitor is even 'more' safe now, though he was safe anyways? In all cases, in fact, the visitor is perfectly safe, it appears. Not incidentally, on the same page as this article is a panoramic photo subtitled 'Cromwell Barracks, Inishbofin. Built by the Protector as a safeguard against the Dutch . . .'. In British chronologies, perhaps, Cromwell is referred to as 'the Protector'. But in Irish nationalist history and popular culture of this time, he was seen in anything but such a kindly light. Or perhaps we have an explanation in the previous issue of the magazine: 'When Cromwell drove the 'ancient Irishry,' as they were contemptuously called, 'to hell or to Connaught,' he unwittingly preserved Irish tradition in the most beautiful part of Ireland' (*Irish Travel*, October 1925: 29). It becomes clear: Cromwell was the Protector of Irish tradition, and conveniently enough for the tourist seeking to consume it, his choice for a reservation was the most beautiful part of Ireland.[12] In any case, the combination on the page of excessive assurances with a reference to Cromwell as 'Protector' is a signal to the anxiety behind the project of the ITA to assert normality to its English readers.

Another signal to this anxiety are the continual warnings to Irish hotel workers or all other workers that come into contact with tourists. For example, a note signed 'a Hotel Manager' urges hotel workers not to 'commit indiscretions'. For if they do, they will thus constitute the 'weakest link' in the tourism industry. He has trouble understanding how such 'indiscretions' can occur: 'Many hotel employees, sane in other matters, apparently fail to appreciate the result of their actions ... and I marvel at it' (*Irish Travel*, June, 1925: 34). Exactly what kind of behaviour he is referring to is unclear but this is apparently a reference to latent hostility towards English visitors among hotel workers. In another example, the editor reports how the policing of proper behaviour takes place:

> The [ITA] have at heart the welfare and interests of the visitors, and they will not allow anything to interfere with their comfort – complaints of discomfort are immediately investigated by special inspectors and serious notice is taken thereof and punishment awarded if necessary: (*Irish Travel*, August, 1925: 42)

There is later a warning to the drivers of cabs and small hotel owners, in a later issue, that sounds even paramilitary in tone. The 'Tourist Protective Organization', as it calls itself (probably a non-entity fabricated for the article), will deal with those who overcharge tourists or treat them badly otherwise: 'and the few individuals who are foolish enough to refuse a "square deal",' will have, in a very short time, practical experience of the Association's protective powers' (*Irish Travel*, February, 1926: 113). Does this mean the deployment of 'Special Inspectors' who will come and 'adjust' the violator's 'rates'? The tone here is important because it expresses an overdetermined anxiety to assert and police normality in the places tourists come into contact with Ireland.

The policing of 'tourist comfort' at this time can be evidenced as well by activities outside of the 'powers' of the 'Tourist Protective Organisation.' For after the state was founded, for example, begging and loitering laws were tightened at tourist locales. Begging was allowed freely in places like Killarney under the colonial regime (though laws had been passed against it, they were not enforced). There is evidence that this tightening of anti-begging laws took place swiftly. In the same report in *The Irish Independent* in which Howard Harrington's charge against the Killarney boatmen appears, for example, it is also noted: 'All the old abuses which did so much harm to Killarney have disappeared including the begging pest' (*Irish Travel*, October 1925). The anxiety to 'clean up' or sanitise tourist locales is also dramatically illustrated in one scene that H.V. Morton (1931: 183) describes: two Free State Guards dress up like tourists and arrest an old woman attempting to sell poteen to tourists in Killarney's Gap of Dunloe. And as John Gibbons (1931: 54) hears from a bus-driver in 1931, police generally do not ticket automobiles with British plates. In fact, in the *Irish Free State Official Handbook* (1932: 305), the first thing it mentions, in the 'Ireland for the Visitor' section, written by Stephen Gwynn, is that 'Ireland is now the motorist's paradise'. The ITA's project is a mass-cultural correlative to these state practices, an ideological form of policing rather than the actual policing of tourism amenities – that is, unless the 'Tourist Protective Organisation' was not a fabrication.

While the ITA set about advancing its project of sanitising, modernising and depoliticising the post-colony for tourists – at least textually – it also introduced a campaign that attempted something rather different. This campaign was announced on the covers of every issue of *Irish Travel* until the mid-1930s. It was summed up in the slogan 'See Ireland First'. Directed at all Irish people who could afford holidays, i.e. the new bourgeoisie and those of the petty bourgeoisie with some disposable income, this campaign argued for Irish people to tour their own country, rather than to go to the continent for their holidays. Declan Kiberd, writing in 1991, notes that during the period of modernisation following the 1970s in Ireland, Irish people were treated to similar slogans. Kiberd (1991) states:

> So rapid were the changes that the native Irish themselves began to take the place of absent foreign visitors, in an attempt to exhume on a fortnight's holiday their all-but-buried past. Tourist slogans which, a generation earlier might have been beamed at a British or American audience, were now directed at the Irish themselves: 'Discover Ireland; it's part of who you are'.

The ITA's 1925–35 campaign significantly predates the 1980s slogans Kiberd cites, making it possible to see the phenomenon of Irish internal tourism as historically rooted.

Of course, one of the first great descriptions of the question of internal tourism in the early 20th century is that of James Joyce in *The Dead*. Joyce's story is nothing less than a detailed accounting of the mentality of the colonial petty bourgeoisie. Its chief character, Gabriel Conroy, represents exactly the petty, intermediary, vision-less member of the class that will eventually take over the state and its bureaucracy. His encounter with Molly Ivors dramatises the confrontation between one fragment of that class and its dominant grouping. The encounter should be rehearsed for what its details can tell us about this intramural class conflict. Ivors invites Gabriel and his wife to stay on the Aran Islands for a month. Gabriel waffles. The confrontation follows as such:

> It would be splendid for Gretta too if she'd come. She's from Connacht, isn't she?
> – Her people are, said Gabriel shortly.
> – But you will come, won't you? said Miss Ivors, laying her warm hand eagerly on his arm.
> – The fact is, said Gabriel, I have already arranged to go–
> – Go where? asked Miss Ivors.
> – Well, you know, every year I go for a cycling tour with some fellows and so –

– But where? asked Miss Ivors.
– Well, we usually go to France or Belgium or perhaps Germany, said Gabriel awkwardly.
– And why do you go to France and Belgium, said Miss Ivors, instead of visiting your own land?
– Well, said Gabriel, it's partly to keep in touch with the languages and partly for a change.
– And haven't you your own language to keep in touch with–Irish? asked Miss Ivors.
– Well, said Gabriel, if it comes to that, you know, Irish is not my language.
. . .
– And haven't you your own land to visit, continued Miss Ivors, that you know nothing of, your own people, and your own country?
– O, to tell you the truth, retorted Gabriel suddenly, I'm sick of my own country, sick of it!
– Why? asked Miss Ivors. (Joyce, 1993: 134)

Gabriel never answers her question. And moments later, she whispers in his ear, 'West Briton!' Crucial in this exchange is the fact that Gabriel seems to know, before Ivors presses him, that the kind of touring that he has done in the past on the continent was by now a contested practice among many in his class. He feels guilty for doing it, so evades the issue of exactly where he will be cycling. In short, the character of Gabriel gives us a glimpse into the sort of thinking prevalent among members of his class, and the way that they are entrenched against the more radical cultural nationalism registered in the figure of Molly Ivors. This entrenchment is so deep, in fact, that Conroy even cloaks the fact that his wife is from Galway by saying that only 'her people' are from there – a deliberate evasion meant to sever any direct connection he may have to an Irish-speaking area. When pressed as to why he is so entrenched, why he is so 'sick of' his country, he cannot find an answer. It is a thoughtless paralysis, the lack of conviction characteristic of the post-colonial bourgeois-to-be, that we see in Gabriel Conroy.

Aside from its highlighting this mentality, there is another reason that I have included this confrontation with Molly Ivors here. For Joyce's likely model for the character of Miss Ivors is, in fact, Hanna Sheehy-Skeffington, the radical women's suffragist and republican.[13] Sheehy-Skeffington joined the board of the ITA in 1927 (*Irish Travel*, July 1928: 525).[14] She contributed several articles to *Irish Travel*, three of them of substantial length. Her influence on the board almost certainly helped to pressure the publication to step up the internal tourism campaign, 'See Ireland First'. Furthermore, with the help of Frank Ryan's fluent Irish, the publication of articles in the

Irish language – starting in 1928 in the pages of *Irish Travel* – can be attributed to her influence. 'Miss Ivors' was now a board member. No longer an outsider or representative of a class fraction, she was expressing her 'politics of tourism' in practice.

The conditions of this politics of tourism are multilayered. For the appearance of internal tourism promotion would be the result of several factors. These include at least the following three: (1) the expression of resistance it meant to Ryan and Andrews, (2) outside criticism that the ITA was simply selling Ireland to English tourists, and (3) Sheehy-Skeffington's undoubted influence. In the publication of articles in Irish and the campaign to 'see Ireland first', the resistance of Andrews and Ryan to the idea of tourism as 'national mendicity' shows itself. We can read them as expressions of discontent. The defamiliarisation effect, for example, of having the words 'An Ghaoltacht 'na h-ionad Saoire' in Irish script, as a headline in a tourist magazine sent to England must have been significant (*Irish Travel*, October 1928).[15] Two pages of Irish later, the holiday-maker would be wondering where the stereotypes he had expected had disappeared. The presence of pages of Irish in a holiday magazine represents a radically defamiliarising oppositionality, an intractable otherness in the presence of the deeply familiar. Yet, these are minor resistances within the bureaucratic structure dominated by the new bourgeoisie. But they are, nonetheless, moments of resistance, expressions of dissatisfaction. In 1927 articles in Irish could be published in the ITA magazine partly because Ryan and Andrews were there to write them and saw them as expressions of dissatisfaction but also because outside pressure was brought to bear on the ITA – pressure the two would likely welcome secretly but pressure to which they would have to respond officially in more guarded tones. In response to the board's campaign for full state funding of tourism promotion in 1927, criticism of its purpose surfaced in several journals and newspapers. An article in *Irish Travel* (March 1927: 1), 'Ireland for the Irish Holiday Maker', probably written by Andrews, explains:

> The recent campaign of the Irish Tourist Association for the allocation of National Advertising Funds revealed some curious viewpoints, at least one of which deserves immediate attention. It was seriously contended as an argument against such expenditure that the efforts of the ITA are directed solely towards the attraction of foreign visitors. Our programme is to develop travel to and in Ireland – the attraction of foreign visitors and the popularisation of Irish resorts with Irish people... Thousands of our citizens wish to see London, largest of the world's cities, and to these Ireland offers no substitute. Neither can Ireland enter into competition with the highly developed resort

where niggardly nature requires the support of hobby-horses and distorting mirrors to increase its attractions. The basic fact, however, remains that our country offers a choice of holiday resorts and facilities sufficient to meet the requirements of the great proportion of holiday makers. There are those who speak in exalted fashion of the antiquity and splendour of the Celtic civilization. Have they ever explored the wonderful relics of that civilization to be found in every corner of the land? . . . Irish resorts must be made 'fashionable' for Irish people. There lies the chief difficulty. Travel – for pleasure at least – follows fashion. Ireland, as a holiday land, must be brought into the first line of fashion . . . Let us finish with a final appeal to our members and helpers throughout the country, 'For your Holidays – See Ireland First'.

At first this article is defending the ITA's programme, suggesting that it had always been its practice to encourage internal tourism and that charges against it are unfounded. The defence is a deception. It was not among the goals of the ITA to promote internal tourism before 1927. Proof of this can be found in several places but most clearly in its mission statement in 1926: 'What is the Irish Tourist Association?' its heading asks. Its next heading is: 'Its Objects are: 1) To attract Visitors to Ireland, and to cater for their comfort and pleasure. 2) To secure Fixed Minimum Tariffs in all Catering Industries. 3) To improve Transport and Catering conditions' (*Irish Travel*, September, 1926: 21). And that is all. No mention is made of internal tourism in any way. It has only just now, in 1927, adopted internal tourism as a goal. It adopted the stance of the Johnny-come-lately, who had 'all along' been doing precisely the opposite of what it has been accused of neglecting: in fact, it was promoting internal tourism before its critics even thought of internal tourism. These are the lies it must tell its popular critics to hide the fact that it is truly catering directly, and almost exclusively to English tourists.

Next the article seems to change registers entirely. It begins the 'Molly Ivors' argument: that Irish people should tour Ireland before they go to London or the continent. At the time, this must have seemed well worn and almost unnecessary to say. But nonetheless it is a strong argument in post-colonial conditions – if not for its economic importance then for its cultural political value. Then it presents a standard criticism of 'modernisation' in English resorts with their 'distorting mirrors' that artificially enhance their 'beauty', and a by now clichéd version of the Irish countryside as naturally beautiful (as if beauty as a concept was not 'artificially' constructed or enhanced). Then it argues that such natural beauty be made 'fashionable' among Irish people themselves – or rather, to the 'thousands of our citizens' who would rather go to London for their holidays. It is a rather simple and well-rehearsed line of argument.

Yet this single article, with a few scattered articles in Irish, are the only substantive pleas made to Irish people to tour their own country in the entire publication history of the magazine.[16] In it, the writer is trying to convince not only his readers but indeed himself that he is fulfilling a legitimate and respectable function in a new state. The only trace of the direct promotion of internal tourism to remain, aside from the Irish articles and this single appeal, is in the slogan 'See Ireland First', that the magazine continued to print on its cover until many years after C.S. Andrews resigns at the end of 1930, and after Sheehy-Skeffington leaves the board. In later issues, even the *slogan* 'See Ireland First' is evacuated of its original meaning entirely. First, in June of 1930, an article appears headed 'See Ireland First: Broadcast over Station W.G.B.S., New York City, NY, U.S.A.' (*Irish Travel*, June 1930: 227). Its meaning is reduced simply to 'see Ireland before you see any other countries in Europe', Ireland being the first European point of disembarkation for many American tourists travelling on luxury liners. And then later, the meaning is further fumigated in an article entitled, no less than 'An Open Letter to the British Holiday Maker'. The article argues, at one point, that 'hundreds of thousands of British citizens' spend their holidays on the continent:

> They go abroad because it gives them a change but an equal change is to be found in Ireland and Ireland has a prior claim on their patronage. British holiday money spent on the Continent is money completely lost to your country. Spent in Ireland it will go back in the ordinary course of trade. In 1929 the Irish Free State bought British goods to the value of £41,762,536

The article is signed,

Yours Faithfully, 'SEE IRELAND FIRST'! (*Irish Travel*, January 1931: 1).

The article parades Ireland's economic dependency on Britain as being its claim on British tourist money. Since Ireland 'faithfully' buys English goods, rather than making them itself, it should be rewarded with English tourists. 'See Ireland First' because it is your loyal neo-colonial market. The meaning of the slogan becomes so trivial as to lose all of its cultural-political inflections. Depoliticised, the slogan is harnessed to a fawning 'national mendicity'.

The history of tourism promotion in the Irish post-colony is marked by a contradiction. The board of the ITA, post-colonial bourgeois to a man (Sheehy-Skeffington being the only woman ever on the board, and whom I do not regard as a vested member of the same class) brought its stunted vision and guarded interests to the fore and into the pages of *Irish Travel*. These interests were met by the staff they hired with scepticism, a few signs of resistance to them and then finally resignation – in both senses of the word. Resigned to writing depoliticising clichés, Frank Ryan eventually resigned his commission in 1929; Andrews left in 1930; it is not clear when Sheehy-Skeffington left the board, but it was probably in 1929 when she joined the radical Republican newspaper, *An Phoblacht*, as Frank Ryan's assistant editor. The project of policing the representation of normality, of making Ireland appear upright, respectable and post-political could thus proceed.

Notes

1. Throughout my analysis I use the term 'post-colony' to denote the Irish Free State, which consisted of 26 counties of the island of Ireland. It is the most accurate expression for the condition of these counties. Terms such as the Irish Free State, or 'Ireland', or 'Eire' do not accurately denote the fact that Ireland as a whole had not undergone decolonisation. The term 'the Irish post-colony' is semantically flexible and also more accurate than these other denotations.

2. '"Visit Ireland": New Forward Move in Free State: Tourist Traffic Development.' The organisations were the Tourist Organisation Society, the Irish Tourist Association of Cork, and the West of Ireland Tourist Development Association. The first contributed seven members of the ITA board, the latter two each contributed three.

3. 'He was involved in the Prize Court litigation in England, France and Germany until 1921. On completion of this work Mr Harrington determined to make his home in his ancestral Co. Kerry, and in that year he acquired Dunloe Castle, Killarney, where he now resides.' Harrington's position as President of the ITA was short-lived, however. For in 1926 he fled the country to avoid income taxes.

4. 'Mr. H.S. Harrington . . . in tendering his resignation of the Presidency of the Executive Committee [the board] stated that it was with the deepest regret he had been constrained to take this course, but a recent ruling of the Income-tax authorities rendering him liable for Income-tax in Ireland on his total income in U.S.A. left him without an option in the matter.' Harrington was, in all likelihood, sheltering his income from taxation from the United States in Ireland before this ruling – though this can only be speculation.

5. Some articles appeared in the *Saturday Evening Post, American Heritage*, the *New York Daily News* and other middle-brow gazettes.

6. After the IRA cease-fire in 1923, most members of the IRA had very difficult times finding employment. In the case of the ITA, its secretary, J.P. O'Brien, had been a family friend of the Chairman of the ITA board, J.C. Foley (a close friend to the new Irish Prime Minister, T. W. Cosgrave). O'Brien had been an IRA volunteer in Ballyporeen during the civil war. Foley had hired O'Brien not because he knew of O'Brien's politics but because he was, simply, a family friend.

7. 'One day in October 1928, CID detectives raided the Irish Tourist Association's Office at 14 O'Connell Street. In Frank's desk they found papers on a court of inquiry set up by the IRA and letters addressed to the Adjutant-General and the

O.C. of the Dublin Brigade. Ryan was tried in the Circuit Criminal Court . . .' but for some reason found not guilty of membership in the IRA.

8. For a detailed account of IRA activities in these years, see the standard Tim Pat Coogan (1994: 34–8).

9. See O'Loughlin (1987: 58) for a detailed account of Ryan's printing of his 1927 revolutionary newspaper. He used back-door contacts in printing presses he knew in order to get it printed. It is very well a possibility that he used the ITA office supplies and layout equipment to produce it.

10. i.e. hunting guides.

11. Ryan's authorship of this particular introduction to a guide is almost certain. However, room for doubt remains in the fact that the ITA let the contents of the guide sit unpublished until 1930, after Ryan had left the organisation. There are continual announcements of the guide's impending publication from 1927 to 1930 in *Irish Travel* but no guide is actually published until 1930. Yet, it is fairly certain that no part of the guide was altered between 1929, when Ryan left the ITA, and the summer of 1930 when the guide was published.

12. The misfortune of Ireland being beneficial to the tourist is a continual theme in 20th century Irish tourist discourse; for example, see the introduction to the 1962 *Ireland Guide*: 'Another great advantage of Ireland arises from a misfortune of her economic history which has proved a blessing in disguise. Here is a country which has not been over-industrialised. The scenery is never marred by screens of smoke from batteries of chimneys such as beseige the skyline in cities and towns of the manufacturing countries . . . The Motorist, the Walker, the Climber, Everyman finds in Ireland the road clear in the least populated country in Europe. That in itself is probably the supreme advantage.' Depopulation, the guide asserts, caused by the Great Famine, which lead to the transformation of Ireland into pasture for cows and sheep, is the 'supreme advantage'.

13. This is according to Terence Brown (1993: 310 in his introduction to Joyce's *Dubliners*). Richard Ellmann (1982: 246) suggests that the model may have been her sister, Kathleen Sheehy. But neither critic knows for certain.

14. She was the Dublin County Council representative to the board. Sheehy-Skeffington was a leading resistance fighter in the struggle against colonialism and patriarchy in Ireland; she was, with three other women, the first to use the tactic of the hunger strike to protest against state repression, a tactic much emulated by male anti-colonialists in years to come (Kiberd, 1995: 397). She was, furthermore, opposed to the partition of Ireland. In the period after the Civil War, as Declan Kiberd describes, she and her republican comrades, 'were now portrayed as cranks in the popular press. The exodus of talented writers left them no more than a peripheral force.' Her pacifist husband, Francis, was murdered by the British Army in 1916 as he tried to stop looters in Dublin. See Margaret Ward's (1997) *Hanna Sheehy-Skeffington: A Life*, for a detailed exposition of the activist's life after partition.

15. 'An Ghaoltacht 'na h-ionad Saoire' means 'The Gaeltacht as a center of rest / relaxation' in English. The article that runs under this heading is, actually, a string of clichés. But it guides Irish-speaking visitors to the West to various holiday centres.

16. Except during its publication during the Second World War, when all international holiday travel was illegal and it was directed toward the Irish audience as a last resort.

References

Andrews. C.S. (1982) *Man of No Property*. Dublin: The Mercier Press.

Coogan, T.P. (1994) *The IRA: A History*. New York: Robert Rinehart Publishers.

Cronin, S. (1980) *Frank Ryan: The Search for the Republic*. Dublin: Repsol.

Deegan, J. and Dineen D. (1997) *Tourism Policy and Performance*. London: International Thomson Business Press.

Ellman, R. (1959 & 1982) *James Joyce*. Oxford: Clarenden Press.

Fanon, F. (1963) *The Wretched of the Earth*. London: Grove Press.

Ford, J. (1953) *The Quiet Man*. New York: Republic Pictures.

Gibbons, J. (1931) *Tramping through Ireland*. London: Methuen.

Ireland Guide (1962) O'Connell Street. Dublin: Irish Tourist Board.

Irish Tourist Association (1927a) *Wexford and its Historic Sights*. Dublin: Irish Tourist Association.

Irish Tourist Association (1927b) *Welcome to Cork*. Dublin: Irish Tourist Association.

Irish Tourist Association (1930) *Ireland*. Dublin: Irish Tourist Association.

Irish Travel (1925–58). Dublin: Irish Tourist Association.

Irish Free State Official Handbook (c.1931) London: Ernest Benn Ltd.

Joyce, J. (1993) *Dubliners* (Terence Brown, intro. & notes). New York: Penguin.

Kiberd, D. (1991) *An Crann Faoi Bhláth*. Dublin: Wolfhound Press.

Kiberd, D. (1995) *Inventing Ireland*. Cambridge, MA: Harvard University Press.

O'Loughlin, M. (1987) *Frank Ryan: Journey to the Centre*. Dublin: Raven Arts Press.

The Irish Independent (1925) 25 October.

The Irish Times, 3 March, 1925.

The Irish Times, 23 March, 1925.

Ward, M. (1997) *Hanna Sheehy-Skeffington: A Life*. Dublin: Attic Press.

Index